CW00321462

WANT SOME AGGRO?

WANT SOME AGGRO?

CASS PENNANT & MICKY SMITH

JOHN BLAKE

Published by John Blake Publishing Ltd,
3 Bramber Court, 2 Bramber Road,
London W14 9PB, England

www.johnblakepublishing.co.uk

First published in paperback in 2007

ISBN: 978 1 84454 403 5

All rights reserved. No part of this publication may be reproduced, stored in a
retrieval system, or in any form or by any means, without the prior permission in
writing of the publisher, nor be otherwise circulated in any form of binding or
cover other than that in which it is published and without a similar condition
including this condition being imposed on the subsequent publisher.

British Library Cataloguing-in-Publication Data:

A catalogue record for this book is available from the British Library.

Design by www.envydesign.co.uk

Printed in the UK by CPI Bookmarque, Croydon, CR0 4TD

3 5 7 9 10 8 6 4

© Text copyright Cass Pennant and Micky Smith

Papers used by John Blake Publishing are natural, recyclable products made from
wood grown in sustainable forests. The manufacturing processes conform to the
environmental regulations of the country of origin.

Every attempt has been made to contact the relevant copyright-holders, but some
were unobtainable. We would be grateful if the appropriate people could contact us.

Dedication

This book is dedicated to my mum and dad and my brothers. I would also like to personally thank Darren who runs the 'In The Know' site – http://www.network54.com/forum/181218.

I also need to thank my wife for all her support while writing this book. If I was you, Annie, I would have walked away long ago. To my kids Chris and Kelly: I'm glad you never had to grow up in those times. While they were great for me, I shudder at some of the things we did.

To all the lads from that era – in particular my old friend Steve Morgan RIP – and whether you are enemy or friend, many thanks. Lastly, to all the West Ham fans worldwide, remember: 'We're West Ham ain't we' – and never forget it.

Cheers,
Micky

Contents

Acknowledgements

MICKY SMITH:

I only write about what I saw – which brings me to some of the lads I ran with and have met over those great years. I can't remember all the names and will use nicknames if possible, but many thanks for the good times and the back-up always. A great load of lads:

The two Royal Green Jackets.
Cass or Cas or Cazz – I remember back then.
Stevie M – that was some long head of hair.
Wardie – top lad.
The Gatties – pure nutters.
The Spicers – don't know what a backward step means.
Yorkie – great times, mate, some not so good. Have you jacked in the hodcarrying?

The two lads from Didcot – solid West Ham lads who travelled everywhere and never let us down.

Vince – the Bryan Ferry lookalike.

Johnny H – solid lad, never let us down. Are you still collecting the programmes, John?

The lads at Harold Hill – some top lads. I can't remember all your names, but cheers anyway.

The small firm from Collier Row – some good laughs, thanks also for the back-up.

The Chelsea lads – Babs, the twins, Dickie and Reggie, I think.

Stuart – the newspaper boy. You were lucky in your court case and came across as a lad led astray. We know the truth, don't we?

Sammy Sykes – nice having a pint with you even if our teams hated each other, but that night we had another enemy. The lads with you, once the hangers-on were gone, were quite a handy crew.

The Arsenal lads – never got to know many, saw lots of them doing a runner and have been turned over by them. God knows what you are like now with your recent successes. I bet there are more women than anything at your games. Shame you never had a good pop at us, as some of your fights with your mates the Yids are legendary.

The Kippax boys – great lads.

Millwall – get fucked, south London gypos. The Mancs – well, the least said the better, but thanks for coming down and getting your heads kicked in. Cockney Reds – wake up to yourselves, simple as that.

ACKNOWLEDGEMENTS

CASS PENNANT:

I would like to express my debt to the following for valuable assistance and contribution made while researching and writing this book.

Book preparation is down to the efficiency and dedication of Charlotte Fitzpatrick.

Assistance in the book's production and design: our gratitude to Michelle Signore and John Blake Publishing.

The authors also thank the *Newham Recorder* for their kindness in supplying FA Cup celebration pictures along with further photographic illustrations contributed to the picture section from various sources. We thank: The Press Association, *News of The World*, Camera Press, Julia Skeggs, Timmy Dorsett, Tim (Slim) Conlan, Tallman, Bimbo, Nig Brewer, Steve Barone, Bob Mayer and *Skins* author-photographer, Gavin Watson.

Taped recordings regarding confirmation of past events – I need to thank Mouthy Bill, Alfie Barker, Bimbo, Ted and Simo, plus Tonbridge Cliff, who shared their stories, thoughts and memories.

Further sources of excellent research: I would thank the staff of The Newspaper Library (Colindale) Archives and Local Studies of Stratford, Southwark and Lewisham Libraries plus historian John Helliar's *Book of Match Facts, West Ham Utd, The Elite Era*. Also, Simon Inglis's *Football Grounds of Britain*.

Finally, to my family and friends for the encouragement and support – you know who you are.

Both authors would like to express their gratitude to Hammers fan Bef.

Foreword

FOOTBALL VIOLENCE HAS always been around. Sociologists and anthropologists could point you back to comparable behaviour in medieval times. In its heyday, the politicians, the courts, authority and the reporting media were forever throwing up their hands and asking the question: why? Why did we do what we did? The question today is: is it back?

It appears the passage of time has made it accepted that crowd trouble is very much part and parcel of football and at times is reckoned to be unavoidable. The old West Ham chairman Reg Pratt once stated that, 'The root cause was the near hysteria of a certain type of youth today. We hope it's just one of those phases, because how do you prevent it? If someone wants a punch-up there is no power on earth to stop it.'

These were the words of one very frustrated football club chairman and the day that prompted his comments was Boleyn

'Black Saturday' 6 May – wait for it – 1967. The Busby Babes were in town along with a travelling invasion of Manchester United fans, all hoping to see victory that would clinch their team the English League Championship. A fans' battle for the North Bank broke out and developed into the worst football riot ever experienced in the south of England. The fighting went on the whole day, even causing the underground network to grind to a halt. The average age of those arrested turned out to be a mere seventeen. Football had just witnessed a new youth cult attach itself to soccer. The bovver boy was born on the North Bank, West Ham.

How the memory fades … Skinhead, suedehead, boot boy; the denim, flares and cherry reds – plus, of course, your tatty and frayed favourite Super Irons scarf. They date back to a time when Mungo Jerry, Dave and Ansell Collins and Harry J Allstars had hit records blasting out all over grounds from the public address system during the half-time interval.

The cropped hair grew out and by the time rock music took over in the Seventies it was bushy sideburns and ridiculously long hair. Those early years of aggro were the times remembered by 'working-class' lads as WE RULE OK. Sporting your first pair of Doctor Martens and a Ben Sherman shirt with a pair of braces, you just felt untouchable as you walked the street doing the skinhead bowl. The much-referred-to 'spirit of '69' saw everyone get into Prince Buster, and the Trojan reggae sound was heard on every council estate in the land. The skinhead movement was kicking off big time. Now was the time to join the lads behind the goal in your Home End and be somebody.

Since the introduction of the old football special trains, we had discovered the freedom of travelling to football matches in the name of our club. They brought with them the inevitable punch-up along with the opportunity of a good piss-up. It was a scene that was fast becoming the done thing nationwide: from Charlton to Burnley, every club had its hooligans. Everywhere seemed to be kicking off, with a sort of 'See what happens' attitude from the fans. Sociologists will say this is a means of escape for discontented youth, yet most of us honestly thought we were just having a laugh with our mates. The sense of adventure, the loyalty and enthusiasm, together with a real passion in defending your club's honour against rival fans, was just all part of the day's atmosphere and excitement. It was all what we called a buzz.

The buzz in going to football had a beginning, long before what became the notorious ICF. This is a story of those very first guv'nors, as told in the words of Micky Smith. You would remember the likes of Micky from those bovver boy days when you just tagged along wearing all the right gear with people and mates you were only ever really on nodding terms with; with no crowd segregation, a bit of aggro was bound to be on. It was part and parcel of being young. A bonding of common interests, like you didn't know anything better, would see you follow the rest in invading the pitch or the end behind the goal, to have it with their mob. The crowning triumph of it all was hopefully to see it all captured by the TV cameras and the whole show seen again on Brian Moore's *Big Match* highlights with the famous commentator screaming, 'GOAL!' to the background noise of fans chanting, 'West Ham aggro, 'ello, 'ello! West Ham aggro ...'

Fashions change, as does taste in music. But the one thing you could never change was your family and the team you support. I like to remember that bygone era which belonged to the bovver boys well before all the 'erberts ever went casual and attracted designer label thugs wielding Stanley knives and flares – the ones you fired, not the baggy ones everybody wore on to the terraces during the Seventies. Remember those loud trousers? The further north you went, the higher the waistband went. Back down south, the hard men of the terraces had these real long cardigans, almost coat length, complete with a woollen belt, while it seemed like every fan was into the hooped-arm zip-up jumpers in club colours. Even so, the North remained a backwater in the fashion stakes: grown men with 'taches took to wearing tight-fit jumpers that had a huge star on their front. Just imagine getting chased by someone dressed like that. Sad, well sad.

I remember the songs and chants still – you might remember even more of them – but I've never come across anyone who recalls that period of time as well as Micky. Maybe it's because that is his lasting memory of the shrine we called Upton Park. For towards the end of the Seventies he emigrated to Oz, and from then on became a Hammer in exile.

So how, and why, have I teamed up for Micky's account of who those first guv'nors of London's terraces were? Firstly I felt there was unfinished business when I wrote *Congratulations You've Just Met the ICF*. What were the ICF building their reputation on? When was this reputation first established, and by whom? These are questions that today not every West Ham fan can answer. So for the benefit of many readers I included several references to the early Mile End years in my book, including, in one complete chapter, tales of the famous Mile End and their battles with Millwall. These accounts entailed some graphic stories of real terrace warfare that established West Ham and its East End support as the hardest firm around. Some of the older members that also became part of the ICF thought of those stories as vital accounts, particularly as they go a long way towards explaining why certain vendettas between rival clubs' fans have carried on over the years.

This presented a problem. I had realised by then that, although the Mile End stories were important and had been told by those I had come to respect on the terraces, I couldn't put them all in the book. These accounts were from entirely different periods of time that would take something away from each other. Indeed, they were separate history, and I now had at hand the possibility of two books.

The ICF were still terrace legend, while the Mile End era – because of the passage of time, those involved at the head of it must be approaching their fifties now – had all become a forgotten episode. A total myth to the new generation of supporters who cannot even imagine what those times must have been like.

Whilst putting together *Congratulations*, I realised by way of conversation with fans from all over that it would be an in-demand book. Then why not use the earlier years of West Ham, in what was a real violent age? The more I thought about it, the more I conjured up images of my early teenage years: my first pair of Martens, being a skin and thinking you're the bollocks. Taking down old Enid Blyton books and Beano comics from the bookshelf and replacing them with every one of Richard Allen's books. Bunking in to watch Stanley Kubrick's *Clockwork Orange*; remembering how eager your classmates were to leave school at 15, with the sole ambition of being able to buy their own fags and a pint.

The more I pushed on with the ICF story the more I came across events linked to earlier times; this book would definitely need a prequel. Then this bloke Bef tapped me on the shoulder in the Prince one home game, shoving me a contact number for someone writing a book in Australia about the lads.

'He's known to you, Cass, and is keen to get in touch with you regarding your book.' At first I couldn't think who he was, especially with the surname Smith. But Bef seemed pleased he had handed me this scrap of paper. So, out of courtesy to a fellow Hammer, I decided I would make the contact. Soon I was talking down under to a Micky Smith. And you could forget the fact he was in Australia: right then we could have been standing in the Queens down Green Street sharing a pint – only the year would have been '72.

Some of the names Micky was asking after hadn't been seen over West Ham in decades; one in particular, I informed him, was no longer with us. The conversation was over the fact both of us were writing a book which both of us thought was a first, featuring West Ham fans. But where Micky was coming from – his last memory of seeing West Ham at Upton Park – was really back to the Seventies, when he left England for Oz. Aside from Micky catching up on news of fans and what happened to the 'bad old days', we really were old mates. Micky, my senior by some four or five years, was part of the most well-known gang outside the Mile End mob who gathered in the South Bank. This firm also travelled to as many away games as possible during times when you really did know each fellow supporter by sight and name. This would be the same gang I was virtually shanghaied into after an away game at Wolves, a chapter I cover in my autobiography, *Cass*.

Me and Micky were sharing memories that only the gang could tell, like the time we got trapped on the Paxton with our backs against the wall. But the real urgency behind our contact was we were both writing about our exploits following West Ham and were concerned at the risk of taking an edge off each other. Word was out there was going to be two books on the ICF at the same time. Micky was also concerned I had gone on to be rather well known in West Ham circles, which would take away the interest from him a little. I assured Micky this top-boys, main-face business is something bestowed on you by others, mainly through your actions and the firm you chose to run with. At the end of the day you can only ever be yourself, as names and reputation are always things that can go beyond your control.

The main thing was, we knew we were both there and were both West Ham. The real issue here was that our own expertise lay in different periods of time. Coincidence had us going head to head to be the first fan author with the West Ham story but in the end, as with any book of this nature, it would come down to credibility.

The ICF era would be unknown territory to Micky, but the bovver boy years that started in the late Sixties would be much more up his alley. The obvious thing to do, as we had both got some way down the line with our own projects, was to come together at a later stage and pool our resources, contacts and research. And that's what we did: Micky erased the ICF stuff that didn't relate to his time and I didn't use all the early years stuff I could have in *Congratulations*.

This book is presented as a diary and tells of a lifestyle from 30 years ago. It recalls many events and images about which little has ever been written. What is described has certainly influenced today's supporter, in baseball cap and Stone Island gear.

In this book, I believe we have managed to take you back to those times of the yesteryear bovver boys of Upton Park. Plain old-fashioned terrace aggro from men to boys, boys to men. No big names, no mobiles, no gang's dossier, no prearranged meets and certainly no bloody internet warriors. It was simply those that wanted to think they were hard were amongst those who were hard. And as the boots went in, that was when all the fun started.

As Micky says somewhere: don't knock it, these were the lads that kick-started whatever fun you had. Look back and recall your own era, whether it be second-generation skins, punks, new romantics or the best of the lot, the football casual. Everybody had a crack at it some time in going to football, for you can only take so much shit from gobby rival opposition fans.

Cass Pennant

Introduction

'WANT SOME AGGRO' – kinda in yer face, ain't it? But please read the book and draw your own conclusions. A couple of things I would like to tell you.

Firstly, I am no superhooligan or main man. I'm just a West Ham fan brought up in the East End – West Ham being my team of choice, as it was for my father and grandfather before me. It was bred in me. I am no big fighter, but at the same time I would not back down. Many times I wished I had. Other people talk about getting an odd slap here and there. I reckon that's bollocks, as if you were involved in those times there was a good chance you got the odd kicking – and I don't mean a right hander. We often did, but we always came back for more.

I don't claim to be a founder or even a member of the ICF. In fact, it started after my time, though it became more or less a household name. Many new firms have started up since then, but I believe the way we travelled and went about things at games led up to their start. Many firms may have been bigger or even harder at home, but the way we went about business was the talk of every team in the land. A meet-up with us would guarantee some action. As I said, we at West Ham had one thing in common – that was, not letting your mates down. This was the key to our success and many may laugh but any lad around who has come up against West Ham fans will know what I mean. Many other firms had some top lads who were well up for any action, but they were nowhere near as well planned as us. We learned a few things from other firms and used them to our advantage. This book will hopefully shed some light on those great days. The attire of the fan on the front cover is to me a sign of those times: the Sixties and Seventies. Those who were around will know what I mean. We never had video players; photos were black and white; some lucky people had colour TV – but computers, well they were non-existent. When you consider the computer system that landed man on the moon covered something like five storeys of an office building and the PC you have today is in fact 10,000 times more powerful, your own pocket calculator is more advanced than the *Apollo* mission computer that landed men on the moon, and that is a fact.

I decided to write a book for many reasons. One was to more or less tell about what the scene was like before the all-seater ground, and maybe to give some idea to the younger fans that turning over a pub is not a result. Events depicted in this book are ones I was actually at or involved with. Some fans from this era will remember some of the clashes in this book, some won't, but unless you were standing beside me, your view may be different. The opposition fans may not agree with what I have written, but I was there and it is true. At some of the games I heard about various events but don't comment much on them here because I never saw them. I have left names out of this book as I don't want anyone tied to any one incident.

People might have a go at my writing, but I don't claim to be an author and I write the way I think and speak. I don't want to be a spokesman for football hooligans or a so-called expert on the subject. I was only ever a fan who followed West Ham. But what I do know is that I did run with some great lads who never let me, or their mates, down. We were one big family at West Ham and I like to think they are still the same today.

Don't knock the older lads – they kicked off the fun you are having now. I know some teams' fans will say what I have said couldn't be true about their firm, but it happened, like it or not. I'm telling you what I saw and was involved in.

There were always fights between rival fans, long before my time, and there always will be. From what I remember, it was from 1967 on that things became different. The aim was always to take the opposition fans' end. That was the prize, no more or less. Anything else was a bonus.

Nowadays, with the all-seater and all-ticket matches, this has become nigh on impossible to do. You still had aggro outside back then. Being a London lad, you sometimes found knowing the tube system well acted as your best friend, but it could also get you a kicking as well. You had to be cunning, and that cunning was proven at our ground many times. The away fans' preferred method of travel was by coach, as the tube, if you think about it, could be a nightmare, especially for those teams from outside London. That short walk to West Ham's ground from the tube station was only five to six hundred yards, but it was a real gauntlet for visiting fans. Any who have been there know what I mean. So, if you are reading this book, stop and think, remember what you see and when you get home write it down. Keep a diary and who knows? In fifteen to twenty years' you could be writing a book and thinking that those young lads today don't have a clue.

On my internet site one lad asked me how you know who to hit when you steam into a large mob of a few hundred. I told him it was simple: hit the ones hitting out at you. We have given out loads of slappings and I remember nearly all of them. But to say I can remember every punch or boot I put in would be bullshit. I can remember the ones I received and still have some of the scars to remind me. Writing this book brought back many painful memories as I relived some great and not so great rows I was involved in.

Some lads who were there will have different versions I'm sure, but all I can say is if you have been involved in any way in the football scene, can you remember every punch or boot given out? You might know the results you have had against other mobs, but I bet not many of you will own up to being run by them. At any major off you were involved in and have talked about after, you would have heard different versions. In all fairness to any fans it may have happened, a lot of stories would have been blown out of proportion. I have seen this with our lads and they were just as guilty. Stories like the size of the mob that got run or given a slapping in reality may be a couple of hundred or more, but by midweek it has done the rounds, and the mob who you done or who ran you is now more like ten thousand. In any case, the excitement and adrenaline of it all keeps you thinking all the time and you can't wait to have another pop at this or that firm. It was all part of the scene in those days – and I believe still is.

As a West Ham fan – and therefore being a bit one eyed

when I say this – if I had my time over, they would be the lads I would like at my back, as I knew I could trust them. I met some great lads over the years that I was 'active'. Even met a few good ones from the other side.

Even if I got a good kicking (and I had a few), I would be back the next week. It is in your blood and even now, approaching fifty, if I could do it all again, I would. Trouble is, though, things change at football. Even when I left for Australia, things like knives and CS gas were becoming the weapon of choice of many firms, including West Ham. My opinion is that the sooner knives are left at home, the better. Even in the days when the kids carried bike spokes around, it was mainly for show. Fans are getting killed now. The ICF of later days were known to go tooled up to a game. I never went tooled up, but used the resources around me if I had to. With a bit of thought it doesn't take much. I have taken the odd golf ball to places like Chelsea, where you knew you were going to be pelted, but that was about it really.

So I hope you enjoy this book, and I look forward to getting some flack on the internet sites. And remember, my writing is my opinion only, and while I may slag off your firm and sound well biased, don't be put off by that. Things have changed a lot since those great days – for me, anyway.

Micky Smith

CHAPTER 1

1967

NINETEEN SIXTY-SEVEN was a special year for me, one that changed my life forever. I had been with the old man and his brothers to the football many times – I went with them and saw West Ham do the treble in '64, '65 and '66: FA Cup, European Cup Winners Cup and the World Cup. West Ham was my life, but from the day I went to Upton Park on my own, things took a very different turn. That day Manchester United came to West Ham and if they won, they would have the title.

The famous Busby Babes were in town. A lot of fans of all age groups had some respect for them, for the way they had rebuilt after the Munich '58 air crash, and just ten years later they were going to win the title with great players like Charlton, Best, Stiles and Stepney. West Ham had the famous trio of World Cup winners – Hurst, Moore and Peters – and it promised to be a big day, one that I never forgot.

As usual I left from Mile End tube station about 11 a.m. for the short journey to Upton Park, but things were different. Everywhere you looked Manchester United fans were to be seen – mobs of about a dozen or so singing, carrying on. All the way on the tube to Upton Park, there were Manchester United fans and not many West Ham around. I was alone that day and lost my scarf to a Man U fan who was in need of a trophy on that trip. I wasn't the only one – many kids had theirs pinched by that mob. Real big men taking a thirteen-year-old's scarf – there were so many of them I could do nothing, and it would have been silly to as I was so young. I was a skinhead and jack the lad, but nothing prepared me for this mob. They took the piss out of me and the way I was dressed (all the fashion at the time in London). From that moment on I hated Manchester United.

My hate was soon to turn to hatred with vengeance. Arriving at Upton Park, there were many more Man U fans along Green Street and women and girls everywhere with George Best rosettes and pictures. It was like a mini Wembley with all the colour around. Further towards the ground, there was a massive police presence. There were fights all over, mainly isolated ones.

Normally I went on the old Chicken Run with my old man and his brothers, but today I was told to go on the North Bank, as I would be safe there and amongst my own. The queues into the ground were nearly back to the gates. I met up with some mates, who were also on their own. When we got into the ground the North Bank was full of Manchester United fans singing and the bars were full. We made our way up to the back of the North Bank, climbed up the back wall and hung on to the girders. As a youngster it was the best view of the game and we were too old to go behind the goals.

Then I saw something that has stuck with me till this day. About five or six hundred West Ham fans came in a run, charging the Man U fans. It was on. West Ham were trying to claim the North Bank back. There were men fighting all around – five hundred-plus of them kicking, punching, shouting. I had never seen anything like it. The Man U fans held their own and I watched as they lashed out with red-and-white walking sticks and banners, only to meet with a hail of bottles from the West Ham fans. The police, who were trying to establish a dividing line between the fans, were powerless.

The fighting went on for ages. A hail of pennies being thrown by Manchester United fans at West Ham was like something out of an old war film with the English archers all letting go of their arrows at once. Pennies and bottles were thrown back and in front of me I saw one Man U fan with a dart in his shoulder. His mates took it out and threw it back at West Ham fans. The screaming and singing was something to see. The Man U fans beat back the West Ham fans, mainly because of the sheer numbers they had. More and more bottles came over towards the Man U fans, who were now shoved down behind the goal. I saw one West Ham fan, with a Man U coloured walking stick, hitting into the fans. This walking stick looked to have barbed wire wrapped around it.

West Ham fans were at their side and back and the police were slowly forming a line. Hammers fans were lighting newspapers and chucking them down on the Man Utd fans; it made an eerie sight to see paper on fire floating down on to them. More and more bottles and pennies were being hurled; the crowd was surging back and forth, but as the time for the game got closer, more and more Man Utd fans came in. There were thousands of them – I have never seen so many at West

Ham. More West Ham fans came in, about three hundred from the Chicken Run side, and ran at Man U's fans, but were beaten back by the sheer numbers. Some Man U fans our age tried to climb up in the girders with us but we kicked the shit out of them as they climbed up. The whole of the North Bank was full now and some West Ham fans were jumping in from the Chicken Run to help, only to be turned back by Old Bill.

The South Bank (which was for away fans) was covered in Man U fans. The North Bank was gone as well. They covered the whole centre of it down to the goals and two-thirds up to where the police were, and then there were West Ham behind. Groups of West Ham were attacking the sides of the main mob, but police moved in quickly and as soon as one fight was stopped, another load of West Ham fans would attack somewhere else. More bottles were thrown, more lighted paper was sent down – I saw fans in pain with blood streaming out of their heads, swearing at the cockney cunts.

The Man U mob's plan was simple – get in early, in numbers, and hold on and take West Ham by surprise. They succeeded.

I don't remember much of the game, except women and girls screaming for Georgie Best, and we got thrashed 6 – 1. One incident I remember came soon after our full-back John Charles (the first black player I ever saw) smashed in a long-range shot through a ruck of players to score our goal. He was then involved in the most dubious of penalty decisions, which went United's way after it was alleged he pushed Denis Law in the box. The legend Law took and scored it himself for United's fifth. During it all, as the West Ham defence protested, the Man U fans chucked bananas on the pitch at Charles, and this kicked off more fighting, more pennies and more bottles. Man U were chucking back broken glass and anything else they could at

West Ham. As much as they threw, twice as much went back. Man U had taken the North Bank, but not without a fight. I saw Man U fans crying, walking about in disbelief. The kids who had a go at us came back with some older lads and tried to get up to us but we kept kicking and spitting on them and some older West Ham lads soon joined in. We had a result, our first real 'off' with fans, and we were kings of the world. The blood and excitement were rushing to our heads; we wanted more.

I had seen quite a few punch-ups at West Ham, mainly in the Chicken Run with the older fans, and mostly with other London supporters, but nothing like this. I did not know why my old man and his brothers missed this one, but I found out later.

The game over, Man U were champions and, their fans stayed behind to celebrate. The North Bank half emptied. As we got out as well, we went on to Green Street, where a huge West Ham mob was waiting, thousands of them, for Man U to come out. Lots of fans headed off towards the Barking Road to find the lot from the South Bank and the coaches. We stayed with the main mob. The police were lost as to who to follow, and tried to set up a line between us and Man U by the gates. Still no Man U fans. They were still inside. I saw West Ham fans with half bricks, stones, bottles, sticks, you name it. If it could be chucked, they had it.

Some half an hour later and the Man U fans were still inside. A lot of us moved off towards the tube because we knew they would have to change at Mile End, and there we would wait. As we got halfway up Green Street to the tube, near the market, they came out of the ground and it was on. West Ham turned and charged as Man U ran towards them. The police were powerless, with only a few on horseback keeping up, and black marias were everywhere trying to separate the fans. More missiles were thrown from both sides, and fighting went on for ages until the Old Bill got some grip on it.

I saw a couple of coppers being helped away injured. Someone had seen to them, as one had blood streaming from his temple. It calmed down a bit with the Old Bill getting in between the fans, but then the mob that had gone down towards the South Bank came back, so Man U were in the middle. More bottles and bricks were hurled – I saw one front garden fence being pulled down for ammo. If Man U thought they had come down to take the piss out of West Ham, then they weren't going to do it easily. They still had to go back on the tube yet, and many fans left for the station. We tagged along on the train. It was full of people screaming abuse at Man U. Tempers were up, and wearing red and white was not a good idea. On our carriage, nearly every one of the overhead handles was gone, taken for weapons. People were carrying bottles, sticks, poles, anything that could hurt.

At Mile End we got off the train to be greeted by many West Ham fans already there waiting for Man U. One train-load turned up, and as the doors opened it was on – bottles were being thrown; a chocolate vending machine was lofted by three or four blokes into one carriage. They had no chance. West Ham stormed the train, kicking and punching as we went. I had my first real result – a Man U skin my age picked me out. He had a quart bottle he was going to hit me with but I got in first, so it was him or me. I hit him with a bottle of Tizer I had and laid the boot in as he went down in a heap. A whole lot of others seemed to converge on him like locusts. He was left lying there battered. Police started coming in to the station from outside but never had a hope. I saw a couple of Man U fans jump the centre tracks trying to get away. How they didn't get killed I'll never know. That train finally left and the police tried moving us off the platform. Then the next train came in, this time with loads of Old Bill on it. Out came the Man U fans, being a bit brave with the police around. Missiles started flying again and many were beaten back on to the train.

The police had the numbers now and were moving us off the station. I lived near Mile End so me and my mates called it a day. We walked home and talked all the way about what had just happened. The game? Who cared – the season was nearly over, roll on next season. This was football violence and I was hooked for life. I wanted more and my friends agreed. From that day West Ham was my life. I always went on my own from then on in and looking for other fans was all part of the fun.

That was the last time the North Bank was taken – and the first, I'm told. Chelsea tried later on in 1969, and the Yids (a name for the Tottenham team and fans, even used by the fans themselves) in 1976–77, but no one else dared try. Coming to West Ham was always a hard one for away fans. The location of the ground, the tube and above all the reputation of West Ham made most away fans think twice.

The next day the Sunday newspapers were full of what happened at Upton Park. Front cover stuff, splashed all over: 'Thugs! Hooligans!' the headlines read, with pictures of bleeding fans being led away.

My old man and his brothers were at the game, but were mainly in the Boleyn drinking until the kick-off. I found out much later they had been in the North Bank lot. Your ears flap when you are young and some of the things I heard that went on that day, I was surprised – no wonder they did not want me around. From what I can gather, about forty of them, mostly all dockers, were having a day out and it was adults only.

From that day on I learned a few things, some of which were to carry on for years afterwards. Never wear scarves home or away and, later on, the way we travelled. This was mainly after a trip to Ipswich one year where the train that brought us back had quite a few carriages destroyed. Stay with your mates and never let them down. Let them know what was happening, where to meet and spread the word. Strength in numbers, and remember you are West Ham always.

Manchester claimed to have taken the East End. In truth they got most of the North Bank for a few hours and they had won the title, but at a cost. Something that we never let them forget every time they came to West Ham. The season was not over with two more games against the Yids and Man City. The Yids played us on the Tuesday night following the Man U game. They won and it was a piss-poor turn out from the Yid fans. Would Man City bring a mob equal to their neighbours for the last game of the season? Alas, it too was a non-event.

Being brought up in Limehouse, West Ham was your team. God help you if you chose Arsenal or Chelsea, and if you were Man U after that game, your life was made miserable.

From that day on the skinhead movement was kicking off really big. I had left school and started as an apprentice bricklayer. Some of my mates faded into the hippie scene of The Beatles and Dylan. The rest stayed on at school to get 'O' and 'A' levels. My new friends were West Ham, people who I became friends with, travelled with to away games and knew I could trust in a fight to back me up.

Gangs of skinheads were starting all over. The Mile End Mafia was one in our area. Although I never personally knew any of these, we knew of their reputation and looked up to them as heroes. They were much older lads, and loved to have it off with rival gangs from south London or up the West End. The Man U game at Upton Park that day seemed to be a breakthrough for hooligans – things were different at games from then on. You were a skinhead or greaser or mod. As the greasers were a dirty lot most around our way went the skinhead way – the smart clothes, the look.

The National Front tried to get West Ham fans involved, but never succeeded. There were many blacks at West Ham – in fact, we had one playing for us – so it wasn't a race issue.

But the Asians, now that was a different story. They were not liked. They never mixed; you never saw them at football or in the pub buying a pint. They would not let their kids mix with us and they isolated themselves from the East End community, which is the real working-class community of London. Many Asians would buy up a corner shop or something similar, work every hour God sent and end up looking down their noses at ordinary working-class people, something which wasn't taken lightly in the East End. They had their own class system and were the worst snobs of all time.

Paki bashing became the rage in the East End and the papers were full of how innocent Asians were attacked by mobs of skinheads. I was involved in Paki bashing at the time, and anyone who was a skinhead or football hooligan at the time who says they weren't are liars, or have a selective memory. Some Asians youths tried to fight back, but had no chance; the skins were too well organised.

Dress of the day was Ben Sherman or Brutus shirts (the short-sleeved red check being a favourite), Levi sta-press trousers in white or off grey turned up to the top of the high-leg Doctor Martens boots, or American officer dress boots, sleeveless jumpers, thin red or black braces and a decent overcoat or sheepskin coat – or, if you could find it, an American leather flying jacket. On match days it was boots, either Doctor Martens or steel-capped cherry reds, Levi jeans and a decent sweatshirt, braces and a flying jacket or monkey jacket. It wasn't cheap being a skinhead, but it was the scene, and I was part of it.

With the new season looming, all talk was on who was going where and wondering what team was bringing the best support to Upton Park. I was planning to go to London away games and get some trips in further afield. Attending every away game wasn't possible with the money I was earning as an apprentice, and there were always clothes to buy. Being dressed like an Eric (now called 'anorak') was not an option. If you were part of West Ham and the skinhead movement the clothes were as important as the team itself and if you did not have the right gear it was soon pointed out to you.

It was during this period of a lot of racial tension that I acquired the name Micky, after an affray at Mile End tube station one evening. It was when I was thirteen years old, and dressed in all the skinhead regalia, along with a shaved head.

I was standing outside the tube waiting for some mates when three Asian lads had a pop at me because of the way I looked. Being only young, and these lads being grown men, I must've seemed like an easy target. One had a pop at me and got slapped for his trouble, then his two mates decided to join in. Being three to one I evened up the score with an old soft drink crate (the wooden type) from outside the kiosk at the tube. Well, I hit one with it and nearly clocked the second; the third one just legged it. I dunno if it was because I stood but a couple of my mates showed up and it was all over. The next thing I know the police arrived and were saying all sorts of things – the lad who legged it had claimed it was a racial attack. Fortunately for me the railway inspector, himself of West Indian descent, told the police what had happened and we were let go. My mates reckoned I was mad to go at them with just an old wooden crate, but I said it served them right for taking the mick! From then on the name sorta stuck, with variations of 'Mile End Micky' bestowed on me even to this day.

CHAPTER 2

1967–68

THE NEW SEASON was here. Tottenham were the cup holders, having beaten Chelsea 2 – 1. This started a hate relationship between the two groups of fans. QPR were League Cup winners, but all the talk was of that game at the end of last season.

At Upton Park, the North Bank had seen some changes. A police tunnel made of crash barriers was put on the North Bank to the left of the goal and ran all the way up to the back. At home games this was packed with police – they weren't going to get caught again like they had been with Man U. The bars around grounds sold you beer, but poured it into paper cups – no more bottles. Body searches going into the ground, and if you were carrying a soft drink bottle you were stopped. No more walking sticks or banners or flags that had poles or sticks. Things had tightened up. By doing this the Old Bill were saying that the football hooligan was here permanently. West Ham was one of the first grounds to get this treatment, but others soon followed.

If you were on the North Bank and the Old Bill picked you out as a trouble maker or did not like the look of your face, you were grabbed and hauled down the dividing tunnel, being punched in the neck all the way and with the odd ankle kick thrown in. The police liked grabbing you by the collar and pushing you all the way down to the front with their fist clenched in the back of your neck – a bit of payback by the Old Bill. Then you walked around the outside of the pitch, through the players' tunnel and, depending on what you had done, your name and address was taken and you were let go. Otherwise, depending on the copper, you were chucked into a black maria and made to wait till the game was well over before being released. I saw a couple of lads fight back, before going into the maria, and the Old Bill gave them a good hiding. It's hard to fight with your arms bent up your back and two or three Old Bill thumping into you – real brave. Not many were charged in those days, as the Old Bill was judge, jury and executioner. You never heard of anyone being hauled up in court. The coppers used to go mad every time that song 'Harry Roberts is our friend, he kills coppers' was sung. They hated it, we loved it.

Many West Ham fans now got on the North Bank early. Only the older ones came later, after drinking in the Boleyn or other pubs around the ground. If there was another mob challenging they were soon there, but it was up to the younger ones to sort it till they got there.

The season started off with us losing at home to Sheffield Wednesday and the following Monday beating Burnley 4 – 2 at home. Come Saturday and we had the first away game of the season against the Yids.

Going to White Hart Lane was going to be special. The Tott fans had taken the piss out of West Ham over the Man U game and now it was their turn. The word was: if you were not at Mile End, wait at Liverpool Street station. We got to Liverpool Street about eleven o'clock along with many other West Ham lads. At Liverpool Street there was a huge mob milling around, some in the buffet bars, the rest just waiting until about 12 o'clock when we all moved off and got the British Rail to White Hart Lane. Rumours were going around that Tottenham would be waiting at Bruce Grove station; they proved to be false.

The main target was the Park Lane end, the home of the Spurs mob. We were going to storm it no matter what. Once inside the ground, most made their way on to the Park Lane and many stayed under the main stand having a drink. White Hart Lane was a good ground for a mob on the prowl – unlike West Ham where, when you went in there, you stayed in that part of the ground. At Tottenham you could walk from one end at the Park Lane to the Paxton under the main stand, no problems. This was handy and came in useful for many a game. Not long before kick-off a massive West Ham mob gathered on the Park Lane, pushing the Yids away. The Park Lane was ours. The only hiding we got was on the field as the Yids hammered us 5–1. Did we care? The easy way we took their Park Lane was the result we were after, and we rubbed it in all the way back to Liverpool Street.

All thought was now on the upcoming fixture with Man U, our next Saturday home game, and we were ready. We lost the game but had a fair bit of payback for the season before. There were loads of Man U fans around, but nothing like the year before, and the Old Bill were everywhere. They weren't taking a chance this time. We went early to the ground so as to get on the North Bank – they weren't going to pull the same stunt again. On the tube down from Mile End people were fighting, little mobs of two or three. It wasn't a good idea to wear red and white on the tube that day.

At Upton Park we got on the North Bank to find the South Bank was full of Man U fans. Most came by coach and the women were screaming again for George Best. One part of the West stand was all women in red and white. We lost the game 3–1 but we left early, a large mob from both sides of the North Bank to meet up at the back of the South Bank.

The police were mainly watching the coaches and tube station. Only a few Old Bill were outside on horseback and they had no chance of handling the mob that was running down the back of the old Chicken Run. When we got around to the South Bank, the rest of the North Bank came around. We had a massive mob and steamed right into the South Bank. The Old Bill tried to stop us but never had a chance. West Ham fans were kicking and punching at Man U everywhere. They showed little resistance and we had them now. More and more police came in from inside and outside the ground. The police from the North Bank dividing tunnel came across the pitch to help and the crowd swayed back and forth. More fighting, this time no bottles, but pennies and halfpennies were being chucked from both sides. There were cut heads and people being led away. Police were trying to break it up. This went on for about ten minutes until the police got some control and formed a line between the fans.

These Man U fans never had the bottle of the ones the year before. They got a bad hiding and a lot of them still had to get back to the coaches. Many West Ham split up and went to where the coaches were parked, down Central Park Road. The Old Bill had a massive presence across the road but there was a back way in down St Martin's Avenue and off there was another side street. The Old Bill never sussed this out for ages, and many a surprise attack was done this way.

A few coaches lost the odd window, and a few Man U were done over real bad. I saw one lad have a go and then his mate jumped in and helped. Then they were swamped and went down under a hail of Doctor Martens – it was like a feeding frenzy and when it had finished they just lay on the pavement like limp pieces of rubber, bleeding and moaning. The Old Bill moved up and I saw those blokes going into ambulances. Fuck them, they got what they deserved.

But that was not enough. On to the tube. If you have seen a mob of a thousand-odd skinheads running along a road all dressed much the same, it can be a frightening sight. Into the tube gates we rushed. No one ever paid on the tube, and what inspector was going to challenge a mob like this? On the train there was the usual 'Knees up Mother Brown', with the whole carriage full of skinheads jumping up and down, the train rocking from side to side. Mile End and all out, talk of going to Euston and finding more Man U or any other fan that was around. I called it a day; we had done them again, outside the ground. Only inside the ground under police protection could you hear Man U fans. Even now I reckon they are the gobbiest in the land. They have the numbers, but are all gob. At home it's different, but who isn't at home? True then, true now.

After those few matches, West Ham was never the same. If you came to Upton Park, you were warned. No mercy was shown for away fans and many a time when London derbys were on at Upton Park we would go in search of the away fans on their turf. You always kept your pennies and halfpennies for big games. They were not very big but any older fan would tell you if you were hit by one it would split your forehead open or give you a nasty bump on the head. They were the perfect weapon. Police could not stop you taking them in to the ground. If they searched you they were easy to conceal but it hurt like fuck if you were hit by them.

Our next home game was against Wolves and it was a no-show by their fans, which was a disappointment. We had heard they were well up for it, but in truth not many fans had the money or could be bothered to travel to away games. In those days a London family would go to Clacton or Southend for their holidays. Not many would travel the length of the country to watch a game of football and maybe get their heads punched in while they were there. The same with the northerners – Blackpool or Morecambe for the holidays, why go to London for a day? It was seen in those times as a major excursion by those both from the north and south of England. Most away game trips in those days were saved for FA Cup ties or shorter trips to the Midlands. If you lived in London and it wasn't on the tube it wasn't worth going to – with the exception of the Yids.

Our next away game was Fulham. West Ham fans were getting their act together. A large mob gathered at Mile End for the tube trip to Fulham. District line all the way, no stops. Rumours were going around that Chelsea would be waiting at Earls Court station. We arrived and no Chelsea, but there was more West Ham, who had also heard the rumour, and plenty of Old Bill.

On to Putney Bridge and the whole train was full of skinheads. We got off and waited around for any Fulham fans

and the so-called Chelsea mob. The next train arrived and more
West Ham skinheads got off. The roar was incredible and off we
set to Craven Cottage, about ten to fifteen minutes away. Most
of the mob were running down the middle of the road, traffic
was stuck and anyone who blew their horn had many a boot in
their car panels. Many drivers just sat there, and I didn't blame
them. We turned off the main road and down towards the
ground. Once at Fulham we got on the Fulham end, and a small
mob of their lads had legged it – they wanted no part of us! We
had taken their end and we weren't moving. We won 3 – 0 and
the whole day was a knees-up – not that there was any fighting,
as there was no one to fight with. After the game we went back
the same way, but with a police escort. Only the horses could
keep up, and many an Old Bill were jumping in a maria and
speeding up to the front to warn and stop traffic.

Back to Putney Bridge station, and we piled in through the
gates. The ticket inspector gave up. The first train came and it
was filled in a instant. Talk of Earls Court again, but nothing –
no Chelsea. It was a story or they bottled it, I reckon. They
would not stand a chance with the mob that day. Back to Mile
End and some lads were going further down the line to look for
Millwall. Nothing was heard, so I figured they weren't to be
found. A great day out. We had gone away, won the game and
taken their end unscathed. It seems that nothing would stop us.
We were getting bigger and more cunning each game and many
other fans knew this.

Our next few games were non-events. A draw to Leeds,
getting done by Stoke 4–3 at home, away to Liverpool and we
lost again, and next home game was Southampton. Again, no
show by any of these fans, though there were a few stories of a
handful of West Ham lads getting done at Anfield.

The next big away game was at Chelsea, which had a large following of skinheads. We could not wait – the rumour mill was working overtime. One such rumour was that Millwall was going to team up with Chelsea. We wished it would happen, they would need all the help they could get. Some said the Yids were teaming up with us and meeting at Liverpool Street station. I went with many from West Ham to see if, in fact, the Yids were there – not to join up, but to give them some as well. But no show – typical Yids, all gob. West Ham fans hated the Totts and whoever started that rumour was well out of order. We got back on the tube for the trip to Fulham Broadway and Chelsea. There were loads of West Ham on the train, and as we got closer to our final stop we were ready for Chelsea.

At Fulham Broadway there was no Chelsea mob to be found. We made our way round the Shed enclosure and there was a huge mob at the Rising Sun pub opposite. We thought at last we had found them, but they were West Ham. When we got there we started singing, 'UNITED!' and made our way into the Shed.

The Shed was well named. It was a semi-circular stand with a big Shed up the top. They used to have a running/dog track at Chelsea and when it rained heavily the place flooded badly. Hence we called it the Duck Pond, as at one game a few ducks settled down on the track outside the pitch.

There was a huge yard outside the Shed End that day, and it soon filled up with more and more West Ham fans pouring in. Many jumped the turnstiles to get in, including me. Once inside we found most of the Chelsea mob right up in the corner, mouthing off at us – only the police barrier saved them.

A hail of pennies came down and also light globes, torch batteries and tin cans. They were brave fans stuck up in the corner behind the Old Bill. We had all the Shed except the one corner bit that was Chelsea. More and more coins and cans came over, I saw people pissing in the cans and chucking them back. Then we found out that some of the Chelsea coins were filed down to sharp edges. That was it, we charged them. They weren't up for it. The Old Bill could not hold us back. We got over to their side and most of them legged it. Those who did not were kicked all the way down to the front. Chants of 'WE GOT THE DUCK POND!' went out, followed by a hail of coins and cans and anything else that could be chucked at them.

We had come to Chelsea and taken their manor and we won the game as well, and in the end we all got out. No Chelsea were to be found. We heard a big mob had gone to the Fulham Volunteer on North End Road and loads of West Ham made their way up there. The pub was between five and ten minutes walk past the station but once there, nothing – all bullshit again. We made our way to Victoria station looking for them, but nothing. We had walked all over their turf and they could not stop us and the police failed as well. The day was West Ham's and we were on top of the world.

Our next home game we had Man City. Like us, Man City hated Man U. They had a fair crew down on the South Bank and there wasn't much trouble. We had respect for Man City and I think they had the same for us after the show we gave them in '67. We lost the game and we were told that Man U were going to be well up for it if we showed next time. At home their ground was a fortress, but the Man City lads were saying they would be along – not for West Ham but because they hated United too.

After the Man City game was over our next big test in London was Arsenal at Highbury. Their North Bank was going to be stormed by us and we heard tales that they were ready.

It suited us. We felt nothing could stop us and Arsenal weren't going to be a problem. West Ham were getting together now with trips, meeting at certain stations and being mob-handed. London was ours.

Arsenal heard we would come. We met up with a large mob of West Ham at Mile End station about 10 o'clock. We heard a lot were going to go Finsbury Park. Our lot went to the Arsenal station and we later joined up at the North Bank. At Liverpool Street more and more West Ham were on the station, with quite a fair size contingent of Old Bill. We arrived at Arsenal station to be met by a small mob of Arsenal boys who saw our numbers and legged it. The rest of West Ham joined up and off we went to Highbury. At the North Bank we met up with about another two hundred West Ham who got off at Holloway station and walked from the Seven Sisters Road looking for the Arsenal. We rushed the turnstiles and I jumped them again, along with many others.

Once inside we found the Arsenal boys. They weren't hard to pick out, as they were all wearing red and white. We charged them and they held for about a minute or two until more and more West Ham swarmed in on to them. We had taken the North Bank and many Arsenal legged it into the kids' enclosure and around to the Clock End. We had heard that they were well up for it and had done Tottenham many times, but with us there was no chance. They bottled. In fairness to some of their lads they stood longer than most, but sheer numbers done them – something we learnt from Man U.

The game was a draw and there had been a few scuffles on the North Bank, but Arsenal shit it. We were the kings of London. We had done nearly all London teams in the First Division and it was their turn to bring it to us. Would they?

The next few games were Sheffield United at home, Coventry away, West Brom at home and Sheffield Wednesday at home, then the Yids at Upton Park – something we looked forward to. Would they come with a mob?

The day had come – the Yids were coming and we were ready. We got to Upton Park at about ten in the morning and hung around looking for them. A few came out about 12 o'clock, mainly older fans from the glory days silly enough to wear scarves. A few were nicked as trophies, all the rage at the time with the younger lads. About 1 o'clock and still no show, so we moved off to the North Bank – and still no sign. The game started and Spurs scored, their fans went up, hundreds on the South Bank and loads in the west stand seats. They had slipped in and we weren't happy. They went straight to the away end and gobbed off. With the game nearly over and us 2–1 up loads of us left early to make our way to the South Bank. They had to get out and we would be there to meet them. A massive police presence was outside and blocked off the way for us.

We waited for them to come out only to find that most had left early and talk was that Liverpool Street station was the meet-up. There was one Yid fan in particular who was a black bloke and the so-called leader. I had seen him a couple of times and always with Old Bill around him and loads of younger kids. I reckoned he was their father figure, because with some of the stories that were going around about him, he appeared to be some kind of superman. Well if it was his crew, he didn't find enough phone boxes to change in – they had bottled it and the same at Liverpool Street station. When we arrived at Liverpool Street only a handful were around and many quickly hid their scarves. Loads bolted out of the station towards Bishopsgate police station, hoping they were safe there.

Again the day was ours; the Yids were shite. We thought they would show something against us as their fights with their most hated neighbours were legendary, but not with us.

The next few games were much the same, with only a handful of fans turning up. We played Leicester home and away over the Christmas/New Year holiday, then Man U away. I didn't go to Old Trafford that season, but West Ham had about a hundred lads up there and they got slaughtered by hundreds of Man U fans. In one way, a bit of payback. Stories of the Old Trafford trip were going around and I wasn't going to miss it next season.

I went on my first away game outside London to Molineux, the home of Wolves. We got the coach from Laceys on Barking Road. About four coaches were going from there, a mixed bunch of fans, and we quickly all changed coaches so most of us were together. The older fans going for the game were happy with this and it suited us.

At Molineux we met up with about a hundred West Ham, in all about one hundred and fifty to one hundred and eighty of us. We got into their North Bank and we were quickly sussed out. They had skinheads in the Midlands, but no pride in their dress and we stood out like dogs' balls. The Wolves fans charged us and started laying in to us. We fought back and never stood a chance. I got a lovely one in the eye and was kicked many times. The Old Bill split us up, more for our protection than theirs. We chucked coins at them, but none were coming back. We reckoned they were picking them up and keeping them and we took the piss out of them, but they were to have the last laugh. We won the game 2–1 and about ten minutes from the end their North Bank fans nearly all left. We thought they'd spat the dummy and had gone home. How wrong we were.

When you leave Molineux you go under an underpass by a cemetery or under it, and this is where they were waiting. They stormed us and beat the shit out of us; I got bruised ribs and had a few days off work. They ran us back to the coaches and there were more people going back on the coaches than came up. Most of us had got a bit of a kicking and not many did that to West Ham. Wolves did – they knew their territory and used it well.

The Wolves game taught a few of us a lesson and showed we could be beaten. If we were going to beat them we had to play them at their own tricks and have strength in numbers away from home. We came, we tried and they did us. Never underestimate your enemy away from home, no matter what town or city they are from.

Our next home game was Fulham. They were woeful at home and we weren't expecting any down to the Boleyn. We flogged them on the pitch 7–2, a great result, and – as expected – no show from the fans. We were in the next round of the cup after beating Burnley at Turf Moor. Not much happened at the game, except we won, but the next round was away to Stoke, a game I was not going to miss. Leeds away was the next league game and from what I was told nearly fuck all West Ham fans showed up, and nothing happened.

Stoke in the fourth round of the FA Cup at the Victoria ground, my second trip up north and many made it. I went with Laceys coaches and we left about eight in the morning from Barking Road. There were twenty-plus coaches going up and God knows how many went by train. Many a pub around the East End had coaches put on for a beano.

When we got to Stoke we met up with a massive mob of West Ham who had got the train or came by car. It was a great sight for any West Ham fan. We went round to the Stoke end, called the Boothen End, and we got in and a large mob of Stoke were already on the terraces, about fifteen hundred of them. Once we had the numbers we moved on and into them. They tried but had no chance. We kicked them down to the front and left of the goal. One Stoke fan had this big wooden cut-out of the FA Cup painted in silver, and that was our target. As we surged into them the bloke was hitting out with it, but was soon overpowered from a continual hail of punches and kicks. Their fake cup was ours. They tried to fight back but had no chance. Many were fighting, but Stoke were outclassed. The numbers were about even but we had a point to prove: the Boothen End was ours. We won the game 3–0 and Geoff Hurst missed a penalty at the other end – he hit the bar with Banks in goal. Toward the end the whole ground seemed to be singing 'Bubbles'. There were West Ham all over the ground; it sounded like a home game. What a day – we did Stoke, took their end and won the game. I have to say Stoke at least had a go, not like some London teams such as Chelsea and the Yids. They had a bit of bottle. They tried to come back at us at the coaches but were run again, and that was the last of them we saw. By this time Old Bill had moved in and were pissed off that the cockney boys had turned Stoke over – not many did that and they weren't ready for us. They held up the coaches for nearly two hours and when we finally got off, our first stop was an off-licence to party on the coaches; a good whip-round for the driver saw him OK. It was nearly 12 o'clock by the time we got back to Barking Road, but who cared? Another result under our belts. As fate would have it, Stoke in the league was our next game away and we lost. Hardly any West Ham fans went up and a few who did were telling us they had a massive police presence there this time. They were ready, but we never showed.

Next away game was the Dell at Southampton – the scummers, as they are known. A couple of hours by train and about three hundred skinheads made the trip up. We took their end with hardly a blow being struck. Where were they? Some individual fights were breaking out with some of their fans, but were soon finished. Southampton was one of the shittiest grounds I have been to. It's a funny shape, with one end like a wedge-shape stand. The fans had no bottle. Some Portsmouth fans who hated the Saints fans and wanted some action told us that they would be waiting for us and came along to join in and kick a few Saints fans' heads in. They told us it was normal for them: all mouth and no show. We drew the game 0–0, a boring affair and all round a shit day out. On the train back, some of us started throwing the seats out of the train and anything else we could. A few windows were broken and the communication cord was pulled off once. Many fans were taking their frustrations out on the train. Not surprisingly, the buffet bar closed.

The papers next day carried headlines along the lines of 'Football animals destroy train'. In fact, we reckon we gave it a face-lift. The seats were fucked and needed replacing and the whole service of the train was fucked. If they had kept the bar open, maybe it would not have happened, but they treated us like hooligans and we responded. Simple.

Chelsea at home was next and we reckon they would come in force after the Stamford Bridge incident. They showed but only when tucked up safely on the South Bank. They did a Spurs and sneaked in – the same gobby lot who were well 'ard with Old Bill around. What a bunch of wankers. Lots of Chelsea fans were National Front members as well. I know West Ham had them too, but it was never shown at games as we had quite a lot of blacks, most born in the East End – second-

or third-generation Englishmen – and we had a black player. Also, Asians were not tolerated at West Ham, which makes me wonder why they chose to settle down there, as they had a rough time of it during those first years of the skinhead. Chelsea scored and soon we found out how many there were on the South Bank. About half of it was Chelsea, the whole centre bit. They had slipped in well, but they had to get out yet. We lost the game 1– 0 and most of us left early. A big mob left to go to Mile End to wait for them. We left the North Bank through the side which came out behind the school, near the main entrance, and went round to the South Bank, via Green Street. When we turned the corner, a large mob chanting, 'CHELSEA!' was coming towards us. They soon stopped singing when they heard the 'UNITED!' chant go up! We ran straight at them and loads turned and ran but were blocked by Old Bill behind them, who were expecting us to come from the other way. We clashed and punches and kicks were being exchanged. I had about three Chelsea laying into me and a couple of West Ham jumped in, then more. We were killing them. They tried to run but could not. The Old Bill were trying to stop it and then more West Ham came around. Chelsea was ours and they were gonna pay. I saw one Chelsea lad waving a razor blade at us. It was held in a matchbox. No one got cut, but he got a kicking. The police finally got us apart but we wanted more: these were the Chelsea boys and we wanted to smash them all over the place. With an escort and more and more Old Bill turning up to protect Chelsea, they started gobbing off. Only moments before most had tried to run from us. They got to Upton Park station and the gates were closed to allow Chelsea to get away. Little did they know there was a big mob at Mile End waiting for them.

I was not at Mile End, but some of my mates were. They steamed them and rode the train with them, some all the way to Victoria, on their manor. We had done them good and proper. Chelsea had some lads who stood and fought, but many shit it and were only good gobbing off at home. Once again we had proved we were the kings of London. Only Arsenal to go at Upton Park and that was the following week.

Arsenal came down much the same way the Yids did and sneaked in and on to the South Bank. We had heard they were coming with a large mob to claim our North Bank, but they never showed. They had a lot in the South Bank and the game was a draw. We tried our attack again like we did to Chelsea but the Old Bill were well clued up this time and we got nowhere near them. Most West Ham left for the station to try and get them on the way. It's only a short walk to the station, five to six hundred yards at the most, but it can be a long walk for an away fan. We got the tube up to Liverpool Street, as we knew many Arsenal would change there and waited. Mobs of four and five came through, some singing, but the songs soon stopped when we showed. We were about fifty strong and growing and we were having a go at any mob of Gooners that came through. One mob had a go back and I got hit with a waste-paper bin and had stitches in the head. They got a good kicking for their trouble. I don't think they meant to use weapons, I think they were just scared and trying to protect themselves. We had done Arsenal home and away and we let them know it. We were getting more and more cunning every game and some of the methods we used totally fucked the other side, Old Bill included.

Our next game was Newcastle. Nothing happened that game. There was the odd punch-up, but not many Geordies turned up and those who did were based in London. In fact, we had a couple of Geordie lads that ran with us on game days. Home again four games in a row. Notts Forest – not many fans turned up, only older ones, and we weren't interested in them. Next away game was Man City. I did not go, but I am told the Kippax boys made about two hundred West Ham welcome. No big trouble. Some United fans wanted a go outside but Man City chased them off with the West Ham mob. In being fair to Man U, I'm told that there was only about two or three hundred there and as their team was away that day West Ham was their target. Wrong target.

The day we played away to Man City, about thirty of us went across to White Hart Lane. Chelsea were playing there and we knew these two sets of fans hated each other. We left Liverpool Street station about 12 o'clock to make our way to Tottenham's ground. We had not seen any sign of the fans from either side. We took a walk up towards the ground and we had a pint in the Corner Pin pub. This was a Yid pub and if we were going to have any bother it would kick off here. We got some strange looks as people in the pub were trying to suss us out. We heard remarks about how shite Chelsea were and so on. We did not bite. Who cared? They never knew we were West Ham and I think it was just as well. These were 'the boys', not kids, and if it was going off we would have had a fight on our hands. My mate wanted us to sing 'Bubbles'. We were all up for it when a massive Chelsea mob came past chanting, 'CHELSEA!' There were thousands of them, and they kept filing past. The Yid fans who had been gobbing off before hid their colours and tried to look like they weren't there. Some of the Chelsea came into the pub, turned over a few tables and did a bit of swearing, but Old Bill were right on top of it. Typical Chelsea, I thought: make a noise when they know the Old Bill's around to stop it.

We finished our drinks and tailed on to the Chelsea lot. They walked right around the ground chanting, 'CHELSEA!' and 'YIDO!', letting the Totts know they were there. All the time the Old Bill had them under control. We talked about this mob and wondered where they were at Upton Park when they played us. We went into the Paxton End and made our way to the bar under the main stand to see what was happening. No sooner had we got a drink than a massive mob of Yids came charging through, running, screaming for Chelsea blood. They ran to the Paxton and seemed to stop, I don't know why, there was only a couple of Old Bill there. Most of them were on or down the front of the Paxton. They could have stormed on and had a go at Chelsea and Chelsea could have done the same. It was like a Mexican stand-off, both sets of fans chanting at each other, but that was all. We were disgusted. Had one of them steamed in we would have been with them, Spurs or Chelsea, but they both shit. Near the kick-off, on the Park Lane some fighting broke out and that was us. The Yids had sussed us out. By rights we should have been killed but as the crowd swayed, more Chelsea joined in. It was what they wanted – someone to start it, and it took West Ham to do it.

I saw the so-called Yid leader with his little mob around him. He looked smug and safe. I remember it well. He had his arm in plaster and was gobbing off something fierce. We met a few Chelsea that day and they never impressed us. We were not supermen, just West Ham and we stuck by each other. The fact that we went all the way to White Hart Lane, drank in their pubs and bars and weren't sussed out till we kicked off the trouble in the Park Lane was a great result for us. Chelsea fans were all scarved up as well as the Yids fans – easy targets, home or away. We had proved we could get on to their manor, under their noses and it wasn't even our fixture. I thought Chelsea had some bottle against West Ham but they had no hope, home or away. I thought they would put on a show with the Yids with the mob they brought to the game, and vice versa. Both sets of fans went way down in my esteem and to this day, when I think of those days, I laugh when people tell me Chelsea are a top firm.

With only a handful of games to go, our next game was Nottingham Forest away. I did not go, but heard that nothing much went on. Then we had the Scousers at home. Liverpool were coming to town; surely they would bring some lads down?

Liverpool had some boys around and many were much older than us. A few got a bit of a slapping in the Boleyn for taking the piss. Most thought we were like Alf Garnett in the then popular TV show *Till Death Us Do Part*. Many were in London working and came out for the game. We caught a couple outside Casseratis, a cafe next to the Boleyn. The tea was bad and the food not much better, but many a West Ham player used it on non-game days. Still, it was better than some of the food being sold by some vendors. Wimpy bars were gourmet meals compared to that lot and the stuff inside the ground wasn't much better. And it wasn't just our ground. If you wanted a good pie and mash or fish and chips nearby, the Queens market was the place.

Anyway, the Scousers got a bit of a slapping and had their scarves taken as trophies. I don't know why scarves were taken. We would not wear our own colours, let alone a nicked one. Many were burned or just chucked; some fans kept them as a sort of trophy and built up a collection.

The Liverpool fans to us were gobby arseholes. The way they talked and moaned about the beer, the food and anything else. It was 'great' in Merseyside. If it was so good, fucking stay there – simple. Based on trips to Liverpool later on I reckoned I was lucky: being working class in the East End was a luxury compared to that shithole. Newcastle was much the same but at least the people were real, not like these cunts. We viewed them as thieving half-Irish gypos and we weren't far wrong. If The Beatles hadn't formed, not many people would know where it was, simple as that.

They had a mob down of about two hundred mixed. The Scouse women were more up for it than the men. Not many real big offs but a fair few. The infamous Liverpool kiss was handed out to many a Scouse to show them that if you come to West Ham, be prepared. We beat them 1–0 and nothing much happened after the game. A few lads went up to Euston looking for more, but many Scousers had their colours well hidden by now.

Next game was Sunderland and they had a fair mob down. Not really skins, but genuine fans. Most came by coach and apart from a couple of idiots who got a slap from both sets of fans, they were left untouched. The game ended in a draw and that was basically it with the Mackems. The next away game was my last away one for the season: Sheffield United at Bramall Lane. We went by Laceys coaches and left about 8 a.m. for the boring, slow journey up to Yorkshire. When we stopped on the way for something to eat we bumped into a mob of greasers at a café. They were well up for it until they found out we were West Ham and then they just backed down. We had the numbers but they were a lot older. It seems we were getting a bit of a name. That alone was a result for us, but not long after that things changed.

We went straight on to the Shoreham End at Bramall Lane. It was a cricket ground then and their main end had these huge steps on it, twice as big as West Ham. Great for watching the game. There was about fifty of us and the song 'YOU CAN STICK YOUR KNIFE AND FORKS UP YER ARSE' was going up by us. We were taking liberties and no one troubled us till the game was over. We all started to leave. Behind their end there was a sort of hill that the terraces were built on. Those who have been there will know what I mean. The toilets were there and this was where it kicked off. A mob of about one hundred and fifty Blades lads had a pop at us and we fought back but they ran us down the hill, where another smaller mob was waiting. We just ran straight into them, kicking and punching, but there were too many. They were laying into us. We fought back but they had the day. Not long before this they had knocked us out of the FA Cup at home and we wanted revenge, but we never got it off the field. They had fuck all fans at Upton Park and took a liberty at their manor. We weren't going to forget easily. We would not fall into that trap again. Back on the coaches we compared injuries. The worst was lots of bruised legs and backs where they were punching or kicking into us. My mate had a split lip, self-inflicted from a head butt that went wrong. We were surprised at our injuries. A few lads had said the Old Bill were there and simply turned their backs. The coaches were left untouched and things just went sterile. If that had been at West Ham, they would have gone home with more than a couple of sore bruised legs. Just for the record, we beat them 2–1. Geoff Hurst, the king, scored twice.

Next game was away at WBA. I never went and from what I heard nothing much happened, except we won 3–1. Then the last two games at home. Coventry was first and the most exciting thing that happened was the game was a 0–0 draw. Then came Everton.

Everton brought a fair few down. Lots of mixed support.

There were a few lads down and we noticed they were not wearing scarves. Word had got out. The Toffees were different from their cousins, whom they hated. Not so gobby and well up for a laugh and a fight. There were a few stand-offs, mainly with the younger lot and the odd missile being thrown, but really no big scenes. The season was over – Everton went on to the FA Cup Final and lost to West Bromwich Albion. Out of the two sets of fans from Liverpool, it was Everton who had our respect.

The season over, we reflected on a few things for next season. Skins were still the thing, but the 'suede' look was now in – it just meant having a little hair on your head. We were kings of London and had proved it. Only Millwall were capable of having a go and as they weren't in the same division as us, we never really found out. We had had a couple of run-ins with some of them and most times we came out in front, though not by much. We had given out many a hiding and received a few back away from home. All par for the course. After the train incident coming back from Southampton, Chelsea fans wrecked a few trains. They wanted the attention and they were getting it. They had a big mob but no bottle, as I had seen at their ground. Fulham weren't even worth mentioning. Arsenal had a go and the Yids were about the same as Chelsea: all mouth. Some of the stories we heard that Chelsea did this or the Spurs did that – where was it when we played them?

Out of the northern mobs only Man U had the numbers and after the '67 affair, which taught us loads, they weren't anywhere near as good. Most of their fans were based all over and their main lads were rarely seen at Upton Park. As I've said, Man City were a good bunch of lads and Everton weren't bad either. We hated them, but not as much as their red cousins.

Wolves were well up for it, but only at their ground, as were Sheffield United. It was all over for another season. We finished twelfth in the League, got knocked out of the FA Cup in the fifth round and had a bad loss in the League Cup to lower-league side Huddersfield. A few supporters tried taking the piss about this but it soon stopped. On the terraces we were number one, so it was on to the next season.

CHAPTER 3

1968–69

THE NEW SEASON was here and many of us planned to go by train to Newcastle, untried territory and first game of the new season. About two hundred of us made the trip up to St James' Park. We hadn't had any trouble with the Geordies at West Ham and for many of us this was our first trip up this far. At Carlisle loads of Old Bill got on the train, about six in every carriage, and stayed with us to Newcastle. At the station there were loads more Old Bill around. We thought it was for us but it was to protect us from the many Geordies that were waiting. A mob of five to six hundred were there. Scattered about were more and they were up for it. We had never expected this and we had an escort to the ground. In the ground we were put into the uncovered side stand. Their lads were on the Leazes End and taking the piss something shocking. If we were ever going to get a hiding we had come to the right place.

Nothing much happened inside the ground and the police

had us where they wanted us. The game was a draw. In one way I was glad – had we beat them, I think we would have been killed. If we were going to make an impact on the Geordies we would need a massive mob and then some. At home they were untouchable and most of their lads were men from the docks and shipyards, not kids or skinheads – although they had a quite a few. The clothes and dress sense wasn't the same. You could spot a Geordie skin a mile away, as many of the northerners were all the same: scruffy cunts, no pride in their appearance, not like the London boys. We got out of there in one piece with only the odd bottle being lobbed at us outside the grounds, but the Old Bill had things under control. I believe it is still the same up there to this day.

We had Stoke midweek away and then a home game with Nottingham Forest. They brought a fair mob down of mixed fans on the coaches and about a hundred came out of the tube station. Most of us by this time were waiting outside the Queens pub next to the market and had a drink, or just waited to see who was coming out of the station.

They came out about 1 p.m., singing and cheering, most wearing red and white, showing us who the new boys in town were. When they came down the small hill from the station some went straight into the pub for a drink. Wrong move! The others just tried to get past. I think one of their fans woke up because some started crossing the road in front of cars, not even looking. It was on – these were skinheads and we wanted them. I saw one West Ham come charging up and hit this Forest fan so hard he went straight down. That was the signal. Some tried fighting but were soon giving up. Their fans were holding heads spilt open by bottles; some crouched on the ground like snails, taking a kicking. The blokes in the pub were being thrown out, holding their heads as blood flowed from their faces. Many ran and left their mates there. The Old Bill moved in and things calmed down, but Forest had got a slapping. They came down being cocky and went away with their tails between their legs. We done them on the pitch as well, 1 – 0 – a double result.

We had Everton next in a midweek game and got done 4 – 1; nothing happened there. Next away trip was Coventry, again a new manor for me, and we were told that they normally didn't cause any trouble. We hoped to change that.

Highfield Road must have been another one of the worst grounds in England at that time. It was about twenty minutes' walk, maybe more, from the station. We walked up through the town. There was a lot of new building going on.

Hitler had flattened this place during the war, and the joke was: why rebuild it? This lot looked like they were used to living in ruins; no wonder they let Hitler bomb it down. Up to the ground and on the corner outside their end was a pub, the Mercer Arms I think. About twenty of us went in for a drink and to suss out what was going on. It was like stepping back in time. We were sussed as London boys from the off and the landlord told us that he wouldn't have trouble in his pub. We all laughed – as if he could have stopped us! More West Ham came in and many locals left; only a few old blokes stayed. That publican did well out of us: forty-odd lads, all having three to four pints each, not bad for a couple of hours or so.

Kick-off came and we went on to their end and joined up. We gave a 'UNITED!' chant and let them know we were there. Nothing happened, just a 'CITY!' chant back. We were shocked – we had walked into their pub, on to their end and a punch had not been thrown. We started looking for them and the Old Bill were grabbing some of us and chucking us out. The Coventry coppers are some of the worst I have ever dealt with. Dirty bastards, they kicked and punched like they were the hooligans. You did not get to walk around the pitch here. Straight out the back, down the steps and through the gates with a few choice hits and kicks on the way. The funny thing was if you paid again you could come back in through another turnstile. One lad I know got done four times. I think they gave up on him. I got slung out once and came straight back in. We reckoned they were having a bet to see who could throw out the most. We never saw any City fans go, just the away ones.

The game over, we left for the station. We went down this long hill from the ground back towards the shopping centre. We stopped about halfway down when we realised a mob of Coventry were running behind us. We turned and ran at them and they legged it. Old Bill on horses were trying to get us back to the station. They weren't up for it and we got back to the station without seeing any more of them. The highlight of the day was being chucked out of the ground and the only injuries some of us had were dished out by the Old Bill as we were thrown out of the ground. Mainly bruised ankles and corked thighs and sore necks – they knew where to hit. The train copped a bit of a hiding, mainly the odd seat going out of a smashed window.

The next game was against Burnley at home, a midweek game. Nothing happened and we won 5 – 0. Their fans were few and far between and, as they wear the same colour as us, would have been hard to find. West Brom away was next. I did not go and from what was said not much went off. A small mob of West Ham went and Old Bill rode the train all the way. Calls were going out now about trains getting wrecked. We had damaged a few but Chelsea fans had also smashed some up and had brought a bit of attention to themselves. The public was shocked at the way the youth of England was going.

Man U away was our next game and I got the train up with about a hundred-odd fans, not enough if we were going to take on Man U on their own manor. As the train pulled in to Manchester we decided to have a look around their Piccadilly and maybe have drink. Drinking was not a big thing at West Ham and normally we would not touch it on away games, maybe a pint or so. That was so you had a glass or bottle to use. We figured we would stick together, about twenty of us. We would keep our heads down and see what came along. We had no hope with the amount of lads we had. We talked about what part of the ground we would go to and, as I hadn't been to Old Trafford before, I just followed on. We went on to the Scoreboard End and met up with the rest of the lads. Some had a bit of a go in a couple of pubs near the ground. A couple of coaches made the trip, mainly older fans. I saw my first sight of the legendary Stretford End – it was a big end but half of it was seats, something you never saw on the telly. On match day the noise of the place was loud and we could hardly be heard when we chanted. A few Man City boys linked up with us and were cheering on West Ham. The game was a draw and when Hurst scored a hail of coins came raining down on us from all over. I got hit by a couple and had some nice lumps on my head. I would have to get a trilby, something which some of the lads were already wearing.

After the game we made our way back to Piccadilly. We

walked right through a massive mob of Man U and they never sussed us, dumb fuckers. We were nearly at the station when some Man U bloke asked the time. When my mate told him and he heard the accent it was on. About three hundred of them steamed in and we got a good going-over. We got a few back, but this was their turf and they had the numbers. I think they were surprised we fought back as they stood off for a while and the Old Bill moved in. I was glad to see them for once and as usual Man U started gobbing off. I dunno why they do it. Man U and Chelsea are famous for it. They had a bit of a result, it was their day, so why gob off? We got escorted back to the platform and the Old Bill stayed till the train left. We met up with the other lads. A couple had got turned over but nothing serious, mainly bruises and the odd black eye. We did not seem to have much wrong with us, considering the size of the mob and the way they steamed in. Maybe it was because we fought back, I don't know. I had only a few bruises; my mate had a cut lip. The worst of the lot was a black eye, and a real good one. We thought if that was Man U, then if we had a decent mob we would get a result there easy. I couldn't see the Stretford End being taken, mainly because it was full three to four hours before the game. There were enough Man U around to get a result if we came with a big enough mob, all together up there. Next trip would be different. We talked about how they sussed us by asking the time. It wouldn't happen again. We reckoned if a few of us had Man U scarves on, we would have a right piss-take.

The Yids at home were next and as expected they sneaked on to the South Bank, a fair mob with loads of older fans in the seats. The game was a 2–2 draw and not much went off. The Old Bill had the South Bank sewn up and we could not get in there; many left without being touched. A few got a seeing-to at the market, though. They were wearing scarves and that was their mistake. A load of us went on to Liverpool Street station to see if we could pick up some there. We went into the downstairs buffet bar, the one near the steps that lead out to Middlesex Street (Petticoat Lane) and had a pint. Some had a walk around; others just milled about on the platform. We had got our beers when my mate was hit with a glass in the face. We never saw it coming. About fifteen Yid fans were in there and as there were only about eight of us they had a go, and a good one. When it kicked off more West Ham came in to help and the Yids were trying to block the door while the rest were laying into us. They had the surprise and the numbers and our trick of not wearing colours backfired on us. There was also the fact that we were very cocky and weren't expecting them. They hit us, and good. We fought back and were well up for it. I got a massive whack across the back with a chair and went down, then got a fair kicking and managed to get up. A couple of my mates got some as well, mainly hit by bottles and kicked when down. Finally the others got in and the Yids bolted right though them. The other West Ham lads thought we were the Yids as we had been done and it was West Ham escaping. They had a result – not a big one, but still a result. We could not believe it. We were never so cocky again. I had a few days off work as my back was hurting like fuck and I had bruised ribs again, which I reckon is worse than broken ones. Any sudden movement and you know all about it. And laying bricks at work wasn't going to help.

The following week we had another big one at Chelsea. I wasn't going to go and I was still sore but my mates talked me into it and said as it was only Chelsea, I'd be all right. I pointed out the previous week it was only the Yids but they had had a result, if only a small one. But my mate, who was hit with a glass and had twelve stitches put in his forehead, said he was going, so fuck it, why not.

We decided to get to Fulham Broadway early and have a look around North End Road for some Chelsea and, if we got lost, meet up at the Rising Sun. At the back entrance to the Shed, on North End Road, there are loads of pubs and a market which was open on Saturdays. Most were closing up as it was sort of half day and a London derby. I reckon most were going to the game. There was supposed to be a gang of lads called the North End Road Gang from the council estates near Olympia. If there was, then they never showed that they existed because we walked right up to West Kensington station and had no trouble. We stopped in the pubs, grabbing a light ale as the bottle always came in handy, and after a few drinks we headed off. We came across a few lads with scarves but they legged it as soon as they saw us. We were about forty strong and could not be missed. We grabbed some tomatoes at one fruit and veg stall – I think we paid for two and walked away with loads. If there was no Chelsea we would at least have some fun and chuck a few tomatoes at those few who saw us and legged it.

We made our way back to the ground and went straight into the Rising Sun. As soon as we got in, glasses were being chucked at us. At first Chelsea thought it was only a few West Ham but then realised we were a bigger mob than they sussed. We steamed in, bottles and glasses going all over. There were about thirty of them and one caught me with a boot in the stomach. I was fucked and it hurt like fuck. I still had bruised ribs from the Yids and I went mental, as did most of our lot. More lads came in and we thought we were fucked as it was too early for West Ham yet, but it was indeed more West Ham. The place filled and loads of the Chelsea jumped the bar and escaped that way. Many got a kicking – one was picked up and thrown through a window of the pub. He got up and legged it – unhurt it seemed, or he wasn't hanging around to show it.

We heard Chelsea chants, looked across to the Shed and there was the Chelsea mob, chanting and urging us on at the top of the steps that led to the terraces. It was funny, because at that moment a massive mob of West Ham turned up and they just kept coming, thousands of them, all singing, 'UNITED!' and 'Bubbles'. It was great to watch the Chelsea lads, who had been baiting us earlier, legging it into their corner. It was like a vanishing act. West Ham piled in and kept coming. With most in the ground, we went in to find Chelsea right up in their corner bit once again, gobbing off at us. The rest of the Shed was West Ham and a massive police presence made sure we would not get at them. Coins were being chucked, as well as batteries and – a new one – golf balls, which quickly went back and set us off more. Old Bill were grabbing loads of West Ham for chucking things at Chelsea, but hardly any Chelsea were getting tugged. The exchange of missiles went on all game and many a West Ham fan got whacked with a coin or golf ball. I saw a light bulb bounce over me and my mate and smash on the back of a bloke's neck. If that had been in the face he would have been cut really badly. He went mental and rushed towards the Chelsea. This started a massive charge towards them. The Old Bill held us back and cleared an area between us.

We got talking to some lads – they had come from Harold

Hill and firms from Collier Row and all those new areas that people were moved to from the East End. West Ham's hooligan following was growing. Many wanted to be a part of the football scene and West Ham were kings in London, so for many the choice was easy when coupled with their East End links.

Chelsea scored first and their celebrations were met with a hail of coins and whatever else we could chuck. Whatever they chucked, twice as much went back. Bobby Tambling scored, I think, and we looked like we were going down. Then, not long from time, Martin Peters brought us level with a headed goal. We went mad and the missiles rained down. We did not care. We all started a 'Knees Up Mother Brown', though as jumping up and down hurt my ribs, I just watched. I will never forget that. I knew we had a massive mob but I did not know how big it was until they all started singing and jumping up and down.

The game finished in a draw. The Old Bill tried to keep us back, but gave up and we got out and went looking for Chelsea. Most of their Shed mob waited back with the Old Bill and would not come out. We all went round to the tube station and many went on to Victoria to carry on. I did not go as I was in no state to fight and made my way back to Mile End with thousands of other West Ham lads. Chelsea had shit again and I found out West Ham had walked all over Chelsea's manor at Victoria and no one showed. Again, all gob inside the ground with Old Bill to protect them but against West Ham they bottled. But we did have some numbers that day: Chelsea's gate of 58,000 was their highest of the season.

I missed the next three games and gave my ribs a rest. I had been warned at work that I was losing too much time. I had only lost my sick time and a few days and had a doctor's note to cover me. It wasn't bullshit and trying to lay bricks with bruised ribs was painful.

Sheffield Wednesday was next, but I never went to that game. They had been promoted, while their neighbours had gone down. I did not hear of any trouble, as not many of their fans showed. I missed the Burnley away as well, but from what I heard nothing happened there. The next away game was Leeds and I was up for that. I was missing the football and I had never been to Leeds. We debated whether to go by coach or train. It was decided to go by coach as the station at Leeds was a fair walk from the ground and if we weren't mobbed up it was dodgy ground to be on. The season before about a dozen of us went across to Fulham to watch them play Leeds. Their fans, about three hundred, ran the small mob of Fulham and they even won the game 5 – 0. Alan Clarke had just signed with Leeds from Fulham and he scored a couple, if my memory serves me. The main thing was the Leeds fans bragging that London was theirs. They were fucking joking.

Leeds never brought many to Upton Park. What few did come you never saw until kick-off, and they were on the South Bank. So they were new ground for a lot of us. We had no hope of getting on their Spion Kop as the Old Bill sussed us out from the start and with the small mob we had it was probably just as well. Leeds had a fair mob, but they were the scruffiest bunch of blokes we had ever seen and it wasn't hard to spot us. On the away end at Leeds we had a few scuffles, nothing major, more like the locals getting upset because we were taking the piss out of the way they talked. We lost the game 2 – 0 and we left early to go back to the coaches, only to find a big mob of Leeds waiting for us and not many Old Bill around – we were on a hiding for sure. They lobbed bottles and stones at us and when we chucked some back they seemed to lose interest. Probably lucky for us, as we were well outnumbered. Still, to this day I wonder why they never steamed in. They had us at their mercy, hardly any Old Bill around, it was perfect for a ruck. Had it been vice versa we would have killed them.

The next game was Sunderland at home. They had fuck all fans down and we beat them 8 – 0. The highlight was Hurst scoring six, one with his hand at the South Bank end. Even Bobby Moore scored, a bit of a rarity, while Brooking scored the other. No action here but the Yids were at home to Man U that day and there was bound to be some fun at Liverpool Street station.

We went up to Liverpool Street about twenty-handed and well chuffed at our result. When we got off at Liverpool Street on the Central line we walked up a long tunnel to the British Rail platforms. It was here that about fifty Man U came down, singing and carrying on. They walked straight into us and never realised who we were until they were halfway past us. Then it was on.

Nothing could be chucked in that area and it was boots and all. Many legged it; some stood but had no chance. We were jumping over Man U fans cowering on the ground, covering their heads as we laid the boot in. Another dozen or so lads came up. They were West Ham and had the same idea as us. They all joined in and it was great – no Old Bill around and they were trapped by us. That went on for what seemed for ever. When we had finished, about seven or eight were on the ground screaming and crying, and many had legged it back up to the platforms. We just left them there and ran up to the main area, just as about half a dozen Old Bill were coming down. Some Man U fans were pointing at us, so we legged it out of the station and across to Dirty Dicks, a pub right next door to the police station. We kept our heads down there for an hour or so and moved off back to the station. We came across a mob of Yids, slagging off some other West Ham lads so we chanted, 'UNITED!' and ran at them. The West Ham mob thought we were Man U, as did the Spurs, and both lots legged it until we shouted at the West Ham. Then they stopped and turned and joined in chasing the Yids. Most jumped the platform gates and got on to the platform. The Old Bill swarmed in and it was over. We headed off and, after the hiding we had already given them in the tunnel, we thought we would leave Euston out as Old Bill were everywhere. The Sunday papers the next day carried on about how a massive gang fight was at the station and related that some dozen or so fans from both sides were taken to Guys Hospital. We wondered what we missed and then we worked out that it was us. Massive gangs, what a load of bollocks hyped up by the press. At most there had been about twenty-five West Ham and fifty-odd Man U, and most of them legged it and went for the police. From that day on we never believed what the press wrote, and to this day I still don't.

Next game away was at Arsenal – the London Irish as some called them. The main West Ham mob met up at Mile End at eleven o'clock and two or three trains later they were all away and planned to meet up outside Arsenal station or the North Bank. We went to Finsbury Park, about thirty of us, to have a look around on their manor. We went on to the Drayton Park Road and went into a pub known to be full of Arsenal fans, the Drayton Park Arms. It was full of Arsenal, mainly older men having a quiet drink before the game. No luck there so we made our way back to Highbury. No one challenged us and we went on to the North Bank to find we had missed most of the action. Arsenal had got on early; they were going to hold their North Bank but were overwhelmed by the sheer numbers of West Ham. We took the North Bank, Highbury again and the Arsenal were pushed down to the front, to the left as you look towards the Clock End. We took the piss all game and not once did Arsenal try and take it back. We were the kings again. We had heard so often that Arsenal had a tidy firm and were well up for it, but we never found them. The game was a drab 0–0 draw and the best laugh of the day was when we all ran back to Arsenal station and the Old Bill tried to keep us in order. The odd window went in and we went straight on to the station. Arsenal had been done again at home and we had proved there was no stopping us now.

QPR at home was next, and the best thing that happened that day was that we won 4–3. It was said that if you were a QPR fan then you carried a handbag. They had been promoted that year and only the older fans turned up – and most of them were in the seats. So, a non-event, but plans were already being made for the next away trip and how we were going to handle it.

Wolves away next and we owed them from the year before. On the train up we told many how they got us last time and made plans to get them back. We took about four hundred up by train and coach. No drink on the train, but that did not worry us – we could drink later. A few Old Bill were travelling with us due to Chelsea smashing a train up on one of their away trips. The press called for cattle cars to be used to take fans to away games and really gave us a slagging in the press. Not long before we had been headline stuff after the Liverpool Street station incident. Anything to sell papers, we reckoned.

As we made our way to Wolves' ground we never saw any of their lads. They were on their end, the North Bank. We moved on and tried to take it. A few scuffles broke out and Old Bill kept us apart. We knew what their plan was and about fifteen minutes from the end loads of West Ham moved off while the rest stayed, to come in behind them at their underpass ambush. We lost 2 – 0 and they seemed to stay a bit longer until, as expected, they moved off without knowing we were following them. When they walked into the underpass the first lot of West Ham steamed in at them. We came in from behind and it was on. They didn't know what was going on; they were fucked and many Wolves fans were trying to leg it out. We kept kicking and punching and soon they legged it. We nearly steamed the other West Ham by mistake, that's how quickly they bolted. A few were crouching on the ground screaming and we linked up and went after them. The Old Bill were caught out – this had never happened before and we totally surprised them. We chased them for a short while but they weren't up for it. Their little trick had backfired on them and they were fucked.

Back on the train we compared notes. Some lads had bought those big 'party seven' cans of bitter and we played up a bit. Only a couple of Old Bill were on the train and they were walking up and down the different carriages. 'Harry Roberts is our friend' was sung every time they stuck their heads in our carriage. A few lads were comparing injuries – nothing much, the odd bruise and my mate had got a nice shiner again. He was unlucky – always getting one in the eye

To the skinhead bovver boys, the look was as important as the team.

A West Ham skinhead displays his loyalty.

Above: Skinhead gangs started to appear in many places around 1968-9. The one in our area was called the Mile End Mafia.

Below: Doc Martens and drainpipes: the uniform of the bovver boys, long before the casuals ruled the terraces.

Above: The boys are back in town: bovver boys head to a match.

Below: Fans only really started to travel after the introduction of the football specials.

On match days Old Bill would make you remove your laces and
sometimes do a stamp check for steel toecaps.

Top left: Blood on the terraces. An injured spectator is carried away by two policemen during the battle for the north bank after Manchester United claim the league title at Upton Park in 1967.

Top right: A fan in a headlock being led from the pitch.

Below: Crowd trouble between the same team's supporters breaks out after a pitch invasion halted the play for 18 minutes at Upton Park during the 1975 season.

Today it is B for Beckham. Back then it was B for Best, alongside our own legends Hurst, Peters and Moore. Affairs were just as bruising on the pitch whenever champions United came to town.

In 1975, the Hammers hooligans were condemned in the local press. The model pictured posed with a baseball bat used on the terraces.

– and we all took the piss out of him and told him to close his eyes in future. We had come to Wolves and had pulled their favourite stunt on them and it had worked. We had done them. I hear that to this day they still pull that one on unsuspecting fans and get away with it. They never banked on West Ham, though.

Leicester at home and all I saw of their fans was a couple of lads who got chased into the yard area of the flats at the back of the Chicken Run. Both got a good kicking, mainly by younger lads after scarves. We won 4–0 and it was another non-event. Some were going up to the stations to look for northerners; I didn't bother and heard nothing about it.

The next game was Ipswich away, newly promoted and referred to by our lot as 'the end of the road'. We took a huge firm up there and took the piss all day. We took their end and sang 'Keep right on till the end of the road'. They hated it but only a few were up for it, squaring up like boxers. They were soon rushed by willing West Ham and had the shit beaten out of them. The Old Bill kept them safe and we had a laugh. This one copper was saying we were the worst he had seen at Portman Road. He said he thought Millwall were bad but now, having seen us, he was shocked.

The game was a draw – 2–2 – and we got back to the station. Then, on the train, we carried on – windows were smashed in and seats thrown out. There was one window that nearly all of us had a go at but would not break, despite flying kicks and people swinging off the overhead racks to hit it. This one West Ham came screaming through with the sink ripped out of the toilet and hurled it at the window. It smashed and we all cheered. Near Liverpool Street station the cord was pulled and we stopped. Soon under way again, we got taken to the station and there was a massive police presence waiting. Many jumped off as the train slowed and we all jumped out before it stopped and ran the gates. The Old Bill never stopped us. A few of us were grabbed but we nearly all got out and into the tube. The next day's papers carried pictures of the train: eight out of ten carriages had been damaged in an orgy of destruction. It was totally wrecked and calls went out again for cattle cars as football specials. Chelsea had done a few trains that year and the next season saw the introduction of the 'football special'. Stories were going around that the Old Bill had photos of some who did damage to the train and some people kept their heads down for a while, mainly staying at home games or going by coach to away ones.

Man City at home next and once again not much trouble. They had a fair mob down and went on to win the league that year. They never tried the North Bank and went on to the South Bank. I have never seen much aggro between the two sets of fans. I don't know if it was because we both hated Man U or what, but there was a bit of respect there. We beat them 2 – 1 in a great match. They had some good players at the time, like Summerbee.

Liverpool away next and our lot never went – not many West Ham did, only a few coaches and then mainly the older fans. We heard nothing and all agreed you would need a tidy firm up there as they had great home support. But Everton were the boys to deal with.

Leeds at home next and only a few coaches and stragglers on the train showed. It was getting hard at West Ham to find the other fans. Many had learned not to wear colours; the short walk from the station to the ground could be scary for an away fan. If you changed at Mile End and were unlucky enough to get a train with a load of West Ham then your best bet was to get off or bury your head in a paper. And God help you if you were wearing a scarf.

The game was a draw, 1–1. I didn't go to the next two away games at Sunderland and Southampton. We were keeping our heads down and we didn't fancy going by coach to either place. The third round of the FA Cup was here and we had drawn Bristol City. We were surprised that they brought quite a few lads down, all carrot crunchers. A day out in London was their big event. We never expected them and they went on to the South Bank and never even tried for the North Bank. It seemed word had spread – don't try the North Bank, stay off or you will pay.

I was in the Boleyn having a pint with some mates, when about a dozen or so came in – colours, the lot. They must have come off the coaches, as they would not have got that far down Green Street like that otherwise. It wasn't long before they were taking the piss out of the beer and the East End. Many ignored this and gave them some mouth back, like 'Oooohhhaaaarggg' – taking the piss out of their accent – and calling them wurzels. One lad said to give them all a length of straw to chew as the beer was going to their heads. We all started laughing. Then one of them said that Bobby Moore was a cunt and that Hurst's goal at the World Cup should not have been allowed. The place went quiet. Whether it was a goal or not, this was Geoff Hurst they were slagging and to slag Bobby Moore, well he was the god! I'll never forget this bloke of about forty sticking the head on him and dropping him. The rest of the Bristol lads were saying come outside and have a punch-up and waving to us in that West Country accent. They never made it outside. We steamed them and it seemed most of the pub joined in, no matter what age. I heard one bloke screaming at them and smashing a bottle over one bloke's head – 'Never slag Bobby again,' he kept screaming, along with 'West Country cunts'. They never had a chance and were taught a lesson that, to this day, I hope they haven't forgotten. We beat them 3–2 and I saw no more trouble that day. They went home with their tails between their legs. Some of us went to Paddington station looking for more of them and caught some in the buffet bar. One glass was thrown and they bolted out of the buffet bar and on to the platform where some were complaining to the Old Bill. We left and went home – all in all a good day and a laugh. If lower league teams wanted to play in the big league with the real fans, they should learn the ropes first.

Next league game away was QPR at Loftus Road. We took a large crew to Loftus Road and when we got out of White City station the Old Bill were pouncing on groups of lads and putting them up against a wall and searching them. People were dropping golf balls by the bucket load and this one lad had a large ball-bearing the size of a golf ball. He dropped it and you could hear the thud as it hit the pavement. The Old Bill never sussed it or worried about the golf balls, and moved on to another group of West Ham.

Many of us had brought golf balls. The target was a big drum at their ground that a bloke used to bang nearly all game. Now and again he'd even walk around the pitch with it. Our aim was to smash that drum. We thought it was fucking annoying, and I'm sure QPR fans felt the same. We stopped for a drink in the Springbok and it was full of West Ham, most dressed the same. American drill trousers were the gear for a game: turned up to your boot tops, small turn-ups and neatly pressed. Cammo jackets were in and Aussie bush hats were the thing to put on your head. We had a couple of pints and went into the ground. The Old Bill were telling us if they found out we were West Ham we would be thrown out or we could go straight to the other end. We laughed at this and when Brian Dear scored the whole end was West Ham, one big knees-up. One lad hopped on to the pitch at half-time and tried to get the drum, but Old Bill got him first and he was hauled off. When we saw him next game he said he got a bit of a slapping from the Old Bill and was left in a maria till about six o'clock and then let go. Another London team walked over. We were still kings of the manor and we talked about who was next. We left Loftus Road en masse and jogged back to White City – the odd window went in and traffic was stopped – on to the tube and back home. Some lads went looking at other main stations. We never bothered. Another London team down; we were happy.

We had Huddersfield in the Cup next and nothing happened except some lads had a bit of a laugh. We beat them 2 – 0 and we drew Mansfield in the next round and talk of us going all the way to Wembley was on. We could do Mansfield easy, but we had other games first.

In February a West Ham game was postponed so we made our way over to Loftus Road again. Spurs were playing there and we could have a go at the Yids. I think Chelsea's game was off as well as there was a fair crew on the QPR end. With the Rangers fans the end was split 50 – 50 and we were with the combined mob of Chelsea and QPR. They never sussed us but our target was the Yids. When the game started we gave a 'Bubbles' and many woke up to the fact West Ham was here – not a great number, about a hundred of us, but the combined mob were more glad we were there than having to fight us. That game was one of the worst ones I have been to for missiles being thrown. Loads of golf balls went back and forth, along with coins, and some darts went over. I wondered how they got the golf balls in as we were searched only a couple of weeks previously. Seems our name was bigger than Spurs and we were more of a risk. Chelsea were famous for lobbing things at you during a game and they got through OK. The game was a 1–1 draw and when it was over we all went looking for the Yids. We never found them; it was the best disappearing act I've seen. Maybe the combined Chelsea/QPR with a touch of West Ham did it, who knows, but they bottled. We got on the tube with some Chelsea, who were gobbing off that they ran the Yids. If the truth be known, the Yids ran themselves but that was Chelsea being gobby and claiming a result.

The next two home games nothing went off, as we had Liverpool and Newcastle. They brought some fans, but nothing happened. I missed the next four games, three at home and one away, due to family problems, but I was told nothing major went off anyway so I didn't miss much. I never went to many more that season, only the main ones like Man U and Arsenal.

Man U at the end of March and they were getting wise and hard to find. As expected they brought a load of fans down by coach and bus. A new idea we had was to meet them at Euston and ride the tube with them all the way down to Upton Park. Once inside the underground they were ours and if you did not know your way around the tube system it was a dangerous place to be. At Euston many other West Ham were milling around. We joined up and when the train came in a

large mob of mixed Man U fans got off, all singing and
carrying on. We sussed out who was where and picked a large
mob in the buffet bar. Some of the lads went in, including me,
got a drink and waited. We heard them talking about how
West Ham shit and they were the boys – all gobby talk. When
we had about twenty inside one of us chucked a glass and we
steamed in. The Mancs chucked their glasses at us and we
returned with bottles. More West Ham steamed into the bar
and they were fucked. I was having a go with one Manc when
we fell on a table full of glasses that smashed. He fell on the
floor, and blood was pissing out of him. I later found out he
had many stitches where the broken glass had cut him. As he
had gone down more people laid the boot in, and I even
copped one off a West Ham fan, I'm sure – that's how mad it
was. I saw an ambulance on the station and people being
treated from the buffet bar.

I was sporting a swollen cheek and had blood coming out
of my mouth as we went after the rest who had been
gobbing off. Down into the tube and on the train it was on.
We employed hit-and-run tactics and stayed ahead of the
Old Bill. They weren't expecting us and we steamed in. It
was no contest; we had them fucked. Many piled out at the
next stop, but not before we gave them a good kicking. My
mate was upset that he had blood from a Man U fan all over
his Ben Sherman. We got off and followed them but they
legged it out of the station and we went back to Euston for
another look.

We got back to find a mob of West Ham getting a kicking
from a big mob of Man U. We steamed in and bottles were
thrown as we beat them back. The rest of the West Ham lads
got some revenge. They ran from us down into the tube. That

was a mistake. We piled down after them, fighting as we
went. We had them fucked. Once on the platform the only
way out was past us or to jump down on the tracks and leg it
up the tunnel. We steamed in again and they did not want to
know – loads of them cowered. These were skin-/suedeheads
like us and had all the gear including the 'bovver boots', the
lot, but it was all show. The Old Bill finally got there and
separated us. Then Man U started gobbing off at us and many
were trying to point out who was who to Old Bill. Only
moments before they were cowering; now, with the Old Bill
to protect them, it was different and they were trying to grass
us up. We got on the next train and made our way to Mile
End where we would change to go to Upton Park. We talked
on that trip about how many they had and what a result for
us. We learned one thing: never underestimate the size of
your enemy. We thought one train-load was it, but they had
two train-loads that we knew of, maybe even three. Their
support was from all over and they brought many to an away
game. We would know better next time. They never expected
us at the station, nor did the Old Bill. We surprised them all
and had a good result. We heard Chelsea tried the same thing
but Man U were wise to it and Chelsea got a bit of a kicking.

At Mile End station a large mob of West Ham were waiting
and some steamed on to the train thinking we were Man U. It
was nearly off between West Ham. People soon heard of our
attack on Man U at Euston. Many said next time they were
around they would go to Euston too. After the game, most
agreed to go back to Euston. The game itself was a draw and
not much happened. The Mancs went on the South Bank and
as usual they were gobbing off. We could not get near them
after the game and the South Bank was closed off to us.

After the game the police escorted them up to the station and they sang and chanted all the way to the station. Typical, we thought, with the Old Bill protecting them. Bottles were being lobbed and some lads were chucking golf balls at them. They got on to the tube nearly untouched. Nothing went off at the coaches, as Old Bill had a massive presence there. The gates closed on the station till their train was away. We followed on. A load of lads went to Mile End early, but Old Bill were waiting. They weren't going to get caught again. The Old Bill were well pissed off. The had been caught short with our hit-and-run tactics, which we continued to use for many years. Things were tightened up from then on.

The next game was Everton away and not much happened. I didn't go and the grapevine said we had only a few up there. I missed Sheffield Wednesday away as well and I heard nothing about the game. The next home game was against Stoke and surprisingly they brought a few fans down, a mixed lot but a better turnout than some. A half dozen or so went on to the North Bank but Old Bill got to them first and moved them up the other end quick and smart. Still, they had had the bottle to come on our end; many did not. They got done after the game and were looking for it. I missed it and only saw the aftermath; they had got a good kicking.

Next Chelsea at home. They had a fair mob and were getting bigger, but would they show? Many of us went to Victoria early in the day looking for them, but had no luck. We got back to Upton Park at about 11.30 and we made our way down to the ground. Still no sign of them. We hung around outside the Boleyn and waited. Word soon came back that Chelsea had taken the North Bank, a mob of about five hundred. We ran around to the North Bank and joined hundreds more West Ham fans who had heard the same thing. Once in we found Chelsea were in the middle singing, 'WE TOOK THE NORTH BANK!' And they did – for five minutes. We charged them and they legged down the front, some on the pitch and away from us. We got the North Bank back and they hardly put a fight up. All game they were gobbing off at us, with the protection of the Old Bill. Chants of 'CHELSEA DUCK POND!' went up from us and they replied with 'THEY ALL GONE QUACKERS OVER THERE' and taking the piss because we had lost to Mansfield away in the League Cup.

We wondered how they had got in unseen. It turned out that while we were looking for them they had done a few West Ham lads with scarves and then they'd worn them into the ground. Once in they charged the centre. Only younger West Ham were there and they ran them easily, until we came in. They had pulled a stunt on us by sneaking in with West Ham colours and walking down Green Street, untouched, unseen, in smaller mobs. It appeared West Ham weren't the only ones planning things. Many left before the game finished in a 0–0 draw. Not much was chucked at the game, mainly because we were higher above them and unless someone threw something at us we didn't bother. Chelsea usually loved chucking things at other fans.

As things turned out, Chelsea wrecked a few trains that season. After we wrecked the Ipswich train, it seems they were effectively saying they could do better, or it was just that they wanted their names in the paper. At other grounds they had invaded pitches, mostly while the TV cameras were there, and it seems they wanted the spotlight. We had heard rumours that Chelsea had done this or that to a firm. They never showed us any of that, only gobbing off when the Old Bill had them tucked up safe.

We looked for them after the game and only the odd straggler got a going-over. We rode to Mile End to catch them, and when we couldn't find anyone there, on to Victoria again. We rode the tube for a couple of hours and we had a look at Victoria and the Broadway; some even went for a walk up North End Road, but we found nothing. The day was a let-down after promising so much. Chelsea had bottled it again. They had pulled a stunt on us and it backfired. It wasn't going to happen again.

I missed the WBA game away, but the next one was the Yids at White Hart Lane and word was they were ready for us. We liked that – the more the merrier. I hated the Yid fans and many West Ham fans felt the same. We talked about how we were going to White Hart Lane and many met up at Mile End tube station and Liverpool Street British Rail. We went on before the main mob, about thirty of us, to see if we could find some Yids on our own. We had a drink in the Corner Pin and another one closer to the ground, but nothing. The main West Ham mob came up and went into the ground and they got half the Park Lane; only Old Bill stopped them taking the lot. We had a drink under the stand and sussed things out. We knew a lot of faces there, and with a nod of the head to many, they knew we were ready. In the stands the Old Bill were between West Ham and the Yids.

We caught a firm of Yids at the entrance to the Paxton, about fifty-odd lads who were on the prowl. We steamed in and it was on. They didn't know where we came from and many legged it. We chased them on to the Paxton and some stood and fought. As they did more and more Yids joined in;

some of their main boys were on the Paxton that day. They fought back and it was toe-to-toe stuff for a while. People were crashing through the crowd and more West Ham came in, but not before the Yids had given us a touch-up. I got a whack in the jaw, but it didn't hurt. Maybe my luck was changing. The Old Bill moved in and things calmed down.

One thing we learned this time was to never under-estimate your rival. The Yid lads were hidden on the Paxton and when we followed some of them, we got ambushed. A neat trick, one which we used to our advantage at West Ham. Not much was thrown at the game – that mainly happened when Chelsea were playing. We lost the game 1–0 and we wanted revenge. Outside the ground it was on again with the mob from the Paxton. I remember one Yid bloke waving a blade around at me. He was soon done over as many West Ham came and joined us. By now the Park Lane lot had legged it. We chased the Totts all the way to Seven Sisters Road. We broke off the chase as many Old Bill were trying to keep control and they were succeeding. They walked us back to the station and some escorted us back to Liverpool Street station, where many more Old Bill were waiting. We charged the gate and got through easily. If they blocked the gate, what you did was to run at it and go to the left or right and jump the barrier. If you got caught, that was tough; not many did.

On the whole it was a shit day and most talk was of the little surprise the Yids had on the Paxton for us. I still don't know if it was planned, but most Yid fans will say it was. I reckon they were hiding myself, but it nearly worked for them and we used those tactics next home game, which was against the Arsenal.

The Arsenal game came around and we went on to the South Bank. We knew Arsenal would not go on the North Bank and after Chelsea's stunt many West Ham lads got in early and held the centre – mainly the younger ones, but handy boys in any ruck as back-up. As expected, Arsenal fans came on but, being a night game, there weren't as many as expected. Most were wearing scarves, which was great from our point of view. Not many Old Bill were around, most were on the North Bank and outside. About ten minutes from kick-off we surged the Arsenal fans, about eighty to a hundred of us. We pushed them forward, kicking and punching as we went. We had them and kept steaming in. A few Old Bill tried to get in and chants of 'C'MON NORTH BANK!' went up, inviting our North Bank to join us. Arsenal thought it was their signal for their North Bank. They started fighting back, but the surprise attack had them fucked. This went on for about ten minutes and more West Ham joined in. Arsenal were split into two and we held the middle ground. The Old Bill didn't know what to do and many were called from our North Bank. A load of lads jumped into the Chicken Run and came though that way down to us. A few tried coming across the pitch but were caught by the Old Bill. As more Old Bill left the North Bank, fans were surging forwards towards the pitch. The Old Bill turned back and formed a line across the front to stop them invading the pitch and joining us. Kick-off was held up for fifteen minutes that night. More and more fighting broke out in the South Bank. Arsenal were getting a hiding from us – and we liked giving it to them. The Yids started this trick and we mastered it.

We lost the game 2–1 and that made matters worse. The

Old Bill had to get the Gooners out yet, and stop the North Bank from joining us. Near the end of the game they herded a load of Arsenal out of one of the exits and along down to Green Street which left one mob on the West Side. Many others jumped into the West Side and, they hoped, safety. Some fighting broke out there as well. The game over, we surged towards the remaining Gooners, but most had fucked off. Only a few were left and they got a right going-over from all sides. The Old Bill got in and separated the fans but it didn't matter. We done them again and on the away end, pulling one over on the Old Bill. When we got out on to the street Arsenal were nowhere to be found. They had gone – we totally fucked them that night and they weren't up for a ruck. We felt so good and agreed the South Bank would be the place for us next season. It seems many had the same idea.

Last game was Man City away. I did not go and from what I heard there was no trouble again and only a couple of coaches made the trip up.

This season had been a fairly good one as we were once again kings of London. We had pulled some stunts up north and won, turned over the carrot crunchers, got our name in the papers and pulled some stunts at home that would change the way fans would come to Upton Park for many a year. We had learned what other firms' tactics were at their grounds and had used them against them and won. We lost a few, mainly in smaller firms. In big mobs there weren't many that could match us. The way we started to travel was starting to change as well.

Football-wise, we finished seventeenth, got knocked out of the FA Cup third round by Boro and were knocked out of the

League Cup by Mansfield. Not a great year on the park, but good off it. So on to next season, and a new decade.

CHAPTER 4

1969–70

THE NEW SEASON was here. We had Newcastle at home and they brought a few lads down. A police dividing tunnel of crash barriers was installed on the South Bank. It seems our little trick with the Gooners had worked and the Old Bill were not going to get caught again. The Geordies brought down a good-size crew and many were on the South Bank. As the game got closer there were about three to four hundred Newcastle fans and we were about two hundred strong, but we had surprise on our side. As the teams ran out we got behind the Newcastle fans and surged forward, causing a big wave of bodies. As the Geordies tried to get back up to where they had been standing they were met with a tidy mob of West Ham. It was on and I saw, and was involved in, some of the best fighting ever. The Toon lads were well up for it and steamed back into us. I got a good smack on the head, a head butt I think, on the side. I never saw it and was a bit dazed, then some Newcastle fans steamed me and I went down under a good kicking. I was pulled up and felt OK, a little shocked, but not badly hurt. It was still on and West Ham fans weren't gaining any ground – but they weren't losing any either. The Old Bill stood back for a bit before moving in. I saw one Toon lad waving a meat hook around. This upset the home fans and he was the target. He got a bad kicking and it seemed his mates didn't care. My mate got his usual black eye along with a broken nose. Finally the Old Bill moved in and we were separated. We took stock. A lot of us had been hit but we figured we had hit as many back. The bloke who got me on the side of the head certainly knew how to hit – I had a stinking headache for days. The kicking was nothing, just a few bruises on the back and legs; for once, my ribs were saved.

During the game there was the odd off and we beat them 1 – 0. The game over, their fans turned to leave and as they were going down the centre stairs of the South Bank we steamed them again. This time we had them, they were trapped, but they stood and fought. They couldn't get out because Old Bill was trying to get in. They couldn't get back up the steps because we were there, so it was on. Blokes were spitting down and I laughed when one bloke at the back of the stairs started pissing down on the Geordies. This set them off and they charged out on to the street, past Old Bill, and there they stood waiting for us. We steamed out and Old Bill tried to stop us. More West Ham joined in, lads who came around from the North Bank. The Geordies never ran – they stood and we steamed them again. Fighting was everywhere and Old Bill lost control. They had moved the mounted police in but the rucking was still going on. Finally the fans were separated and the Toon fans were escorted back to the coaches and station. I saw many a Newcastle fan with blood pouring out of his head, along with quite a load of West Ham. All in all they stood and fought and never bottled. I admired them for that. They were solid, but we totally fucked them with the attack on the away end. This trick was working well and Old Bill was caught again. They thought the Arsenal incident was a one-off thing, but it was just the start.

We had Chelsea next at home, a night game on the Monday. Not many Chelsea came down – no real lads from what we saw, anyway. The South Bank trick had been talked about all over London and we had heard Chelsea were gonna try it on the North Stand at their ground. We laughed – they could not hold the Shed, let alone another end. The trouble with Chelsea was that there were some solid lads, but there were lots of hangers-on who never had the bottle for a ruck. They liked wrecking trains and invading pitches but seldom had a result unless it was against a team with shite support. The best they could muster was chucking things at us when they were safe behind a line of Old Bill. We heard many tales about how Chelsea had done the Yids, or done this or that mob, but we never saw any of it, only a gobby mob that once went on the North Bank.

We figured that if we got on the South Bank early and up the back they would find it hard to chuck things at us because they would be below us. We shouldn't have bothered as their turnout was pathetic, with only a small mob down in the corner by the West Side where a load of Old Bill kept an eye on them. It was agreed that if they tried the invasion trick here we would go on after them. We won the game 2–0 and that result was the only highlight of the evening. We looked for Chelsea afterwards and even rode the train to Victoria, but they were not to be found, a non-event. Chelsea were getting worse with us.

Stoke away next and I went up on the train with loads of West Ham. Things had changed: no food or drink on the train and the carriages looked like they should have been put out of service years before. We arrived at Stoke and took a walk around to the ground. We came across a few little mobs, but they all legged it. We went around to the Boothen End, where Old Bill were searching people and asking names. If you sounded like a cockney you weren't let in and were made to go to the away end. They did not want the same trouble they had had in the FA Cup meet a couple of seasons before. We talked to some locals and they told us Chelsea had put on a bit of a show up there. So, to the away end and nothing happened, we even lost the game 2 – 1 and we thought they would be waiting after the game for us. We got out about ten minutes early and there was nothing, just Old Bill waiting to give us an escort back to the station. There were barely two hundred of us. Where were the Stoke lads? There was no mob following us and gobbing off, as many do like Man U. Nothing. On the train back Old Bill was there, about two to a carriage, to make sure nothing went off on the train. The whole day was fucked, the trip, the state of the train, being put on the away end, no Stoke fans showing and the trip back with the Old Bill on board. One lad had a 'party seven' can of beer, which did not last long amongst us. Our only hope was that we would pick someone up at the station, but nothing. We got home very disappointed.

Chelsea away next and we decided to go out alone with a mob of about twenty or so and try something new. We got to

Kensington High Street station and walked the couple of miles back to Chelsea, to see if we could pick up any on the way. We strolled down the High Street to Olympia, the top end of North End Road, and there were loads of council flats where many a Chelsea fan lived. Our first stop was a pub called the Hand and Flower. We had heard many Chelsea fans drank in there but, it appeared, not on a match day when West Ham were around. Next pub was the Fox and Hounds – I think that's the name, anyway – near West Kensington station. Only a couple of older fans there, so a swift half and on to the North End Road market. There are loads of pubs down there and we stopped in the Fulham Volunteer. Still no Chelsea, so round to the ground and into the Rising Sun, which was packed with West Ham. We talked about how we walked right though their manor and no one said anything. If that had been down the East End, it would have been different.

Trying to get into the Shed was getting hard. Coppers were stopping and searching fans and asking where they lived. If you said the East End you were told to go to the North Stand with away fans. Even those they let in were not allowed into the Shed End with steel-toecap boots. If you took them off you were OK, or you could go to the away end. We made it into the Shed along with about three hundred-odd West Ham and kept our heads down. There was no way we could move Chelsea with half our lot on the other end. About ten minutes from the start, Chelsea started singing, 'WEST HAM WHERE ARE YOU?', typical gobbing off knowing that most were up the other end. We thought, fuck it, and steamed in. We totally surprised them and many ran to the other side of the police barrier on the Shed. Some stood and fought but they had no hope as their back-up had legged it to safety. The

Old Bill moved in and many West Ham were pulled out. I was one of them. I had my name and address taken but I told them I was a Chelsea fan and had just got caught up in it. They let me go. Many West Ham lads also pulled this stunt. We went on to the North Stand and joined up with the other West Ham lads. We could see Chelsea had gone back to where we had run most of them before. We looked for the so-called North Stand boys, but they weren't to be found. The game was 0–0, with about ten minutes to go. We decided to move off and around to the Shed End. We had about six to seven hundred. Old Bill blocked the way with marias and mounted, and wanted us to go back to the station. There was no way we were getting through as a large mob. We headed off towards Broadway station and went on to Victoria station, about a hundred-odd of us, and waited. The game had ended in a 0–0 draw and Chelsea fans had started coming through. Finally a mob of about a hundred and fifty Chelsea showed, singing and carrying on. Some were saying they done West Ham. We proved them wrong. Nothing was chucked, we just mingled in with them so they thought we were Chelsea and then we started. We were in the middle of them and they had no chance. Loads ran, many stayed and fought it out. They had no choice. I copped a beautiful head butt from one Chelsea lad and it dropped me. I didn't know what hit me until my mate told me. I went down and got a fair kicking, and I had blood pouring out of my nose, but I'm told the lad who had hit me had got a good kicking as well. The Old Bill came from everywhere to quieten things down.

We got back on the tube and everyone was alive with excitement. At last some Chelsea had stood toe to toe with us. We had found some of their proper boys, the hangers-on had bolted but these stood and gave a good account of themselves. A mate of ours had his flying jacket slashed right across the back and it was ruined. They were hard to get, the Yankee ones. We worked out that it could not have been just a razor blade in a matchbox but something heavier, like a cut-throat razor, to cut the leather like that. We were upset – not only had blades been used, but an attack on the back of a bloke was not on. Just when we thought Chelsea finally had some bottle, this happened.

From then on we hated only the Yids more than Chelsea. Millwall was a natural enemy but we hardly ever met, only the odd off on the tube. More and more weapons were beginning to appear with different firms. Some younger West Ham lads carried bicycle spokes down the seams of their jeans because if they were searched they were hard to find. A short jab with one of these hurt, and if you had a group of ten or so climbing over you, all kicking and jabbing with the spokes, the end result was a totally fucked fan.

West Brom at home next and nothing went off. Hardly any of their fans showed and those who did were mainly the older, in-the-seats kind.

Another night game, another London team, this time Arsenal. Word had gone around about our South Bank trick and a police tunnel made of crash barriers was put on the South Bank. Arsenal did not have a big mob and Old Bill had things well in order. More and more older West Ham fans were on the South Bank and as the numbers grew the away team's numbers dropped. The few who came went into the West Side or the seats above the Chicken Run. The game was a draw, 1–1, and when Arsenal scored there were many fans scattered all over the ground but nowhere near us. We could not find them after the game, they had gone or were well hidden. Another disappointment.

Forest away was next and we decided to go up by coach, about twenty of us. City ground was a first for me and many of my mates. When the coach pulled in the Old Bill met us and escorted us on to the away end. Many West Ham had come by train, a decent mob of about four hundred. No trouble in the ground, but after the game a mob of Forest fans came after us. We stood and then steamed them. They legged it kind of smartly and Old Bill was trying to get in to form a line between us so only the Forest stragglers got a few boots up the arse. When Old Bill took control Forest did a Man U and started gobbing off. We heard a few Forest had been chucked in the river before and others just jumped into it to get away; unfortunately, I missed this. The lads from the train were escorted all the way from the train to the ground. We lost the game 1–0 and we were well pissed off at what had happened.

We decided next away game at Everton we would grab the normal train to Liverpool and give the football special a miss. At least you could get a drink and a sandwich on the normal train, even if it was over-priced. No Old Bill rode the normal train and we agreed we would behave on it this trip and see how we went.

However, before that we had the Yids at home. They brought a fair mob down, but sneaked in and on to the South Bank where they thought they were safe. They had about five to six hundred fans on the South Bank and we steamed at them and pushed them over to the West Side. Many jumped over into the west stand, where some other West Ham lads were waiting and pushing them back but there were not enough of them there. The Old Bill moved in and pushed us back, but we continued to chuck coins at them and some had golf balls. Their main lads, who stood mainly because they were trapped, tried to have a go but we kicked the fuck out of them.

Chants of 'WE'LL SEE YOU ALL OUTSIDE' rang out and all during the game we tried getting at them. I got pulled and had the normal walk around the pitch and down the players' tunnel, this time backwards and with Old Bill on both sides hanging on. The game had not started yet and already they were chucking out. At the back of the tunnel there was the usual: name and address and what team do you support. I was put in a maria for a while. The van had a few other West Ham lads in it and we talked about what we would do when we were released. We agreed to spread the word and meet at Liverpool Street station. Not many Yids were held, only a few in another van, and we kept shouting, 'YIDO!' and taking the piss.

We got let out at half-time and were told to go home. The Yids in the other van had already been let out and I think the Old Bill wanted the room. Fuck that, we went back to the South Bank but the gates and turnstiles were closed. There was a massive crowd there that day, some forty thousand-odd, and we waited around outside till the big gates opened. A few Yids saw us and legged it. Many West Ham fans who had been chucked out were milling around. Near the end of the game the gates opened and we ran back in. The Yids were still pinned down in the west stand corner and there was a massive police presence between them and us. We were 1–0 down and we decided to head off to the station and on to Liverpool Street. About fifty of us left and there were more following us looking for the Yids. We changed at Mile End and were joined by another fifty or so West Ham who had the same idea.

We got to Liverpool Street and decided we would split into

three mobs and meet on the main platform. One lot met up with some Yid lads and got turned over really badly. I don't know what happened, I only saw a few cut heads and loads of blood. It turned out that these Yid lads had some Millwall along with them and were looking out for West Ham lads. They gave this group a good kicking. We went after them but they had gone. We reckoned they would be coming back on the next tube, so we waited. The next tube came in and nothing, but the next one came and a big mob poured out screaming, 'TOTTENHAM!' They never saw us and we steamed them. They bolted back on to the train. We tried to get on but they had those handles from the train and were swinging them at us in the doorway. We tried keeping the doors open but they shut but only after a few of us got smashed fingers. They left and they must have hopped out at another station and changed lines because we never saw them again. We went back up to the platform and waited. We sussed out the buffet bar. We weren't going to get caught twice by the Yids.

We hung around for about an hour and still no sign of their main boys. We decided to fuck off and call it a day. We got the tube back to Mile End and met up with some West Ham lads who had bumped into a mob of Yids and had a massive ruck with them. The Old Bill had moved in and stopped it and escorted the Yids back to Liverpool Street. We hadn't seen them and I can only guess that they had split up into twos and threes so we would not suss them.

My mate got two broken fingers from the tube incident and was upset. He wanted to go all the way up west and find some more fans – anyone. We calmed him down. We still had the return leg to go and we would be well clued up by then.

The Everton trip came around and about sixty of us went

up by Inter-city normal service. We gave the football special a miss. It wasn't that much dearer and a lot less aggro on the normal train. We were into Liverpool before the football special and there was no Old Bill around – they would show later for the other train. We had a walk down Lime Street and then called into a Yates on the street. We worked out that we would go to the ground by bus. Some wanted to walk and met up in the Everton end. Some lads went off to meet the other train, the special, to see how many West Ham made the trip. We had heard about two hundred mixed fans and we did not know how many by coach. At Goodison Park we went on the away end. We would have been killed going on to their end with the few numbers we had. We weren't scared, but we weren't stupid. We lost the game 2–0 and left well pissed off. A mob of Everton fans waited for us outside the ground, about one hundred-odd and we had about the same. We ran at them and they stood; it was on. Everton lads were lobbing bricks and bottles at us but we still went into them. This surprised them and before they knew it we were in the middle of them and Old Bill was trying to get in between us. The Merseyside coppers used to carry these big long night sticks and used them well. They did not care who they thumped and shins and ankles were targeted by many of them.

More Everton fans came along and joined in. I could see we were on a hiding to nothing here, as we were totally outnumbered. The Old Bill got between us and escorted us away and still some bottles came down on us. We went past this big park, Stanley Park I think it's called – Liverpool's ground is on the other side. Loads more Everton were there waiting. We were fucked and Old Bill had lost control. They steamed into us and most of us got a bit of a kicking. We tried fighting back but had no chance. Everton had the numbers and turned us over well. We got back to the station and Old Bill tried to get us on to the football special but we weren't having any of that and slipped off into the buffet bars around the station. We had about half an hour to kill and, with the train gone, so did most Old Bill. Most of us had a few cuts but surprisingly not much damage when you think of the numbers they had. We reckoned Old Bill did more damage with those fucking big truncheons. On the train back we talked to some Everton fans who told us that when you get near the park they always mob up there and just wait for away fans. We would remember that.

We had a good trip home and had a few beers on the train with no Old Bill around. We caused no trouble on the train and we decided this was the way to go in future. It had many things going for it – there was no Old Bill waiting at either end, north or south and none on the train. We could get a beer and some food, even though it was British Rail shit. The only bad things about the day were we got a bit of a kicking and lost 2 – 0.

Sheffield Wednesday at home next and nothing happened. Hardly any fans came down; the highlight was that we won 3 – 0. The next game was Manchester United away and we made plans to go up the same way as when we went to Liverpool, by Inter-city. We reckoned we had about two hundred who said they were going, and then there was the football special, so maybe a tidy firm would make the trip up.

On the day of the game about twenty of us met up at Euston and there weren't many more going by the special. It was a big let-down. Loads of Man U were going up, the so-called Cockney Reds, so we decided to go anyway and have

a good look around their manor. At Manchester we split up
and met at a pub near the ground. It was full of Man U and we
kept our heads down and tried to mix in. We got asked some
funny questions but we conned our way into them thinking
we were London Man U fans.

We heard them slagging off West Ham bad and we bit our
lips. Not this time – we would get killed. We went on to the
Scoreboard End and watched our team lose 5 – 2. When we
scored we all cheered and this got us some strange looks, but no
one had a go. There was only a dozen or so of us and the other
few lads were up in the Stretford End we found out later. They
had a drink in a pub somewhere in Salford and had no trouble
either. We met up at the station and worked out the best way
to get Man U at home was to go on to the corner areas beside
the Stretford End and Scoreboard. 'Alchys' Corner' was the
nickname of one of them, and many of their lads were there.

Unless you had many thousands and got in when the
turnstiles opened, you had no chance of taking the Stretford
End. Besides, it was mainly gobby kids and Old Bill had it well
sewn up. We got back to Euston and we met about fifteen Man
U fans in the buffet bar taking the piss out of West Ham. Well,
enough was enough and my mate hit one with a chair. They
were shocked. We steamed in and in a frenzied attack we done
them. The women working in the bar were screaming. We left
there quickly and made our way on to the tube. As the train
pulled out we could see about a dozen Old Bill coming on to
the platform looking for us. What a day. We had gone all the
way up north, walked around their manor, never threw a
punch or got one back and then back in London we done some
Cockney Reds. The day was not lost.

Burnley at home next and then Stoke in a night game. We

beat Burnley 3–1 and drew with Stoke 3–3. The next away game was Coventry and nothing much ever happened up there, so we didn't go; their fans were shit home and away. We had Wolves in a night game – I never went to that one either and I heard not many West Ham did. Apparently Wolves tried their subway stunt again, but they had no one to fight with.

Sunderland at home and the Mackems had quite a few lads down, a mixed mob and nothing much went off in the ground. In fact, we talked to a few of them and they said Newcastle were waiting for us if we turned up, as they were well pissed off at the smacking they got from us. The Mackems reckoned it was great and we should do it more often. They told us to stay away from any pubs near the ground and go on the away end and we should be all right. Me and a couple of blokes had a scuffle about Hurst's six goals he scored against them before and the one he punched in, but nothing serious, handbags really. The game was a draw 1–1 and that turned out to be the highlight of the day. Next away game was the Saints and I never bothered going – nothing much ever happened at Southampton and the game was a 1–1 draw anyway.

Now, the next home game was newly promoted Palace at home, and this was a new challenge for us. Would they bring a mob? They brought about two hundred hard-core fans and tried to settle in the South Bank – that is, until we ran and split them. A few got a kicking, many hopped over to the West Side and the Old Bill moved in. We noticed more and more West Ham lads coming on to the South Bank – we had quite a team on there and Old Bill was a wake up to us. Palace split up and we could only find a few near the police line. We beat them 2–1 and another London firm fell. We had heard they were well up for it and they had had a few good run-ins with Millwall but, as with most other mobs, they never did it with us.

Hardly any West Ham fans went up to Liverpool, including me. We lost anyway, 2–0, and our next big day out would be Ipswich again – the end of the road. Before that we had Derby at home. Word had gone around that Derby were well up for it, but it seemed not. At West Ham fuck all fans showed, the only highlight being that we beat them 3–0. We would have to wait and see what they were like at the Baseball Ground. Next came Ipswich.

Many of us went by Inter-city to Ipswich as there were loads of Old Bill on the special, mainly because they did not want another train wrecked. The football special left before ours and a big load of West Ham were going up for the journey. This was good, as the Old Bill would meet this lot and there would be no one there at the other end for us. About ninety to a hundred of us left on the Inter-city and most played cards, a few had a beer and on the whole we all had a laugh with no trouble whatsoever. When we pulled into Ipswich we casually walked out of the station and towards the ground. The main mob on the special were already at the ground. We stopped at a big pub in the town and checked out what was going on. A few Ipswich fans were in there and were talking about how the West Ham mob who had just came through would be trouble. It turned out the pub closed its doors until this lot were well away on advice from police. About a dozen or so of us got a drink in. As more and more West Ham came in the landlord looked worried – he had thought the main threat had gone. He had a pub full of the East End's finest, just having a quiet, quick beer, and he was wondering what was going to happen. Nothing did, except a round of our song 'Bubbles'. Many had light ale and some got some barley wine to drink, because the smaller bottle was handy to have.

We walked up to the ground and into the Ipswich end. The other mob from the special was already there and only Old Bill stopped them running Ipswich. We came in behind the Ipswich mob and formed up. Still no one sussed us out. The Ipswich fans were giving it all the gob at West Ham, safely behind the police and screaming they would kill us. My mate tapped one on the shoulder and asked if he would like to kill all West Ham fans. He looked puzzled and said yes and my mate stuck the head on him. His nose went like a squashed tomato and he cried out. It was on. We steamed them, punching and kicking and there was a massive surge down the terrace. The Old Bill was fucked, they didn't know what was going on. The other West Ham mob were surging across and Old Bill was trying to hold them back. We started chanting, 'COME AND JOIN US OVER HERE!' and waving at them. The gobby Ipswich fans legged it and the police were now stuck in the middle of the two lots of West Ham. They soon woke up and moved between us and the remaining Ipswich fans down the front. We had taken their end and they were pissed off. They started being gobby again and we all started singing, 'WE'LL SEE YOU ALL OUTSIDE!' and a song that summed them up. If any West Ham fan was there they will remember it. It starts with 'I CAN'T READ AND I CAN'T WRITE, BUT I CAN DRIVE A TRACTOR'. We pissed ourselves laughing and the Ipswich fans hated it. The only result they had out of the day was that they won the game 1–0.

With about fifteen minutes to go we left and tried to find

some of their so-called crew. No luck, so we headed back to the station and had a couple of beers while waiting for the train. Not long after that the main group from the special came on to the station and a few came into the bar, saw us and thought we were Ipswich. It didn't take long to find out we were West Ham. It was funny: all that way and we nearly got done by our own. We got back to Liverpool Street about 9.30 and we found out some Yids had been waiting for West Ham to return and when the football special pulled in and they saw the numbers, they legged it. We went for a quick drink in the buffet bar, where yet more West Ham thought we were the Yids returning. It was nearly on again but it settled and we swapped stories of what happened with the Yids and the trip to Ipswich.

It seemed many more had decided to travel the way we did, as they liked the idea. Many said they were going to Leeds next away game but we had a couple of home games before that.

Man City at home was next but they didn't bring many down and those who came were let alone. A couple of scuffles, nothing much. We had a fair bit of respect for Man City. Although from the same town as Man U, they were different fans, more loyal. And we had something in common – we both hated Man U. The day passed without incident and we lost 4–0, a shit day all round.

Next home game was Everton and they brought a big mob down. They were champions that year and had a strong away support. A mob of about four to five hundred were on the South Bank and Old Bill had them well sewn up. We would have to pull something special to get at them. More and more older West Ham lads were now using the South Bank and about forty of us moved down in front of the Everton mob. We reckoned if they scored they would surge forward and then we could have a go while they were still celebrating. They did score, the only goal of the game, and as expected surged forward. That was our signal. We steamed back into them and the main mob of West Ham were trying to get at them from the side. We jumped right in against their mob but with our numbers at the front we were slaughtered; they kicked the fuck out of us. I got a nice whack across the head with something and it left me with a huge lump on my head and a headache for days. The Old Bill did not know what to do. If they left the line it would have been weakened and the rest of the West Ham lads would have pushed through easily.

More coppers came in and got between us. A few West Ham were being pulled out and I was grabbed and taken to a St John's bloke. I had blood coming from my head and the copper thought I was seriously hurt. After the St John's bloke cleared me, he then walked me round and through the tunnel, got my name and address and let me go. They asked you time and time again for your name and address and if you gave a fake one and slipped up you were put in a maria to remember. I slipped up a couple of times and had quite a few little rests in the back of a police van.

We all met up after and agreed we wouldn't try that stunt again – attacking from the front and fighting uphill was not easy. We had reckoned Everton would be easy to do. We compared them to Liverpool fans and that was a mistake. Out of the two teams Everton are the lads and are not as gobby as Liverpool fans. They had done us home and away but we still had to go to them. They never went near the North Bank. Not many away teams did.

Leeds away and a fair mob was going by Inter-city; word

was spreading. When we left London for the trip up a couple of West Ham fans were fucking around on the train; they went to smash a bit of it up, but we put them in their place. I had been to Leeds before but by coach only, so the train was a first for me. We knew Leeds had good home support. They had won the title the year before and their fans had a bit of a reputation.

When you go to Elland Road by train it goes past the ground and you think you are there, but it goes on for a fair while before pulling in and it's a fair walk back. We decided to split up and meet outside their North Stand and take it from there. Some stayed and waited for the special, the newer faces mainly. I don't know why they didn't just catch it instead of coming up with us. These few included the lads who we'd had to quieten down on the train.

A good half-hour walk towards the ground and we stopped for a swift pint. One good thing about Yorkshire is that the beer is good and cheap. It is a step back in time though: the flat cap/whippet syndrome. A couple of lads were taking the piss out of the locals and their accents. 'EH BY GUM!' was a popular one and to this day I still don't think they caught on. The pub we were in had whisky jugs of water and large porcelain ashtrays all over. We thought that if it went off we had some handy weapons just sitting there, but nothing happened so we had a pint and left and headed towards the ground. We got around the back of the North Stand and met up with the rest. The lads off the special had a bit of bother earlier on and Old Bill had now wised up to them, so when they teamed up with us we were well and truly sussed.

The Old Bill moved us around to the away end and Yorkshire's finest constabulary didn't mess about – a boot up the arse or around the ankle helped us on our way. A mob of Leeds came at us and we met head on. The Old Bill did nothing – it seemed like they wanted the Leeds fans to do us – but we were West Ham and the fighting was a bit more than they had bargained for. We stood when they expected us to run and they seemed to hesitate when we didn't run and instead charged back. This caught Old Bill by surprise and they waded into us. I wish someone had filmed it that day as it was police brutality at its finest. The Leeds fans had legged it after only a bit of a small ruck. They didn't think we would stand but we did and only the Old Bill had a result. Any fan who has been to Leeds will tell you they look after their own up there and don't like it when the away team get a result. We lost the game 4–1 and expected them to be outside waiting. We also had the long walk back to the station and there were many side roads where they could get us, or so we thought. We were held back at the end, about three hundred of us, and when they let us go they escorted us all the way to the station. Police vans were speeding up ahead and blocking roads to let us through. We expected the Leeds fans any second after the way the Old Bill had stood back briefly at the ground but nothing, just some gobby kids on the way.

It seems we upset them. We found out many a firm was given a hiding like that and most legged it. Not us: we stood and this threw them right out. What upset them most was when about two-thirds of the lads got on to the special and we stayed and waited for the Inter-city. This pissed them off something shocking as this had never happened before, and to have a mob of West Ham hanging around their manor was not liked.

We got the train back without incident; not much of a day,

really. We had run their fans outside the ground mainly because we stood up to them and even Old Bill thought we were on a hiding. It turns out that was their normal trick. Let a load of Leeds fans steam in to you and then the police would move in and nick the away fans, leave them in the police vans till the train had gone so you had a fucking long wait for the next one. Not this time, it backfired and the Old Bill weren't happy. We copped more kicks around the ankles and legs and punches into the back of the head by Old Bill than Leeds fans. We thought the Leeds fans were wankers and the nickname 'WEEDS' was started up. Apparently it was true that they needed Old Bill to help them. No wonder you never saw many Leeds fans at Upton Park.

The Yids away next and we were looking forward to it. We all agreed on the train back from Leeds that Liverpool Street was out, as the Old Bill would be everywhere. Mile End was no good either, for the same reason. The Yids had a couple of pubs up their way – the Corner Pin and the Bell and Hare, I think. We decided on the Corner Pin, about 1 o'clock.

We made our way over to White Hart Lane. There were a fair few West Ham at Liverpool Street station and, as predicted, loads of Old Bill. We got to the pub around 12.30, about six of us. A couple more were already there and a few Yids were in as well and were waiting for the rest. This time we would get on to the Paxton and kick things off before they knew what had hit them – or a least that was our plan. A massive West Ham mob came past chanting and the odd missile was thrown at the pub. We all laughed; we were about thirty-handed by now and by about 2 o'clock the place was packed. By then we had about forty-odd in and out of the pub and were just waiting for an excuse to kick it off. We didn't have to wait long. One of our lot was hit with an ashtray from behind and that was it. We got the cunt who did it and he got a right kicking. Many of his mates legged it and didn't help him. That would never happen with West Ham fans – they always looked after each other, no matter what the odds. The Old Bill came in with some of the Yid fans who had legged it before and moved us on. They had grassed us up to the Old Bill. Only minutes before they were up for it, until they found out our numbers. We reckoned they thought the main mob had passed and they would have a go at a few odd fans on the way. Wrong move. We had met up with our other mates. They had been at the other pub and had had a result there. It seems the main West Ham mob came in and totally fucked the place and a couple of lads were saying that they were nearly mistaken for Yids.

On to the ground and Old Bill was trying to get the main mob into the Paxton, which told us a few things. The incident we had before with the Yids was a one-off and their lads were probably keeping their heads down. Once inside you could walk from one end to the other. The Park Lane was 50 – 50 West Ham and Yids. We went on to the Paxton and their boys weren't there. It seems a few had started going on the Shelf, which was hard to get at unless you went into a separate turnstile. We would know next time. We figured they went on there to keep away from us, but we found out it was a regular meeting place for the older Yid fans as the Park Lane/Paxton was too easy to get on and they figured they held the terraces better there. Not a bad idea – one we would have a look at next season.

We done them on the park 2 – 0 and apart from the bit of crowd trouble at the Park Lane nothing else happened in the ground. We headed off to the station and a mob of about a hundred Yids were coming towards us. This was their boys, we thought, and we steamed into them. They soon turned and ran but only into a large mob of West Ham who were on the Park Lane. They were trapped and had no choice but to stand. We slaughtered them. Many had blood pouring from their faces; the ones on the ground were cowering and curled up like a ball and we never stopped kicking them.

A few of their lads had a go and did all right but the sheer numbers had them fucked. The Old Bill moved in and things quietened down. They had had enough, but at least they had a go, not like some London firms. We admired that and all the talk back to Liverpool Street was about that and how they stood. We had heard stories about how the Yids had done the Arsenal and Chelsea, but never believed them. Maybe there was some truth in it. At least they had a go at us and if they had had the numbers, maybe they would have had a chance. A lot of their fans were hangers-on from the '62 glory days when they did the double, a bit like today's Man U fans. Glory hunters and not up for a ruck.

West Brom away next and I stayed at home – from what I heard it was a waste of time on the fan scene. We lost the game 3 – 1 and had a decent crew up there, but nothing went off, mainly because West Brom weren't up for it.

Notts Forest next at Upton Park and they brought down about three hundred fans. They crept on to the South Bank and started giving it all the gob. About kick-off time we steamed them, a massive surge into them, kicking and hitting as we went. I can't remember one fighting back. They were dressed for the part but that was it – all show. They moved over to the other side of the police line and stayed. Once again we had surprised an away mob. After the game we could not find them anywhere. They had hidden their scarves and disappeared. Many came by coach, so it wasn't worth going up west looking for them. The game ended in a 1–1 draw and that summed the day right up.

Sheffield Wednesday away next and I went up with about thirty-odd lads and more met us at the station. We noticed more and more West Ham lads were giving the special a miss and they were paying the few bob extra and going by Inter-city. On the train a couple of West Ham lads, mainly younger ones, got a slap for being right prats and trying to start some trouble. They were told we did not want the attention and if they carried on they would be thrown off, whether the train was moving or not. They settled down and ended up being regulars on the away games.

Hillsborough is a massive ground, and was one of the best at the time. This was the first time I had been and I remembered the old man saying how good it was when he went to watch the FA Cup semi-final there against Man U. We had won and went on to win the FA Cup, my first game. From what I heard from his brothers it was a big day, with many an off going on. It seems the older West Ham fans in those days hated Man U as well, something the Mancs didn't forget and came for a bit of payback in '67.

But back to Sheffield Wednesday. We had a good look around the town, unnoticed once again. The Old Bill were waiting for the special to arrive. We had a beer in one pub, where the gaffer was a bit worried we would turn him over. He even bought us all a pint, not bad for seventy-odd lads. Some split up and went looking for Wednesday fans. We had our drink and headed off to the game. I still remembered the bit of a kicking I got at Sheffield United before but it appears United had a bit more bottle than Wednesday boys. We slipped in the home fans' end and waited. West Ham scored first and we went mad. The Wednesday boys didn't know what to do. We were on their end and if we had had another four hundred or so we would have taken it. Some fronted up for a go, but that was all. We were well up for it but the Old Bill moved in and wanted to know who was West Ham. We all kept schtumm as we scored again. The Old Bill started grabbing blokes and throwing them out. They had nicked about thirty of us and left us well short if any trouble was on. There were about two to three hundred on the away end. If they had been with us it would have been a right piss-take. Their fans were a joke, one of the scruffiest mobs I had seen. Cheap, no-name-brand jeans, Marks and Sparks shirts, duffel coats – the ones with the wooden buttons. Most had skinhead haircuts, which was not the style any more, while we were all suedeheads now and you could pick our boys from theirs any day. I dunno why the coppers were asking who was what. They only had to look at the way we dressed and they would have sussed us. We reckoned most of us were wearing on us what these prats earned in a week.

Another goal and we went mad. The Old Bill grabbed more and threw them out and we had about thirty left. We thought that if there was going to be an off then this would be it, as they had the numbers and we were well done. It never came and we won the game 3–2. Outside we linked up with the lads on the away end and we started a bit of a run around the ground. Nothing, only Old Bill trying to get us back to the station. Even Sheffield United had had a bit of a go and Wednesday was a bigger, older club. They had the support, but no bottle. Back at the station the football special left and Old Bill wondered why we weren't on it. We told them that we were Wednesday fans and did not want to travel with the West Ham fans. They accepted this and left us alone.

When we got back on the train we all talked about what had happened. The lads who were pulled in the ground were walked around under the main stand and put on the away end. We all laughed. Sheffield Wednesday were one of the weakest we had come across. We had a good drink on the way back, a good laugh and that was the day. We talked about the next game – Man U at home – and some of us planned what we would do. It was agreed most of us would meet up at Mile End and go up to Euston to see what we could find there coming off the train.

The Man U game came around and as planned about a hundred of us met up at Mile End at 10 o'clock. We got the tube up to Euston, some had a walk around, others got some breakfast. The rest just milled around and waited. About 12 p.m. we knew the train was close because Old Bill started to appear and some sussed us out. We told them we were Cockney Reds and were waiting for the main fans to come down as Upton Park was a bad place to go. They seemed to swallow this and, as there had been no aggro on the station, left us alone. We teamed up and decided to get them on the tube as it was too open at Euston and there were too many Old Bill around. Two trains came in and a massive mob of Man U got off, all chanting and letting people know they were there – scarves, the lot. We let the first lot go and joined the second lot. Coming off the platform we all walked down to the tube and once on the train the Old Bill left. They had done their bit and it wasn't their problem any more.

We waited for a couple of stations and then started. One of our lads nicked a Man U scarf and was trying to burn it with his lighter. The Man U fans didn't like this and about six of them fronted him. That was the signal. One bloke swung up on the overhead handles and kicked this Man U bloke in the face. He went down and the rest soon got a good slapping. As the train pulled into a station a load got off; the ones we had done got thrown off. The train moved off and we went down to the next carriage. It was half packed with Man U fans and once we were all in, we steamed in. They were shouting and screaming. We just hit and kicked them and trampled over them. Many were cowering, with nowhere to run. One Man U lad pulled a knife on us, a sort of short kitchen knife. That was a mistake as he got a bad kicking. A couple of mates of mine were really upset and would not leave him alone. He was battered and bleeding badly. One lad was gonna stick the knife in him as a warning, but we stopped him. At Tottenham Court Road station most of them piled out and ran. We stayed on, as we were going through to the Embankment station where we would change and pick up the District line to take us to Upton Park.

We had had a good result so far and we would probably pick a few up on the way to Mile End where we would see if anything was going on there. We got off at Mile End and linked up with some other West Ham lads. We talked about what had happened. Some said a couple of trains had come through loaded with Man U and Old Bill on board. So it seems Man U had run to the Old Bill. We got the next train to Upton Park and, true to form, there were Old Bill on every carriage. We got off and there was a massive police presence at the station checking tickets to see who came from where. We paid at the gate from Mile End, which was the last station for many. We decide to keep out of the pubs as we weren't sure who or what Old Bill were looking for. We walked down to where the coaches were parked and there were not as many as usual, but just as many Old Bill.

We stayed away from the South Bank as there was a group of Old Bill and Man U fans checking out fans as they went in. We didn't know if it was us they were looking for, so we went into the West Side for a change. Once in we had a good look around. A few Man U were in and a couple of fights were going off, mainly with the older fans, more of your traditional punch-up-type fights. Man U had most of the South Bank and, as usual, were giving it all the gob. Someone told us that he had heard on the radio that some Man U fans had been attacked on the tube and some were in hospital, so now we knew what the fuss was about: it was our crew they were looking for. We decided to keep our heads for this game and stay away from Euston for a while. The game was bad as well, a 0–0 draw. We had had our result and the more Man U that had been hurt, the better. Knowing your way around the tube system helped. We reckoned if we hadn't changed at Tottenham Court Road we would have got nicked for sure.

Burnley away next. I didn't fancy it and heard I made the right choice as nothing happened, except we lost 3–2. I was up for the next one, though: Sunderland away.

The train ride up to the north-east is long and boring. Many played cards and had a few drinks. About fifty of us went on the Inter-city and it would have been worse on the special. We finally got to Newcastle and we had a walk around the station and into the city. Sunderland's ground was about eighteen to twenty miles away we were told, so we decided to catch the bus up there.

We got to Roker Park and went into a pub near the ground. I can't remember the name of it but it had a big long bar with a big curved bit at the end. It was a Sunderland pub and the lads in there were not kids. We were soon sussed as cockneys – it wasn't hard with our accents. They had heard Man U fans had got a right kicking on the tube and they were glad to hear it. It seems they hated Man U as much as they hated Newcastle.

In the Thirties Sunderland were one of the biggest clubs around, if not the biggest, and their fans let you know all about it. A few said they had been to West Ham and had no trouble with us, which was true, and I think this stopped us getting a good kicking. The Sunderland lads told us the word was that Newcastle wanted some payback next time we met and that this would be a hard one as they were one of the few mobs that stood against us and looked after each other. Nothing happened at Roker Park. I think we were the only West Ham fans there and the lads we met gave us a few hints about their rivals Newcastle. In fact, many wanted to join up if we came up. They were real nice people the Mackems; one of their lads was a brickie who later came to London to work and gave me a call. The beer was good as well. And on the day, we won the game 1–0.

Southampton at home and like the game – a 0–0 draw – nothing happened. No away fans came. Many took the opportunity to work out who and what we would do if we went to Newcastle. Some had been before and told us to be careful: we needed numbers up there. We worked out that we had big numbers so we would see how many would show up at the station the following week. The day came and about seventy of us turned up, with about another one hundred going on the special. The Old Bill were grabbing those booked on the Inter-city and getting names and addresses. It seemed they had clicked to the way we travelled. Some of the lads who had booked changed their minds and with the small numbers left we decided we were on a hiding to nothing, so we did not go. We had seen their fans and had admired the way they stood at our ground, and with the tip-off from the Sunderland lads, we said fuck it, no point travelling all the way up there and getting your head kicked in. We lost the game 4 – 1. They would have to wait till we could get the numbers up before we would even attempt to have a go at them at St James' Park.

The next away game was Derby and a load of us went. The Baseball Ground was a dump, one of the worst. A new ground for us and we weren't expecting much trouble, but we had heard they had turned over Chelsea. That did not surprise us, as many did. Derby is a middle-class city; some call it Rolls-Royce country. We did not expect too much bother there. Their end is a side called the Pop Side, if I remember rightly, and we made our way on there and waited until the game started. We gave a round of 'Bubbles' to let them know we were there and all hell broke out. They steamed into us and this took us by surprise. They fought as good as any other firm that stood against us. One Derby bloke had a hammer and was swinging it at us. I don't know if he copped anybody with it, but he got a kicking. They kept coming, they had the numbers and the bottle. I copped a good hit in the cheek and it swelled right up. Many of us got a kicking. We had underestimated them – they were well up for it. We fought back but the day was theirs. They battered the shit out of us and we even lost the game 3 – 0.

Their fans had been well up for it and they had proved themselves at home. We got back to the station and nothing happened outside, only inside. The Old Bill seemed reluctant to get in between the fans but once they did it calmed down. Hails of coins and batteries were chucked at us; we were totally outnumbered and outclassed. Once back on the train we all talked about how they had done us. The stories about Chelsea were true. Derby's fans were more of the older kind and were nutters. We had better be prepared next time. My mate got yet another black eye. We all laughed at this as he was only saying on the trip up that he wasn't going to have another one. We worked out that we would have to get into their side (end) a bit early next time and join up before kick-off. Then once amongst them we would have a better chance. But we would need numbers to do that.

Ipswich at home and I never saw any of their fans at the game. We went to Liverpool Street station after the game and saw none there either. The game was a 0–0 draw as well.

Maine Road, Manchester next and I was going again. We got the Inter-city up and had a good laugh with some Man City fans on the way up as well. They heard about the Man U trouble on the train and reckoned we should have done more. Man City's ground is near an area called Moss Side, which had loads of blacks living there at the time, a real rough area in fact. Man City is the only team actually in Manchester, and many wished Utd on the outskirts was on the South Pole. At Maine Road their end is a side like Derby – the Kippax – and we went on there. We never got any bother or looked for any. With the numbers we had we would have been killed. Besides, we seemed to get on with Man City. Many of their lads wanted to know what happened to Man U on the tube. They told us Man U wanted revenge and to be careful next time we came to Old Trafford. This did not worry us: we had walked around their manor, gone into their pubs and nothing had happened. Man City took the piss a bit, but soon quietened down when we beat them 5–1. The game over, we left and headed back to the station and the train home. I was glad Man City fans liked us and vice versa, as they would have killed us otherwise. They had done most other London firms both home and away.

Next game was in London and it was a first: Crystal Palace away. As Palace was not on the tube it was a British Rail job from London Bridge. That's as far as I got. A mob of Millwall had a go at us. There were about thirty of them and we were about ten strong but there were many more West Ham around and soon it was on. All over the station Millwall had tried to hijack us but made a mistake with our numbers. One Millwall lad got me a good one, with a waste bin I think, and flattened me. I got a bit of a kicking, but not much. It seems the West Ham lads were into them. I was helped up and my mate got a bit of a kicking as well but nothing serious. The rest of the West Ham lads chased them off. They had caught us out and I was swearing like mad and then the Old Bill moved in and nicked me. I was put in a maria with a couple of other West Ham lads. We tried telling them we were the victims but being West Ham and with Millwall around, they weren't listening. We were made to wait in the van till nearly six o'clock; they let us out after the game was over and most of the West Ham fans had gone home. The game, we found out, was a 0 – 0 draw. A great way to spend a Saturday afternoon. We were well pissed off. We didn't come across Millwall often and they had pulled a good one on us. At least they were up for it and if they had had more, the station would have been a war zone.

Next game was a midweek one against Liverpool and hardly any Scouse turned up, no mob anyway. Just a few lads, mainly working in London. I saw a couple of offs with some older fans, not anything serious. We talked about waiting for Millwall at our next home game and also their next home game. We would try and catch some of them where the District line and the train from New Cross Gate crossed at Whitechapel.

Wolves were next at home and we wanted them but they never brought a mob down. It seems they were only good for their subway trick and we had tumbled that so they never showed.

One more home game. It was Leeds and they brought a fair few down and got a good slapping on the South Bank. They came down Green Street like they owned the place (but not for long) and were really mouthing off. They just got past the Queens pub and it was on. West Ham appeared from all over and Leeds got a good kicking. I saw some of the gobby ones crying, one was calling out for the Old Bill who arrived shortly, mainly mounted coppers and a few on foot. They got in between us and it calmed a little until the Leeds fans started with the gob again. One Leeds lad had a crowbar and caught my mate across the arm really badly. We steamed him real hard and when we were finished he was just lying there all limp. The Old Bill got to him and an ambulance soon turned up. My mate got a fractured arm and was well pissed off. The St John's put it in a sling and insisted he go to hospital for x-rays. He told them to piss off as he wasn't going to miss the game. The Leeds fans got an escort to the

South Bank and we followed them. As they got in we heard another big off going on. The lads already on the South Bank were hitting them as they came up the stairs. Many of us jumped the turnstile and joined in. We had them trapped and Old Bill could do nothing. If they had opened the big gates, more West Ham would have steamed in and getting down from the police tunnel on the South Bank wasn't easy. They were trapped and they knew it. They fought back and had a real go – what else could they do? The Old Bill finally got some control and were thumping into fans. They did not care who. One gave me a nice kick to the shin which felt like it broke my leg, even with the high-leg Martens on. They finally got up on the terraces and there they stayed, near the police line.

Many were upset and down the front getting treatment from St John's. I saw a couple getting carried out. Chants of 'WEST HAM AGGRO, HELLO, HELLO!' were going up. We had done them badly and could forget about Millwall. Another time for them. We decided to go up west and follow them to the British Rail station. We had given them shit all through the game and many opted to leave quietly and slip away unnoticed. The game finished 2 – 2 – not bad, as Leeds were defending champions. Their fans had got a good smacking and we were pleased. Leeds were only good at home and against teams like Fulham. They came down the East End and learned not to mess with us. One good thing, the Old Bill our end gave everyone a smack, they didn't care who. As I've said before, at Leeds the Old Bill favoured the home side, right or wrong. A few lads were nicked up there and, because of the distance to attend court, pleaded guilty by mail and then were handed out a fine. Probably a good money-raiser up north.

One last game of the season and it was Arsenal away. We were all fired up for this one and their North Bank was the target. We had heard they had given the Yids a seeing-to and were well up for it. Only time would tell. We met up at Mile End at 12 o'clock and many West Ham faces were already there. They told us a large mob had already gone up by tube and that suited us well. We noticed more and more lads were going with us. We had a fair mob and many liked the way we travelled. We decided to take the tube to King's Cross and then get the Northern line to Arsenal. At King's Cross we came across about fifty Arsenal lads. We ran at them and they legged it. We were over a hundred strong and they stood no chance. Old Bill was quick on the scene and went on the tube with us for the short trip to Arsenal. We decided to get off at Caledonian Road station, walk up to Highbury from there, a good thirty to forty minute walk, and see what we could find on the way. About forty of us got off and Old Bill did not know whether to go with us or stay on the train. We walked up both sides of the road and some lads went into a pub called the Sutton Arms. No sooner had they got in than we heard a massive off going on and Arsenal fans were piling out of the doors. We had found some of their boys.

We ran across the road and into the pub, tables and chairs were overturned and some Arsenal fans had jumped the bar trying to hide. Some were having a go but we done them easily. Next thing Old Bill piled in and we were chucked out. A few West Ham were taken away in marias and the rest of us were made to wait. Some Arsenal fans came out covered in blood. It seems as soon as West Ham went in there the Arsenal were chucking glasses, bottles, ashtrays and whatever they could find at West Ham. They came off second best and my mate who had his arm broken reckons the plaster of Paris was the best weapon he ever had. Loads of Arsenal were talking to Old Bill and pointing out who was who. They were quick to grass us up, although they were the ones who started chucking things. Our mates only went in for a swift pint and stumbled on the Arsenal mob. A couple more lads were pulled and Old Bill asked us who were the trouble makers in the Arsenal fans. No one grassed – that was not our style. A few had cut heads from thrown bottles or glasses but nothing serious, mainly a lot of blood that made it look worse.

We were finally let go and about six Old Bill escorted us to the ground with a couple of vans in tow. It wasn't long before we were left with only a couple of coppers as the rest left with the vans to go back to King's Cross station. It seems there was a big off there and Old Bill wanted reinforcements. We decided to start running to the ground and this pissed the Old Bill off but they kept up, we could not lose them. At Highbury we went straight on to the North Bank and West Ham had half of it. Arsenal had got on early and held this time. The police were in the middle with a line about three deep and every time West Ham tried to get at Arsenal they stopped them. Even Arsenal had a go back, nearer kick-off, and we stormed back at them. The Old Bill was in the middle and fucked. More Old Bill came in and bodies were being pulled out. At least Arsenal were having a go back this time and we never got their end completely. Just being on it and staying put was a good piss-take and they hated it. We lost 2–1 and Jimmy Greaves, an ex-Yid player, scored for us. This upset them because Greaves was transferred for what was a big sum of money in those days, in part exchange for Martin Peters, something West Ham fans weren't happy about. To have him score for the Yids' bitter enemy was another good piss-take and they hated it.

The game over, we tried one run at the Arsenal. A lot of Old Bill were waiting outside now; we all started singing, 'WE'LL SEE YOU ALL OUTSIDE' and off we went. Both sets of lads tried to have a go but Old Bill had it well under control. We left for Arsenal station. Maybe we would pick some up there, or at King's Cross.

Some of the West Ham lads went up to Finsbury Park station to try their luck there. We met up at King's Cross and heard reports of only a few offs there. Old Bill were everywhere, so we made our way home to Mile End.

The season had come to an end. We had a bit of a result with the Gooners, more of a piss-take really. West Ham finished seventeenth that season and got knocked out of the FA Cup third round by Middlesbrough. I did not go to that game – only a few did – but we heard the Boro lads were nutters. Some carried hammers and they were well up for a ruck.

Notts Forest knocked us out of the League Cup and again I heard nothing about what went on up there, which didn't surprise me as Forest weren't much of a mob and West Ham took very little up midweek. All in all we had some good results and gave some spankings out. The best was Man U on the tube. We copped a few slaps as well but if you give it you gotta take it and Arsenal grassing us up at the pub was sickening. They liked giving it but were quick to point the finger when Old Bill were around.

We had been caught by Millwall, who in turn did not realise how many we had. The Newcastle lads were good: they never bottled and held their own even when they were outnumbered. The Mackems were good lads, and we never really had bother with them.

The way we travelled was getting popular and more and more West Ham lads were doing the same. We were getting quite a reputation now too, and the Old Bill were waking up to us. But we still had next season to look forward to.

CHAPTER 5

1970–71

A DREAM START to the new season: we had the Yids away, Arsenal at home midweek, then Chelsea away. Three London derbys in a row. We expected the Yids to be up for it as it was a new season and they were at home. We had decided to go on the Shelf at White Hart Lane as the word was that the main Yid lads went on there. We got the train from Liverpool Street and when we got to Bruce Grove we got off and decided to have a look around. Old Bill was well on the case and we met up with about three hundred West Ham lads who had a bit of a run in at the Corner Pin pub. We were going to go there but gave it a miss as the place was full of Old Bill. We went into the ground and on to the Shelf. The Yid fans seemed to have changed ends; the Paxton was their home end now. It did not matter at that ground, you could still get from one end to the other under the main stand.

About thirty of us were on the Shelf and as kick-off came closer we noticed more and more familiar faces from West Ham on there. From the way we cheered when the teams came out I reckon there were about two hundred of us. The Yids hated this and ran at us. It was on and we stood. This brought more West Ham into our mob and we fought back. The Old Bill came in and tried to stop it but it was too late. We were on their prized Shelf and we were not moving. I got a couple of whacks, nothing much. I hit one Yid with the head and saw him holding his head and blood pouring out; he was screaming like a big girl. This seemed to make them think twice and we steamed into them, kicking and punching as we went. They stood for a little while and then most legged it into the crowd. A few of our lads had been hit as well. Some had bleeding noses which looked like they were broken. Many had just been kicked around the legs. We saw a fair mob of West Ham on the Paxton and they were holding their own. The West Ham fans on the Park Lane came around and it left a big space where they had been. They joined the lads on the Paxton and a massive ruck was on. The Yids held their own and, as much as we hated them, they at least had a go.

The Paxton was half and half and Old Bill got in between them. It was good to watch from the Shelf, the constant surging back and forth by the rival fans. It kicked off again in the Shelf when Jimmy Greaves scored. The Yids had been chanting, 'TOTTENHAM REJECT' earlier on, which we reckon was bad, with the record he had with the Yids. We never slagged Martin Peters off like that and, in that transfer, they had the better deal. With Greaves scoring against his former club it was on again and the Yids had re-formed and steamed in at us, this time with a bit more fight. We held, but only just. We copped some decent hits. I saw a mate of mine getting a kicking while he was down and a couple of us jumped in to help him out. We got him up and he was fucked, they had done him good. I saw a few Yid lads in the same way being held up by mates. This was not the Yids we knew; this lot stood and helped each other out, something we had never seen before. We steamed back in and got a few more. A few lads from both sides were just swinging and kicking out, some connecting, some not. One Yid lad hit about three West Ham. He had a bit of style about him and knew how to ruck. We steamed him as our target and he went down under a hail of punches and when down it was like a feeding frenzy, he got the shit kicked out of him. Old Bill moved in and pushed us back, they grabbed this lad and hauled him out, he was more or less carried off by Old Bill.

This seemed to take the steam out of the Yids as missiles started coming over, mainly golf balls that went straight back. I got hit with one and they leave a lump on your head the size of the golf ball itself. It really made me mad and, along with loads of other lads, we charged them again. Old Bill had formed a line and were starting to nick people and throw them out. Things calmed for a while and we saw the Paxton was still having fun, mostly surging at each other. Old Bill had it sussed and were pulling lads out from all over. We sang, 'WE'LL SEE YOU ALL OUTSIDE' and the Yids laughed and made a wanking motion with their hands.

The game over, we tried one more run at them. This caught both them and Old Bill by surprise and we kicked them right out of the ground. They weren't standing this time and we steamed in. I got hold of one Yid and threw him down the stairs into other Yid fans. This caused a surge forward and many lost their balance. We followed through and they never stood a chance. Many were trying to get up and we just laid the boot in and trampled over them.

We got outside and found a large mob of Yids running towards us, about six hundred of them. We thought they had just come around to the Shelf but right on their toes was a bigger mob of West Ham chasing them. Mounted police were trying to get into the middle of it but were having no luck and when we came out chasing the Shelf boys they were fucked and had enough. We wanted more and joined up with the main mob of West Ham from the Paxton, mostly a lot of younger lads but well up for it. The Old Bill had pulled more and more in and were getting a hold of the scene now and only a few small offs were going on, mainly the odd Yid fan getting a kicking.

We were escorted back to the station by a massive mob of Old Bill. The Yids had legged it outside but at least they had a go inside. Talk was that a mob of Millwall had teamed up with the Yids for the day. I never found out if this was true but the way they stood it had to be something different. We hated Millwall more than the Totts and they hated us. If it was true then we would find them at Liverpool Street station. When we got there the Old Bill were waiting at the gates. We charged at them, as many never had tickets, me included and they stood back and opened the gates. There was no way they were going to hold this lot. We went down to the tube, singing all the way, which sounded great in the long windy tunnel down to the tube line. We never found Millwall, if there ever were any to find. To this day I still don't know if they teamed up with the Yids; we heard rumours, that's all. We could not believe it somehow but if they did then they got a kicking and legged it as well, so in a way it was a double result for us. The Paxton had been 50–50 that day and we had done the Shelf and chucked out the South

London gypsies into the bargain; it was a fair result. A round for us and only the first game of the season.

Arsenal at home midweek next and as expected they appeared on the South Bank not long before kick-off. Many came not wearing any colours and just slipped in. They had a few in the West Stand as well and we saw a few disturbances in there. Old Bill were pulling lads out and on the South Bank they stayed close to Old Bill to the left of the dividing tunnel. The game was like the fighting, a non-result 0–0 and it was a real disappointment. Arsenal had the fans but not the bottle, it seems – not against us anyway.

Chelsea at home next and we expected a good turnout from the West London boys. They had won the FA Cup and were on a high. They had won it after extra time in a replay at Old Trafford. We heard they had taken the Stretford End, not hard when that's where Old Bill put you and Man U fans weren't interested. Leeds had played them and stories of how Chelsea had run Leeds at Wembley and Old Trafford filtered back. I could not see it myself. Out of the two mobs I reckoned Leeds were well up for it and although Chelsea had some good lads they had a lot of hangers-on, would-be boot boys, who would give it the large one behind the safety of Old Bill and down the Kings Road. This was a sad fact which was borne out when they went down into Division Two in the mid-Seventies and their gates were shocking. Many of their fans just left and only the die-hards remained.

We decided that instead of going up west and looking for them, we would hang around the Queens pub and market and let them come to us. A few came through in dribs and drabs, then a massive mob came out of the station. We could hear them from the platforms with their 'CHELSEA' chants, as if someone clicked their fingers. A large mob of West Ham gathered and waited, then out they came, about five hundred strong I reckon, and down the short hill from the station towards us. Many were lobbing bottles and golf balls at us; they steamed right into us. We were about three hundred strong and they gave us a fair go. Another load came out and came down towards us; the Old Bill were going mad trying to stop it all. Chelsea had come mobbed up and had got us. Most of our lads were on the North and South Banks, we were totally outnumbered and we fought running battles along Green Street down to the main gates. Chelsea had the better of us and were well up for it at the gates. About half of them split and went to go on the North Bank. The rest stayed and we fought them right around to the turnstiles of the South Bank. Old Bill were grabbing blokes and throwing them into vans but it did not help. As Chelsea lads tried to get in the West Ham lads inside were fighting and pushing them back. Many jumped the turnstile only to jump back out again and we were waiting. I got a good whack in the head and went down. I was kicked as I went down but managed to scramble up again. Chelsea had us on the back foot and they knew it. If they had stuck together they would have run us easy as there were too many of them. The Old Bill restored a bit of calm and we finally got in the ground.

Inside the ground they had half the South Bank but had lost the North Bank. They got run really bad on there and many hopped into the side stands to get away. We tried to get behind them but Old Bill was a wake-up to that and we stood side by side. I had blood coming from my head – it looked worse than it was – and I had got a few boots in my back. Chelsea had started with all the gob again. We wanted them and they were up for it this time. They had totally outclassed us at the station and down to the ground. They had brought the numbers this time. The game ended in a 2 – 2 draw and we left a bit early to try and get the jump on them. It seems many Chelsea had the same idea and it was on again outside the South Bank. We had the numbers this time and fought all the way to Green Street, where a large mob of West Ham from the North Bank steamed in. Lads were jumping over cars and how no one got run over, I will never know. We had them now and they knew it and tried to leg it back to the station.

We chased after them, picking up the stragglers, and they got done bad. There was no sign of the mob that had gone on to the North Bank. At the station a massive Old Bill presence slowed them right up as they tried to get into the station. With us on their backs steaming into them, they pushed their way through. Old Bill shut the gates and a few Chelsea were locked out with us. They got a bad kicking, Old Bill were powerless to stop us. The first train away and the gates were let open. We charged down the steps and the platform was empty. They had all piled on the first train and left. We were mad that we had taken them for granted and they had caught us. We rode the tube home to Mile End and loads went up west looking for them. Nothing was heard about it except that Chelsea reckoned they ran West Ham and they did for a while. It was good to see them stand for a change. I had a badly bruised back next day and needed three stitches in a head wound, which made me think I was hit with something, not just a good hit with a fist. We looked forward to the return trip to the Duck Pond.

Leeds away next and about sixty of us went up by Inter-city. As soon as we got into Leeds station the Old Bill were waiting there and also a fair mob of Leeds fans. We took the piss out of them about Chelsea beating them and they fired up and wanted us bad. If it wasn't for Old Bill they would have killed us. The Old Bill escorted us to the ground and I think we were the only West Ham fans that made the midweek trip up. We went on the away end – we weren't scared of Leeds but we weren't stupid. They would have killed us with so few a number. They beat us 3–0 and we were well pissed off. We went all that way midweek, had the piss taken out of us and got thrashed on the field. It was a long train trip back. To take Leeds on at their manor, you need big numbers, so another day maybe.

We still had another away game on Saturday at Man U. I didn't go but I heard that about two hundred West Ham did and got turned over by Man U really badly. Some of the lads got some of their own back on the travelling Cockney Reds at Euston.

We had two home games in a row next: Southampton and Everton. Southampton fans were a joke and hardly any showed; they seemed to save their energy for Portsmouth lads and from what I have heard never had a result with them.

The Everton game came around and the Scousers had a fair crew down. They went on the South Bank and started giving it the big one. We steamed them, they tried to stand but we ovewhelmed them and kicked the shit out of them. They ran down the front and Old Bill moved in. I was grabbed and hauled out for the customary walk around the pitch and through the players' tunnel. They took my name and let me go. I was surprised, as normally they hung on to you till half-time at least. I went straight into the North Bank and just watched what was happening on the South Bank. A few offs were going on and there were loads of surges by West Ham towards the Everton fans. It seemed funny being on the North Bank again and I met up with a couple of mates and we mainly had a drink and a bit of a piss-take. Everton done us 2 – 1 and we were not happy. We left early to go to the South Bank and try and catch a few coming out. It was too late, loads of South Bank lads had the same idea and had steamed into them. Many were walking around holding their faces and Old Bill was trying to grab lads all over. They got the Scousers into some sort of order and most had come by coach and were escorted back to where the coaches were parked, closely followed by us. We were chucking anything we could find, giving them some of their own medicine. A couple of coach windows went, mainly by golf balls.

We left and looked for the few who came by train. By the Queens market this one Scouse lad, who was bleeding from the face, was swearing and calling us cockney bastards. A load of younger lads jumped him and he went down under a flurry of boots. It was funny in a way to watch a grown man mouthing off and a load of kids about thirteen giving him a kicking. He should have kept his mouth shut. The Old Bill moved in and the kids disappeared like nothing had happened. That was one sore Scouse with a long trip home. We headed off and decided to call it a day at Mile End. Loads of Old Bill were around – it seems another load of Everton fans had got a bad kicking and a couple were being stretchered out. We all laughed; fuck the Scousers. In one respect they weren't as gobby as Liverpool, their neighbours. At least they tried to stand, even if it was in vain.

The Hawthorns and West Brom was the next game. I missed this one and I heard it was just a piss-take and nothing went on. The West Brom fans were hardly contenders in the Midlands. We hoped our next home game against Newcastle would be a good one.

The Geordie lads had put up a good show the year before and we knew they would stand if it came to it. They brought down about five hundred by train and some coaches. The main mob came out together from the station and crossed the road and started walking down Green Street. Safety in numbers, they thought, but they were wrong. As they got parallel to the Queens a load of golf balls and glasses were thrown at them. We tried throwing the glasses against the houses so they would smash and shower them with glass. They had enough and steamed at us across the road and it was on all over. I copped a smack in the chin and laughed at the cunt. I wished I hadn't because one of his mates hit me from the side in the jaw and nearly dropped me. Fuck, it shook me up. My other mates jumped this cunt and he fought like fuck but he went down in the end. Everywhere Newcastle and West Ham fans were holding bloody faces. A couple of lads grabbed one Geordie fan and threw him across a market barrow and they were jumping all over him. His mates came to help him but they got a kicking as well. A couple tried to hide in the pub but came straight out again with some West Ham lads on their tails.

The Old Bill on horses were trying to regain some control and lads were being lifted from both sides. One copper got a nice smack from a Newcastle fan and this spurred on the Old Bill badly. The gloves came off and they were hitting out at anyone. They eventually restored calm to a degree and the Newcastle lads were given an escort to the ground under the watchful eye of Old Bill. They did not want this and were keen to go on with it. They were now outnumbered badly by us but they did not seem to care. We kept lobbing what we could at them and they threw what they could back. As we got to the road which goes around to the South Bank, the Old Bill formed a line and tried to get them into the ground. The Geordies still wanted to go on with it, so we legged it around to the other road, which takes you out to the Chicken Run and South Bank corner. We came around as most of the Newcastle lads had gone in the ground. We could hear it going off inside and we got in as quick as we could and came on the South Bank from the corner entrance near the Chicken Run. A large mob of Geordie lads had gathered in the middle and had joined up with the rest from the coaches.

When we had the numbers we steamed straight into them. More and more West Ham lads joined in but they stood. It was toe-to-toe stuff for a while and I got another smack in the jaw. How it was never broken that day, I'll never know. It was a good hit but I got him back with the head and he went back and down, lost his balance and over he went. We just walked and stamped over him and I saw him being helped out by St John's afterwards. He was fucked, a rubber man. The Old Bill got between us and things calmed down a bit although there was a lot of surging back and forth. We lost the game 2–0 and Old Bill was trying to get them to stay behind. They did not want to but wanted to get out the other exit and the only way to do that was through us. I think they remembered the year before and weren't going to be caught twice. Old Bill finally got them out and they had a massive police escort back to the station. Some of the West Ham lads went down to the coaches but that was a waste of time. They got them into the station and again closed the gates until the train had gone and they let us though. All in all a good day. I admired the way the Newcastle lads stood – not many did and they were well up for it. They kept screaming at us during the game, 'Wait till you come on the Leazes End' and 'We'll have yer, yer bastards.' They kept their promise.

Newly promoted Huddersfield was our next game away and I did not fancy it at all. The name alone suggests it was a shithole, all flat caps and whippets up there. I gave it a miss and gave my jaw a rest. It clicked for ages after that game and hurt like fuck. Burnley at home next and as they were the same colour as us we never knew if they brought a mob down or what. I never saw any. We done them 3 – 1 and the king, Geoff Hurst, got a hat-trick.

Stoke away next and I missed it as I had to work. I heard I didn't miss anything except Old Bill giving the West Ham lads a hard time and a couple of coach windows went in from stuff chucked by Stoke lads. We had the Yids at home next and we were waiting for them. They had put up a bit of a show at their ground and we were hoping the same would happen at Upton Park.

They showed up with a mob of about six to seven hundred at 1.30–2 p.m. They had a large police escort with them and were chanting all the way down Green Street, nice and gobby with Old Bill protecting them. We walked on the other side of the road and the odd missile went over. This brought more Old Bill into it. They got them on to the South Bank and as we went in the police were searching us for weapons or anything else. If you had steel toecaps they weren't letting you in and many a West Ham fan had his foot stamped on to see if they had steel toecaps. They said we could take them off and get them after the game and go in our socks. Fuck that, I did not fancy it. If there was an off, half your fighting power was gone. Loads of us tried to get in the Chicken Run and West Side but the Old Bill were clued up and we could only get in the North Bank, which was the home end anyway. The ground was packed that day and the South Bank was full of Yids. We could only watch from a distance. We saw a few minor offs but mainly the crowd surging. The game itself was a 2 – 2 draw and there were Yids everywhere except near us. There was an off in the Chicken Run – some of the older West Ham fans had a go at a small mob of cheering Yids when they scored their second goal. You could feel the tension in the ground. We wanted them and could not touch them. Loads of us left early and made our way to the tube. We would try at Mile End and then maybe on to Liverpool Street station. It seemed many had the same idea and at Mile End the first train-load pulled in full of Yids and the Old Bill at every doorway into the train. We could not get on and they could not get off. The next train was the same although we managed to get on the end carriages but Old Bill had the connecting doors well guarded. At Liverpool Street we piled out and tried getting at them, but more Old Bill were on the platform.

They tried to turn us back so we jumped on the next train, rode one stop and doubled back. This worked till we got up to the platform where we were sussed. We went after a mob in the buffet bar but the police got there first and we were stopped. Five of us were lifted and taken across the road to Bishopsgate police station. We were printed and had our photos taken and held until about 11 o'clock that night and let go. We wanted to know what the charges were but they said they dropped them and we were told to piss off.

It had been one shit day. The Old Bill were getting well clued up now. They gave fans escorts and the wearing of steel toecaps was banned. On-the-spot searches were becoming common. They would grab you, search you and then move on. It all made for an uneasy atmosphere. It seemed that they were saying, 'We control this manor, not you.' We had to prove them wrong, and many times we did.

Crystal Palace away next and we weren't going to get caught

like last season again. We teamed up at Mile End and about thirty of us went to London Bridge station by tube to get the British Rail out to Selhurst Park. We met up with a load more West Ham at the station and we headed off. We had no trouble whatsoever on the way there. A couple of minor rucks in the ground, mainly the odd Palace fan getting a whack for being out of order, but mainly a quiet day. No trouble on the way back and the game was a 1–1 draw, which was the highlight of the day really. Two London teams in as many weeks and no rucking at all.

Blackpool at home next and that was a waste of time as far as their fans go. There weren't any, not the ones we wanted. The next game was Ipswich away – the end of the road again. Always good for a laugh and their fans were a good piss-take. They had some good lads, mainly blokes off the trawlers, but nothing to worry about and they weren't keen to have a go. It seems some big rucks have gone off up there against Norwich, their closest and bitter rivals, but we never saw any of it. We reckon the strongest thing to come from Norwich was the mustard that was made there, the only tasty thing in those parts.

The Ipswich end was divided by fences and you could no longer take the home end, only share it. Old Bill loved it – they could control us and hold us back after the game till the home fans were safely away. This they did and then you had only enough time to get back and get the train home. This didn't worry us as we weren't on the special so we had a walk around. I reckon if you blinked hard and long enough you would miss most of the town. It did not take Old Bill long to find us. We had found a pub open and slipped in out of the way. We had an hour or so to kill before the Inter-city left so we decided we would have a drink.

The pub we went in went all quiet, like one of those you see in a movie when the bad guy walks in. The barman refused to serve us and this sparked it off. A couple of lads chucked a chair behind the bar and some of the locals had a go at us. That was their mistake. I remember one Ipswich bloke saying to my mate, 'Come outside and have a punch-up,' in that funny accent of theirs. My mate hit this bloke with a beautiful head butt and the turnip sat on his arse, he didn't know what had hit him. We all laughed; no Marquis of Queensberry with us. Next thing Old Bill were on the plot and moving us out. They escorted us back to the station and told us we had missed the football special and we would have to buy tickets for the normal train. They got a shock when they found out we had been going on it anyway.

Our next game was Wolves at home and a small mob of their lads showed for a change. Many never made it to the main gates at the ground. Before getting turned over they came out in a small mob and tried going in the Queens. This was their first mistake. Wearing colours was the second. I was in the pub when they came in and I could not believe it. Many of us looked around in amazement as about a dozen got in and it was on. My mate hit one with a big ashtray on the side of the head and he went down screaming. We steamed them and they were trying to get out but were held up by more Wolves fans coming in. One lad was hitting into them with a chair, they were screaming and people were laying the boot in and did not care. The pure cheek of them, coming in to where we drank! Old Bill arrived and things went back to as if nothing happened. A few Wolves fans were lying on the deck, broken glasses all over, a couple of overturned tables. The Old Bill got them and we followed. They were fucked – they came looking for it and had got it, more than they expected. The Old Bill was telling them to hide their scarves. Most did and Old Bill walked them to the ground where most went into the West Side and only a few went on the South Bank and stayed close to Old Bill in the police tunnel. We only heard them when they scored, which was three times – the game was a 3–3 draw. After the game they could not be found. We discovered that they had come down to show us who were the boys. They did that, stupid fools. I had never seen a mob of fans come into the Queens before – not a good place for a pint if you were an away fan.

Manchester City at Maine Road was next and I did not go to that one. We normally got on with Man City fans, so many of us did not bother. If you wanted to take on Man City you would need a big mob up there as the fans are genuine and loyal, not like their neighbours.

We had Coventry at home next. As expected, it was a no-show from their fans – which was just as well for them as we lost 2–1 and we were well pissed off.

Our next game was Derby County at the Baseball Ground. We decided to get the coach up as Old Bill was giving us a hard time at the main stations. We booked a coach from a travel firm opposite Mile End station. We knew if Old Bill was watching the trains they would have an eye on supporters' coaches as well. There were enough of us to charter a coach, in fact too many, but not enough for two. It did not cost much more per head and the coaches were better than the old things Laceys put on. We could always have a beer on board if we wanted. It wasn't far to Derby and we got up there about 1 p.m. after a stop on the motorway. If anyone has been to the Baseball Ground they will know what a shithole it is, one of the worst I had been to.

We stopped in a pub close to the ground and no sooner had

we got a drink than one of our lads was hit with a water jug for no reason. One Derby bloke started swinging a hammer; they were up for it and it was on. I got hit on the shoulder by the bloke with the hammer, who was swinging it madly. He was our target and we got him and he got a good seeing-to. He was trampled on and left on the floor. His mates didn't even try to help him. We had the numbers but they didn't care. Glasses were being thrown and we finally got them outside. We chased them to the ground and we teamed up with some other West Ham lads. There were about two hundred of us now, so we steamed into the ground and on their end, the Pop Side (it was really a side, not an end – a bit like at Man City). We looked for the blokes from the pub. They certainly had surprised us, even with lesser numbers. My shoulder hurt like fuck, but it wasn't broken. Once we were in and gave it a 'UNITED' chant they steamed us from all sides. They were mad and a lot of their fans were much older than our lot. We copped it bad that day. The Old Bill seemed reluctant to stop it and when they finally moved in they gave many of our lads a whack to separate us. I had copped a few whacks on the back of the head, nothing much, and I also got a few boots as well. The worst affected of us was one of our mates who had been dropped and trampled really badly. His teeth were badly damaged and both cheeks were well swollen, as were his eyes. Old Bill moved us behind the goal, more for our own safety than anything else. Derby had done us well again, they had the numbers in the ground; in the pub they didn't, but they didn't care.

We won the game 4–2 and we got back to our coach under escort by Old Bill. Derby kept lobbing things at us and as soon as we chucked them back the Old Bill would pull the lad who done it. They were giving Derby fans a free licence and this pissed us off really badly. Never had we seen the Old Bill side with fans so blatantly before, but it was fucking obvious to us. When we got on the coach they seemed to vanish; their fun was over. We told the driver to stop at an off-licence. He hummed and hawed a bit but a whip-round soon sweetened him. We grabbed two cases of beer and settled down for our trip back to London.

We talked about who did what and a few mentioned hammers being used inside the ground. I never saw any inside, just the one in the pub, the one I copped a whack with. Our mate who got trampled was missing and a few lads told us he was taken away by ambulance – he was in a bad way. We never took Derby for granted again. They were mad at home. We would have to wait several weeks to see what their away form was like. I had a week off work with my shoulder. I faked it as a work accident so I never got into any hassle from the gaffer. Being an apprentice was hard and you had to do as you were told. The job I was on had a Scouse foreman and he hated me, so a convenient slip and fall off a ladder got me a week off.

I missed the Liverpool game at home as I knew the foreman would be there and I didn't want to get caught. Liverpool done us 2 –1 and I heard that a mob of them came down, about two hundred-odd from reports from my mates, but they were well turned over. I just hoped the foreman was one of them. I would find out soon enough.

I wasn't missing Chelsea at the Duck Pond, which was the next game on. We were looking forward to it, as Chelsea were pulling some stunts on other teams and were having a go back for a change. Against us, would they be the same?

Loads of West Ham met up at Mile End at about 12.30 and

then we were off. We filled up the tube and many waited for the next one. At Liverpool Street loads more tried to get on and we thought they were Chelsea but it was more West Ham. A few got on and the rest waited for the next tube. Loads wanted to get off at Kensington High Street and walk the few miles down to Stamford Bridge along North End Road and turn the place over. Most agreed we would not get far with the big mob on the train, so it as on to Fulham Broadway to await the rest of the West Ham lads that were behind us on the next tube.

We piled out at the Broadway station and rushed the gates. They were trying to stop us and wanted to see tickets but they had no chance. Old Bill were on hand and a few lads were getting searched. They were doing the steel toecap trick but we had wised up to that. I had my American officer dress boots on and as they were going out of style, I decided to get some use out of them. Never again though. I don't recommend the leather soles on the terraces – when you were chasing fans they were slippery as fuck. Suedeheads were the scene by those days but loads of skins were still around and Chelsea had hundreds. Times were moving, though – a few lads had dropped out of the football scene and were only seen now and then at big games where they knew there would be some aggro. And today was one of those days.

Outside the station Old Bill were mob-handed and said they were going to walk us around to the North Stand as the Shed was only for home fans. We all laughed and took the piss and Old Bill tried moving us off. It was then the next train came in loaded with West Ham lads. They did the same as us and charged the gates and out to join us. We were well over a thousand strong by now and Old Bill had lost it. We all started running towards the Shed End with Old Bill in tow. We were all chanting, 'UNITED'; we were going for the Shed and Old Bill knew it. We got around to that yard outside the entrance and quickly filled it as more and more West Ham piled in. Old Bill closed the turnstiles; they weren't having us on the Shed, no matter what. Chelsea fans on top of the steps were chucking golf balls, torch batteries and whatever else was lying around. We saw Old Bill not twenty feet away from this lot and they did nothing. We chucked what we could back and it was obvious we weren't going to get in the Shed this time.

We made our way round to the North Stand and got in there. As we went in loads of Chelsea lads jumped the fence and legged it up to the Shed. The so-called North Stand boys did not want to know and we all started singing, 'RUN CHELSEA, RUN CHELSEA, RUN, RUN, RUN.' The Shed was nearly full and I reckon their lot got in as soon as the turnstiles opened. Chelsea came back with the chant 'WE'LL SEE YOU ALL OUTSIDE' and we all laughed. Once again we had come to their manor and taken the piss.

Talk was going around that we should jump the fence and invade their end but Old Bill must have got a whisper of this, as they brought more and more police around and formed a line across the North Stand at the fences. It never went off and they done us on the pitch – 2 – 1 in a shit game. They had some great players at Chelsea, like Charlie Cooke, Chopper Harris, Peter Osgood and Bonetti the Cat in goal. Being cup holders and showing up at Upton Park that year with a decent mob, we all thought they would be well up for it at home, but they weren't. The game ended and we all went round to the Shed End. Most had legged it; there were a few scuffles but nothing serious. They failed to show and we were well pissed off and headed back to the tube. A load of us decided to head to Victoria station and see if we could pick their lads up there; North End Road was a waste of time.

We headed into Victoria station and caught a few dribs and drabs of Chelsea but one look at us and they legged it. We came on a mob of about fifty Chelsea lads and when they saw us they were off. We chased them towards New Scotland Yard where Old Bill were coming up to meet us. Police vans were driving all over the road and they blocked us off. We wanted to go back to Victoria but they weren't having that, we had to go to St James's station. Again the Old Bill had looked after them. When we walked to St James's we saw about a dozen lads outside the New Scotland Yard and one look at us and they bolted inside. I dunno if they were undercover Old Bill or just scared Chelsea fans, but the uniforms looked after them. We talked on the tube about why they ran in that direction. Maybe they were Old Bill but we never found out. Once again Chelsea had shit with us, after we had heard so much about what they did with other fans and they did have a go at Upton Park.

All in all the whole day was a piss-take. We went to their manor, walked around like it was ours and all Chelsea did was hide behind locked gates or the Old Bill, just gobbing off as per usual.

The FA Cup third round arrived and we drew Blackpool. I didn't go and just as well. I heard that they walked over us on the pitch 4–0, but there was nothing on the fan front. The game was marred by the newspapers blaming the loss on Greaves, Moore and the big black mamba Clyde Best. They had been on the drink the night before in some nightclubs. It turned out Best got the blame but had never touched a drop.

With us out of the cup our next game was Arsenal at Highbury. We planned to go across with a small mob to avoid the Old Bill and get on the North Bank unnoticed. We reckoned there would be about twenty of us, which grew to nearly a hundred by the time we left Mile End station. A lot of lads we had never seen were tagging along and some familiar faces as well. We didn't know many by name but knew they were OK if things went off. Our mate who got the hiding in Derby was there, minus a few teeth, and he still had bandaged ribs. He had spent the night in a hospital up in Derby before coming home.

Our plan was to meet up with some other mates at Tottenham Court Road station about 1 p.m. and head off from there. We got out at the station and when the next train came in a large mob of Arsenal got out. When they spotted us they steamed towards us but we stood. This seemed to scare them and they stopped. We ran at them and they legged it, some down the end of the tunnel and into the tube itself. They were lucky they weren't killed. Some made the exit, a few got done. One Arsenal geezer pulled a blade out and was waving it around; we backed off and tried getting to him. He was going backwards and you could see he was scared, but he still had a blade and, no matter how tough or good you are, you can still get sliced bad. He kept going back and he lost his balance. This was our chance, we all rushed him and he was soon being trampled on. A couple of mates wanted to throw him on the line and let the next train get him but we put a stop to that and jumped on the next train out on the Central line. The platform had Arsenal fans all over it, some kneeling, some lying down, others were just helping. As the train pulled out we saw Old Bill coming on the platform. We had just got away but not before turning over a sizeable mob of Arsenal lads. So much for going unnoticed.

We had about thirty left now that some had gone after the

other Arsenal lads at the station. We jumped off at Queens way and decided to let things cool down. We would have a walk around, have a pint and then jump the Circle line back to change for the Northern line to Arsenal. We went into a pub down Queensway called the Ducks and Drakes. Loads of spades in there but this didn't worry us as they were mostly Rastafarians. Unfortunately a couple of them objected to us being in there, so a mate of ours, who was something like third-generation black English boy, hit this bloke straight in the mouth. He went backwards and it all stopped. I think they were shocked that one of their own had hit out at them. We did not want any bother with the West Indians, it was Pakis we hated, but it was close. We were served one drink and told to leave. We thought about turning the pub over but decided against it as we were supposed to be not attracting attention and so far we had done the opposite.

We walked back up to Queensway station and jumped the tube back. It was now getting close to three o'clock and we wanted to get in the ground. We rode the tube back to Arsenal. The game had kicked off and we were late. We went straight on to the North Bank, only to find most of the West Ham lads were on the Clock End. Arsenal had been leading the table most of the year and their fans seemed to come out of the woodwork. We called them the London Irish as many a Paddy played for them, along with Jocks. Thousands of Irish lived in North London, especially Camden Town way. We teamed up with a few more West Ham and waited around the centre of the North Bank. Arsenal were all over us and won 2–0 and towards the end some Arsenal bloke had a go at one of our lads about something he said. We had been sussed and the Gooners steamed in on us. Boots and punches came in everywhere; we copped a real bad hiding. We tried to get away but we were surrounded. It eased off and Arsenal got their second wind and were back into us. The Old Bill got us out and for once I was glad to see them. Arsenal slaughtered us. They had the numbers and we were stupid going on their end with so few. If we had not been late we probably would have been on the Clock End. We found out the Old Bill weren't letting any West Ham on the North Bank and searches were the order of the day, along with questions like 'Who scored last home game?' – all Arsenal-related questions only Gooners would know. They warned that if you were found on the North Bank and were West Ham you would be nicked. We were pulled out but the Old Bill reckoned we had enough of a hiding and let us go. We missed the main mob of West Ham lads but heard it was on between the two sets of fans and no one ran – Arsenal stood for once. We heard loads of stories about Gooners pulling blades. We had seen it ourselves back on the tube.

The hooligan scene had stepped up a gear. Back on the tube we worked out that we came off lightly. Mainly black eyes, bruised legs and arms; the odd nose had been hit too. We came off lucky for such a wild attack and with the numbers they had. We reckoned it had been just ordinary Arsenal fans and not their main boys because, had it been, we would have come off worse. Our mate who got done at Derby got a badly broken nose and that was all he needed to go with the missing teeth and cracked ribs.

We would get them back, they had their go, now it would be our turn. But it was a few years before we turned the tables on them. A couple of lads who tagged along with us were whining like fuck about the way we had been done but we told them to fucking shut up: if you wanna give it out, you gotta learn to take it.

We looked forward to our next two home games, which were Leeds (as they were current champions they were sure to bring some lads down) and Derby County. Leeds did bring a fair support down, a mixed lot of older fans and women and girls. The few hard cases there mixed in with them and it was hard to get at them. They came mainly by coach and the few that came by train slipped past us unnoticed. No chanting mob, nothing. They were on the South Bank and near Old Bill, which proved to us one thing: they were all gobby shites and needed Old Bill around them to mouth off. Maybe the Yorkshire constabulary looked after them at Elland Road, but the local Old Bill were pulling a few of them out and walking them round to the players' tunnel and the exit. You could see fans in the West Side spitting at them as they went past. They were brave lads at home, but away they were nothing: all gob and no action. We tried getting at a few, but no joy. They knew how to play the game inside the ground and stayed close to Old Bill.

A couple of golf balls went down on them but it soon stopped when the word went around that women and girls were amongst them. We did not want them; it was their lads we wanted, but they were having no part of it. It seems the stories we heard of Chelsea doing them in the FA Cup Final both times were true. Leeds were only good at Elland Road and with numbers; outside that, nothing. I had seen them run Fulham a few years earlier but I reckon a grandmas' meeting could run that lot. To add insult to injury they done us on the field 3–2, a close game; after all, they were the reigning champions.

The next game was one we all waited for: Derby County at home. We wanted their mob badly after the way they had turned us over on their manor. We hung around the Queens and waited for them to come out of the station. A large crowd of West Ham were hanging around the market and pub, just killing time till they got there. We heard a few coaches had come down but they parked way down the other end of Green Street across the road and Old Bill had that well sewn up. A couple of older fans came out with scarves and the younger fans stalked them. All at once a bunch of about six would put the boot in and have it away with his scarf. We watched this a few times and it was funny to watch, like a well-drilled scene from a film. The oldest of these lads would have been about eleven at the most. Now and then Old Bill would grab a kid picked out by the away fan and a search found nothing. The scarf had changed hands many times and, after a few words from the police, the kid was let go. What else could they do? We did the same when we were just kids and we would have bets on who could pinch the most scarves. About ten of you would put a thru'penny piece or a tanner (sixpence) in and at the end of the day the winner would take all.

As far as Derby went it seemed to be a no-show. Another home-only team. We went to the South Bank about 2.30 p.m. and looked for any there. There were only a few older ones and they stood near the Old Bill. They done us 4–1 on the field and we saw a small mob on the West Side. We should have woken up, their own end was the Pop Side and they came on to our side bit. We tried getting into the West Side, but no luck. We went under the South Bank and around to the corner bit where a locked door joined the stands. It took a few boots but finally gave when this one lad gave it a two-legged flying kick. We piled through and it was not long before we came up beside them. They were near the players tunnel, to the right as you look across towards the East Stand/Chicken Run. We waited a while and Derby scored their third goal. That was the signal. They jumped up in joy and we

jumped in boots and all. We had them well outnumbered, a bit
of payback for the Baseball Ground.

They didn't know what was happening. Even some of the
older fans were giving them a smack as they tried to get away.
They were pushed back into us; loads were on the deck crying
and covering their heads. It didn't matter, we just stamped on
them. My mate, who had got done bad up there, was going
mental. He wanted revenge and got it. He went mad, kicking
and punching like a windmill on heat. Some tried getting out on
the pitch but the West Side wall was nearly ground level and
you had to climb, not jump out.

Old Bill got in and were whacking anyone who was in on it –
they didn't care who it was. The police had a good way of getting
through a mob. They sort of teamed up and used their arms in a
pulling and pushing motion, although the pushing was more like
punching. If they got hold of you, depending on the fight, they
would grab you by the collar and back of your shirt or trousers
and push you through the crowd, and too bad for anyone in the
way. I got pulled. It took ages for Old Bill to get through. The
couple at the players' tunnel weren't coming in and just waited
for more to turn up. A load of them came from behind us and I
was yanked out and taken through the back way of the West
Stand along with some other lads. We got our names taken and
were thrown in the back of a maria. They wanted the Derby fans
to lay charges, but none did. A few Derby fans had left by
ambulance – they had been well done. Apparently it was a bit of
a trick of theirs, going on the side bits at away grounds. They
were in for a shock at Man City if they did.

We were driven to the top of Green Street where the police
station was and we thought we were gonna be locked up. Once
in the police yard we were let go and told to fuck off. Some of

the lads who were with us lived in Romford and just got a bus on Romford Road. We walked back to the tube station and talked about what went on. We all agreed next season up there we would have to be on our toes.

The season was going badly for us on the pitch and at the next few games fuck all happened, although a crew at Coventry tried it on but had backed off. That's what I heard from a reliable source but I didn't go so I won't comment any further. We won 1–0 for a change, though. I missed the trip to Anfield as well. Our next home game was a midweek against Man City and nothing went off, although they had brought fuck all fans down because it was a night game. The game was a non-result as well, 0–0 in a boring match.

Nottingham Forest at Upton Park next and surprisingly they brought down a load of fans. Many came by coach and only the odd few by train. They got on the South Bank and stayed close to Old Bill. We had heard they had run Derby at home so we were expecting a bit of a show but it never went off. Only a few scarves were being nicked by the younger fans. We were noting more and more West Ham were coming on the South Bank. The away end advantage had gone; it was nearly all home fans now and the North Bank wasn't dwindling in supporters. We beat Forest 2–0 and that was the highlight, no fighting went off. Another time for them, maybe.

Blackpool away and I stayed home. We drew 1–1 and I heard nothing went on. Our next away trip was something we were looking forward to but before that we had Crystal Palace at home. Their fans were a waste of time. A few said Millwall had teamed up for the day but it was rubbish: they never fronted and the two teams hated each other anyway. A 0–0 draw summed the day up.

The next couple of games I missed. Ipswich at home, which was a non-event, the result a 2–2 draw. The next away game was at Everton and I missed it as I worked. I was in the last year of my apprenticeship and working the odd Saturday paid for the away games. We won 1–0 up there and I heard a few lads got a bit of a kicking. The Stanley Park trick had again been pulled on them. You win some, you lose some, but the next game I was not going to miss – Manchester United were coming to town.

We had a drink in the Blind Beggar in Whitechapel midweek, about thirty of us, and we worked out we would meet at Mile End about 11 o'clock and go to Euston and try and pick a few off. We talked about how Everton had done some West Ham lads the week before and figured we would need a big crew up there next time to make an impact; their day would come. But first, Man U.

As planned, we left Mile End around 11.30 a.m., about a hundred strong. Word had spread and we had a good crew. A lot of lads we knew not by name but by face only and we knew they were sound if it went off. There were quite a few younger lads too, all with one thing in common: they loved West Ham and hated Man U. We worked out that we would ride the tube to Notting Hill and change and get the Central line back to Tottenham Court Road and then change again and get the Northern line to Euston. We would have a look for some Man U fans, then on to King's Cross and finally back to Liverpool Street station and then back to Upton Park from there. We were sure we would pick up some of their fans but only saw older fans and kids. We wanted the older lads, their boys, but we could not find them. We got back to Liverpool Street a couple of hours later and spoke to some West Ham lads, who told us a big mob had been through earlier looking for West

Ham. We headed off to Mile End and found loads of Old Bill on the platform. Man U had been through and turned over a few West Ham lads. A couple were on stretchers and looked like they'd had a good kicking.

We headed off to Upton Park and when we got out there was a massive police presence around. The Man U mob had been through and had caught some early West Ham fans and went straight on to the South Bank when the gates opened, virtually unchallenged. We tried to get in the South Bank but Old Bill were having none of it and loads of lads were being turned away. About ten of us managed to get in and joined up with about another fifty. We never had the numbers and Man U had the South Bank nearly covered. They pulled one on us and we asked a few lads what time they had got there. We said we were Cockney Reds and a few told us they got down early, because they wanted to get out of the station early before the main West Ham fans got there as they hated Green Street. If they had any sense they could have taken the North Bank and we asked why 'we' never did. This bloke told us they had done us at Mile End and Old Bill had escorted them straight into the South Bank after that. I felt like hitting the cunt, as did my mates, but we weren't stupid. Discretion is the better part of valour and with our few numbers we would have been killed.

We moved away and tried getting in the Chicken Run. Old Bill let us in after we told them we had been threatened. The copper gave us a funny look but let us in anyway. He probably reckoned if there were less of us in there it would make his job easier. They had the South Bank and there was nothing we could do, but they had to get out and we would chance it then.

There was a lot of piss-taking at the game and we won 2–1. That alone was great, as it shut them up for a while. We left about fifteen minutes from the end and there was no way Old Bill was gonna let us at them. They had the road blocked to the South Bank and we had to go the other way round the back of the North Bank and to the station that way. We figured we would get them coming up Green Street, Old Bill or not. We walked around and heard the cheer go up for the final whistle. The North Bank was pouring out and I think they had the same idea. It's amazing how fans know what's going on.

By the time we got back on Green Street we had a large mob and as we turned into the street we all started jogging towards the South Bank end. Many other West Ham joined us; we could hear the Man U fans singing and around on to Green Street they came with Old Bill in front. Not many, but as they came round we ran at them and straight into them. The Old Bill was swept aside and we lashed out at them. Lads were going down all over, some stood, some tried to run but most were trapped. One hit out at me and I got a real bad pain in my elbow; I thought he must have hit me with a bar or something. He soon went down, and a couple of lads were screaming at him on the deck about him having a blade; I never saw it and didn't care. Old Bill were going mad and the mounted moved in. The coppers on horseback didn't give a fuck. If you were in the way, too bad. One of theirs had gone down in the initial charge. He was pushed over and when down copped a few boots; nothing serious but they didn't like it. I had never seen the local Old Bill so mad. One of theirs had gone down and they hated it. They jumped in and I got a good smack across the ear from one. He knew how to hit – my ear was ringing and burning. We got pushed back and a line was between us and the Man U fans. Loads of them were on the deck covered up, loads with blood coming out of their faces.

1970–71

We got back to the station before Old Bill and caught the tube to Mile End where we would try again. On the tube one of my mates asked what happened, pointing to my hand. It was covered with blood and I could see no cuts. I took off my monkey jacket and had a look. I had been cut right across the elbow, a real nasty gash. It must have been the cunt with the blade they were giving a kicking to. I was lucky: I'd thought it was a punch and sort of blocked it, otherwise it would have been worse. My jacket was slashed cleanly as well, so it must have been a cut-throat razor or similar. My jacket was fucked and this annoyed me. The elbow could wait, but it was stinging and a lot of blood was coming out.

At Mile End the Old Bill were well on the plot and one pulled me and asked what all the blood was about. I showed him and he said I was going to hospital. I told him I would go later, but he insisted. He got me up near the main entrance and asked for an ambulance to be called. I thought he was joking – it was only a gashed elbow, after all. The ambulance turned up and the crew had a look and reckoned I needed stitches and a tetanus jab. I just wanted to go back to the platform but they were having no part of that. They took me to London Hospital where I seemed to wait for ages – so much for the rush. I nearly left and headed for a pint in the Beggar's, which was two minutes away, when my turn came. They put 29 stitches in my elbow and reckon a tendon was nearly cut – that's why there was so much blood. The Old Bill turned up and asked what happened and who did it. I told them I was rushed by Man U fans near the South Bank and that's all I remembered. It was sort of the truth. I finally got out and went for a pint, but I felt funny and left half of it and jumped a cab home. I was tired and sore and wanted some sleep. Next day my left arm was stiff and sore. My mum changed the dressing and gave me a lecture. I told her I fell over on some glass but I think she knew and let it rest. As for the rest of the Man U lads, I heard they got a bit at Mile End and all the way to Euston they got some of their own back.

Sunday came and I met up with some mates from the game at Charlie Browns down by the West India Dock gates. A bit of a rough hole, but a unique place for a Sunday session. We talked about the day before and a few reckoned we should carry blades. I was against that: you had no excuse for carrying a knife and if you did and pulled it you had better use it or someone would use it on you. A bottle would do the trick, or a glass, and you could not get nicked for having a bottle in a pub. I hated knives. I would rather get hit with a lump of wood or have a good kicking than be slashed again. I know loads of firms carried them but I know none of our little firm did. Loads of younger fans carried them, mainly to impress, and that included West Ham. But if a 12-year-old hooligan sticks you with a knife it doesn't matter that he is a kid, the result is the same. I had seen a couple of blades before, with Chelsea, Arsenal and Yid fans. They even carried razor blades in matchboxes that were meant for slashing, and also the bicycle spoke trick, but actually carrying one was not my style. I said I hoped I would never see another at a game again. I spoke too soon.

I had two weeks off work with my arm. I had some sick time owing to me and picking up bricks with it hurt like fuck. So, Man U fan, if you are reading this I hope one day someone slashes you with a blade. I can take a kicking any day (have had a few and handed out some). I have never complained. I believe if you give it you got to take it, no point whining. But that little injury cost me a few games. WBA at home, won 2−1. Notts Forest away, lost 1−0 and Burnley away, lost 1−0. Nothing special in the fan stakes that I heard about, but nothing ventured nothing gained.

Stoke City at home was on the agenda next. They had a few fans down, mostly older ones that came down on coaches. It was a quiet one; their fans were only good at having a go at home and then they weren't much compared to us. We won 1–0, with Geoff Hurst scoring.

The next game was my last away for the season: Newcastle Utd at St James' Park. I had never been up there before, only to Sunderland, which is about twenty-five miles away. The station is between five and ten minutes' walk away and after a long train trip, which about a hundred of us were on, we were glad to have a look around. We had decided to split up and meet at the Leazes End, the Newcastle home end, and see if any came up by coach or the special. About five of us found a pub behind the ground called the Magpie, if I remember correctly. We went in and asked for a pint. The barman just looked at us. He knew we were cockneys and was wondering if he should serve us. He did, and I'll say one thing for the Geordies: their beer is great, Exhibition, I think it was. I'm afraid the fans weren't as good as the beer. One of our mates got a hiding in the toilets, a good kicking, and things were tense. We decided to get out; we stuck out like spare pricks at a wedding. We were nearly out when my mate at the back got jumped and, as we went to help, they all jumped in. We got with a few bruises and they followed us but Old Bill were around and it never went any further.

We got on the Leazes End and met up with some of the other lads who said they had an off at another pub near the ground. We knew the Geordies never liked us and we had given them a kicking a couple of times at Upton Park but they always stood and fought back on their turf. It was our turn. In reality we should have gone on the away end but we fronted their end, even with the small numbers we had, they knew we were there and we knew they knew. Just when would it happen? If common sense prevailed we should have fucked off. We were getting slagged off and spat on and then Hurst scored. That was their signal. They steamed us; we never had a chance and they gave us a good kicking. I was grabbed from behind and hit in the face a couple of times, good hits; I went down and tried to cover up. I don't mean a couple of kicks up the arse, but a good going over. I don't remember much of who did what but we had no chance. I got off lightly compared to others. I had a pair of black eyes, swollen cheekbone and many bruises all over, where I'd gone down and been trampled on. My mates got the same: a couple had broken noses, one lad had got a real good kicking in the ribs and was coughing up blood. When the Old Bill finally got in they carried him out; he never made it back to the train. That was a long trip back to London.

Newcastle at St James' Park would be impossible to take on. They were hard lads, some of the best we had come up against home or away. I was told the Mackems were the same, but we got on with them. We had copped a good kicking and were saying maybe we should have gone on the away end but a few lads on there got some as well. They were doing a West Ham and waiting for us on the away end. At least no blades were used. I respected them for that but lost that respect later on. Newcastle made you feel like you were middle class coming from the East End. It was a morbid place but it had loyal fans who stood. Our mate had three days in hospital up there before coming home. He had cracked ribs and the hospital thought he had a punctured lung because he was coughing up blood; he was also knocked out cold. He was kept in intensive care for observation and was out of action for the next couple of games, which was just as well. We all were and the season was nearly over.

I missed the Southampton away game, as did most of my mates. We were in no condition for an away game and the last game was against Huddersfield at home. I went to that one not expecting any trouble, and there was none. We never saw any of their fans and we lost the game 1–0, a bad ending to the season. We lost the last home game and had a good kicking to think about during the break.

All in all, it had been a mixed season. We had some great results on and off the terraces. On the field, not so good. We missed relegation but finished twentieth. We wanted revenge for the Newcastle kicking and were dying to meet them again. Anyone with brains would dread the thought of having another go after the kicking we got, but it was all par for the course.

A few things worried me. More and more blades were being used and I did not like this; many other fans hated them as well. We had pulled some clever stunts on away fans and had had a couple pulled on us. All in all, the away day travel on British Rail was gaining popularity; the special for the Newcastle game had been cancelled, as hardly anyone was on it. We used the tube system to our advantage and knowing the underground was an important part of any match plan. We had copped a fair hiding at Derby, and we never took fans for granted again, home or away.

CHAPTER 6

1971–72

THE NEW SEASON was here and many changes were on the cards. My family had moved out to Harold Hill, one of those new council estates. Some mates of mine were shifted to Collier Row. It was all part of a changing East End. The street where we lived is no longer there and all the houses have been pulled down. I did not want to go out to Harold Hill. For a start it was not on the tube and for work and games I had to get a bus to Romford, then British Rail to Stratford, then change and get on the tube. There were a few pubs out that way, but if you wanted anything decent you had to go up to Dagenham or Barking or even Romford. Going up the East End was too much hassle as the tube stopped running at midnight, so getting around was hard if you did not drive or have a car. There were some good lads out there and many West Ham, a few Yid fans and of course the Man U followers.

I hadn't long to go before I was a tradesman and that meant more money, lots more than I was getting. The firm I was with gave you three months when you finished your time then you had to leave for a year at least to gain other experience. I had been carrying a hod for a couple of days a week, to tone up for the new season. Humping bricks and muck all day helped a bit with the fitness and it was a good way to keep in trim and get paid while doing it. I was reminded that I wouldn't be able to do it for much longer because as a tradesman I would be getting a lot more money than a hod carrier and no one would pay a brickie to carry a hod. I knew a few lads at West Ham who worked out in the gym with weights and they looked the part, but it was all show – no natural strength at all, although they never ran. We used to take the piss out of them and now and then have the odd arm wrestle and they would get upset if they got beaten, as they regularly did.

Our first game was WBA at home. They never usually brought any lads down but it was the first game so maybe they would. It was good to link up with some old faces. A few lads had gone over to Germany and Spain to work, many dropped out of the scene altogether and some were courting. No matter how many left there always seemed to be another couple to take their place. A lot of the younger fans were coming through and they knew the score. Nothing happened at that game except we lost 1–0, not a good start to the season.

The next game was Derby away and it was only a few days after the WBA game on a Wednesday night. I didn't go, and neither did many others as it was too far for a midweek game. If I had gone, the time we got back into London would have meant that I'd be lucky to make it home by 1 a.m. next morning. Living at Harold Hill had its problems. We lost 2–0 and Forest away was next. I missed that one too and we lost again 1-0. At the next home game we found out that the Forest fans had turned over a mob of West Ham who went in their home end. This surprised me as they had never been any bother before home or away, but again, don't underestimate your enemy. We were at the Ipswich game when I found this out and, as expected, no Ipswich fans made the trip, probably because it was a night game as well. They hardly brought any on a Saturday, only the odd older fan. We wanted their boys and tossers like that were of no interest to us. We drew 0-0 and still hadn't won a game, or even thrown a punch. That was gonna change with Everton at Upton Park.

We reckoned we should go and meet the train at the station as it came in and take them on the tube. They normally had a decent crew and had a go at least, and we owed them a couple. The meet was at Mile End at 12 p.m. and when I got there about two hundred-odd lads were hanging around. My mates told me a smaller mob had just gone, about a hundred lads. We hung around till around 12.30 and jumped the tube. A few more had joined in and with the mob already gone we reckoned there was close to three hundred and fifty to four hundred lads. We got to Euston and found the place crawling with Old Bill. The smaller mob that had left earlier had made right prats of themselves and as the train came in the Everton fans had run them. We never knew how many but we knew they were on the way to the game.

We all piled on the next tube and headed back. We had got the train times wrong, we thought, and were well pissed off. We got back to Upton Park and went straight out looking for them. They had been and gone and were already on the South Bank. Old Bill thought we were another

Everton mob and wanted to escort us to the South Bank. We thought this would be OK but we were soon sussed and told to fuck off. That would have been a laugh – Old Bill taking us right to the Scousers. There was no rush so we went into the Boleyn for a swift pint and to see if we could meet up with some old faces.

We got into the ground about 2.20 p.m. Everton fans were right by the police tunnel and loads of Old Bill were on hand. A lot of slagging was going on but nothing much happened as they were well tied up and Old Bill made sure we could not get at them. The game was over and we won 1–0, our first victory of the season. All that was left to do was to have a go at the Scousers. They got held back while police were moving us on outside with threats that if we didn't go to the tube station then we would be going to the police station instead. We all laughed: nicking a large mob like that would have been funny but they weren't going to let us near them if they could help it.

The Scousers finally came out with a large escort and many had hidden their scarves. As they came on to Green Street, loads split towards the coaches and the rest towards the station. This threw the Old Bill a bit and this was our chance. We ran at them and they legged it to join the others. Loads went up Barking Road and we chased them. Some gave up and just copped it and were given a good kicking. Old Bill was trying to stop us going after them but running up Barking Road was a waste of time as it only led you into more West Ham. Leaving the game we turned a few over and loads ran across the road and headed back towards the coaches. How they didn't get knocked down I'll never know – it's a busy road. It led all the way up to East India Dock Road and on to

Commercial Road and on to the city area, going through places like Canning Town, the city of thieves.

We headed back to the station and found loads of Scousers being helped by St John's. They had been turned over and Old Bill were well pissed off. They had their finger on the control button for a while but it had slipped. We done a few and loads more were done by other West Ham lads. They had had enough and those who were left were herded into the station and escorted away. There was no point going after them with the police riding shotgun with them.

I headed home and got the tube to Mile End and then back again to Stratford to get the British Rail to Romford and then the bus home. Loads of West Ham lived out this way and I got talking with lots of lads. We always talked about what happened and who was next. It was Coventry at our ground and it was a night game a couple of days later, which we won 4–0 – a non-event as far as their fans go. They had never brought a mob down all the time I had been going to West Ham and this was no different.

Newcastle away next, but I didn't go. Only a few were going and we agreed we would need big numbers up there to make an impact at all. The game was a draw, 2–2, and we saved it for a trip to Old Trafford in a couple of weeks.

Chelsea next and we got to the ground about 11 a.m. in case they came early. My mates were telling me that Mile End station was crawling with Old Bill and they were expecting a large Chelsea mob. We waited at the Queens and only dribs and drabs came out, no real mob as yet. About 2 o'clock we were told that a load of Chelsea were on the South Bank. They had got a bus down and slipped in that way – very crafty. We heard of a few West Ham lads who were turned over, but nothing major. Still, Chelsea were thinking and that was one way we never thought of.

We went on the South Bank and Old Bill were pulling the steel toecap trick again but many had wised up and were wearing normal Doctor Martens. Chelsea had about three hundred and were tucked up on the left-hand side of the South Bank as you look towards the North Bank on the other side of the police barrier. I don't know if Old Bill put them there or they went themselves but it made it hard getting at them. As usual Chelsea were giving it all the gob, chanting, 'WE'LL SEE YOU ALL OUTSIDE!' We all laughed and responded with 'RUN CHELSEA, RUN CHELSEA, RUN, RUN, RUN!' No way a small mob like that was going to worry us. Even a big Chelsea mob were nothing, we reckoned. We had continued to hear stories that Chelsea did this or that but we hardly saw any of it. We won the game 2–1 and big black Clyde Best scored twice.

Chelsea hated this, as they had strong ties with the National Front. Most Chelsea hated blacks and we had loads of black lads who ran with us. It was funny because in later years one of their supposed top men was a one-armed half-caste sorta black – and most know who I refer to here. It was the same as the Yids: their so-called 'top man' was a black bloke, as if supporting a Jewish team wasn't enough.

The game over, Chelsea was held back until the Old Bill cleared us out. Would they go back by bus or get an escort to the station? They took the station route and their numbers were well down on what was inside the ground. Many had hidden their colours and sneaked past. As expected they were giving it the 'CHELSEA!' chant all the way up Green Street to the station. Easy being gobby when Old Bill were there to protect you. I would have been embarrassed and many West Ham thought the same. The odd missile was lobbed into them, but nothing major.

At the station the gates were again locked but a crew of West Ham were already on the platform, about fifty of them. As Chelsea came down they ran at them. We rocked the gates and wanted in and Old Bill pushed us back. The lads on the station got done, but not badly. Chelsea hung around long enough to get the first tube out. We finally got down to the platform and a few lads had been done; nothing major – bloody noses and a few cuts. We went after them but it was a waste of time. At Mile End the police held the train up and ordered us out. They were going to slow us down no matter what. There was talk that the Old Bill knew some West Ham lads were on the platform and had let Chelsea through on purpose. I never believed this, as the local Old Bill wasn't as bad as some of their colleagues in other parts of England. Still, they had a bit of a result and we would have done the same. It wasn't long, of course, before we heard that Chelsea had done West Ham. This pissed us off. They had a result with some lads but to say they had done us was well out of order. Still, they had their moment of glory. Let them have it, we would get square with them.

I stayed at a mate's house that night in Poplar and we met up with some mates for a Sunday drink in the Star of the East pub on Commercial Road. We talked about Chelsea and couldn't wait until we got them again.

The next game was Man U away and we were all up for it. We planned to go by Inter-city and hoped there would be a decent turnout by our lot on Saturday. About four hundred-odd West Ham were going up and we didn't know how many by coach – not bad. Many were on the Inter-city and the football special was packed out with away fans, certainly with West Ham, anyway. A couple of lads were pulled into line on the train for pratting around and chanting. We did not want that; the less attention the better. We finally got away and pulled into Manchester Central station.

We kept our heads down and we were Cockney Reds if any one asked. A couple of lads even had Man U scarves tied around their waists, trophies from another game. A lot of new faces were on the train, but we had seen many of them at West Ham. We split up into smaller mobs and made our way to Old Trafford. Some got the train out to the ground, others were getting a bus; some even jumped taxis. We got the bus out and we would all meet at the Man U club shop about 2 p.m. It was decided to go on the Scoreboard End, as an attempt on the Stretford End would need triple what we had and we would have needed to get on there early, which was a bit hard coming from London.

We met up as planned and a mob of about twenty Man U had a pop at some West Ham lads but they soon stopped when they saw the West Ham lads weren't alone. Mostly we were all there by now and we were getting funny looks from the home fans. Old Bill had us sussed and wanted us in the ground a.s.a.p. We tried the old Cockney Red fan bit but they were having none of it. We moved on to the turnstiles and the Man U lads who tried their luck just before had returned. There were about one hundred of them now, and they were giving it all the gob at us. They weren't keen before but now Old Bill was on the plot they were giving it all the gob. This wasn't their lads, mainly just gobby kids but still a mob, and if six or seven of them jumped you the boots hurt just as much when you were down.

Inside the ground there were a couple of hundred more West Ham fans who had come up by coach. It seems the special was cancelled again due to lack of passengers. The fans inside the ground were a mixed lot and joined us in a piss-take of Man U. We got the usual threats from their lot about seeing us all outside. And they were right, we had to get back to the station; the fun was going to begin shortly. We lost the game 4–2 and Old Bill wanted us to hang around after the game to get us out safely. Most of us objected to this but the lot that came up on the coaches did not mind; they were good West Ham fans but not in it for the fighting. They kept us back for about twenty minutes and when we left the away coaches were outside ready for the fans, but not us. This shocked Old Bill. As the special was cancelled they probably thought they would have an easy day.

We broke away and decided to start walking a part of the way and see what happened. We all started jogging down the road and Old Bill on motorbikes were in front of us. Soon a couple of marias blocked the road, or tried to, and Old Bill was holding us up. They had some buses laid on to take us to the station and we were told to get on or have our collars felt. The choice was simple. Some of us piled on the buses but there were only two, not enough, so they were sent off and we were made to wait for more. A fair-sized mob of Man U fans had gathered now and the odd bottle was being flung in our direction. No one got hit and we wanted to have a go at them but the police had matters well in hand. I got pulled with about four other lads. We were thrown into the back of a van and driven away.

Being nicked up here was a cunt. They would hold you till the train went and then you had a long wait around a strange, unfriendly city till you could get a coach or train home. Surprisingly, they drove us right on to the station and saw us on to the train. My mate was gonna tip one of the coppers for his service but this upset them and he was walked on to the train and copped a couple of ankle taps on the way from the Old Bill. They wanted us out of town and had picked a load out as ringleaders and drove them to the station. A few more police vans pulled up and some more got out; like us, they could not believe they had driven us to the station. A couple of 'Thank you, James, that will be all' remarks were made and it was a good piss-take. The Old Bill were even more shocked that we were on the normal Inter-city service. The buses turned up and Old Bill were keen to get them aboard the train. We finally got off and once again we had come to Man U and not a blow was struck. They had no plan of attack at all and if they had been at Upton Park there would have been some offs for sure.

On the train back we all had a laugh at Old Bill and the taxi service. A couple of lads had been told we were trouble makers and they wanted us off their turf. Once again the police only looked after the home fans. Man U had some hard lads who loved a ruck but their problem was that there were loads of hangers-on and most of them were all gob. Like most of the so-called Cockney Reds, they were just London-based fans that travelled up to games most times. To say they were a mob worth fighting was a joke. You only saw them with a large mob of Man U fans and always they were giving it the gob, until there was an off and they always bolted. We had seen them many times on the tube in London and when fronted they always bottled. Some had a go but always got done.

We noticed on the train that there were no Cockney Reds

aboard. If there was then they were keeping their heads down. The only way to have a good go at Man U was on home turf or on the tube.

Stoke at home next and apart from a couple of coaches, no real fans fronted – not the ones we were after, anyway. Even Cardiff had a bigger following down for the League Cup, but many were Taffies based in London and the game was a draw, 1–1. We had heard a few had gone to Wales for the replay, which we won 2–1, and had got a bit of a kicking. It wasn't big numbers that went but they had been turned over. The Stoke game was a nothing as far as the fans went and we won 2–1. We had Leeds away next and also drew them at home in the League Cup a few days after. I missed the away game and from what I was told it was the same old thing up there with the local Old Bill taking liberties with the West Ham fans. The game was a draw, 0–0, and the same result in the League Cup, 0-0. The replay was being tossed around as a good one to go to but it was a long way up there midweek and I didn't go. Loads of West Ham did, though, and had a bit of a result, if the reports from other fans were anything to go by. We won the game 1–0.

Leicester next at home and surprisingly they had a few down to support them. You could tell by the way they came out of the tube chanting – not many did that unless it was a large mob or they had got there early. There was about one hundred of them and we watched them come down the side of the street the Queens was on. This was going to be easy, they were walking straight into us. As they got down we steamed them, they never expected it and loads were trying to get away. They had a go back, I'll say that for them, but had no hope. The Old Bill was there now and I think they were even surprised at them. Either brave or stupid, I dunno, but they never did it again. They were walked down to the South Bank and Old Bill kept them under wraps. After the game was over, a 1 – 1 draw, they left the same way they arrived, many not wearing colours this time. Not much went off – the odd lad got a smack or two, but that was about it.

West Bromwich Albion next and we decided to charter a coach again. One coach turned into three and we picked up the coaches opposite Mile End station. This was the first time I had been to the Hawthorns, the home of WBA, and I was looking forward to it. They never brought any real fans down to us, so it was about time we took it up to them. Wolves were their nearest rivals and they hated each other. There was a story that their nickname the Baggies came from them being a works team from some industrial area up in the Midlands and the players would turn up to play in overalls. I don't know if that's true, but it's a bit different today. They had beaten Everton a few years back in the FA Cup Final but since then had had no luck with the cups or league, a bit like us really. We had been lucky to stay up for a few seasons but our support was loyal.

The aim of the private coaches was to get in without being sussed out. Also, you could have a beer no problems if you sweetened the driver with a whip-round. We finally got to the ground after many piss stops at pubs. Once we had gone into a pub getting them all out again was a joke. I admit to being one of those on the drink that day. We had a good laugh on the way up and the coaches pulled up practically right outside the ground. We didn't want this, but couldn't care less. The Old Bill moved in and found out who we were and escorted us to the away end. Many of us just wanted to find a pub and carry on drinking. A couple of lads fell asleep on the coach and we left them there. The driver told us they would be all right, so it was off on to the ground and the away end. A few West Ham were there and we heard nothing had gone off. We kept Old Bill busy by staging mock fights and when they moved in we all kept still like nothing had happened. They got jack of this and pulled a few lads out. The game was boring, a 0–0 draw, and the highlight of the day was going to have a drink on the way home. The home end had loads of chanting fans, but no one fronted us. I dunno if they were all show or scared, we didn't care. So as far as the football went, a non-result.

The driver reckoned he didn't want to pull over at the side of the road for piss stops as he wanted to knock off. We reminded him it was ours, a private charter till midnight and so we did a deal with him. One pub stop, we could stock up and he could put his foot down and get home. He agreed and we stocked up at a pub we pulled into and all had a drink. The place was deserted and the landlord thought we were trouble but after we got drinks in and stocked up from his off-licence he was well chuffed. I don't think he had ever seen so much money over the bar in such a short period. He even told us to call back again some time. He helped things along with talking about the father, son and holy ghost (Hurst, Moore and Peters). We never knew who he followed and didn't care – he was West Ham as far as we were concerned.

Back on the bus, we set off and passed a coach full of southern-based Man U fans. We could see their Union Jack flag with the words 'Man U' on it across the back window. We passed them and gave them all the abuse we could, as much as you can give on passing coaches. A couple of bottles were lobbed out at them but smashed on the motorway. A bit further down we pulled into a motorway cafe for a piss stop and as we came out the coach with the Man U fans was pulling in. We all bucked up and walked towards it. The coach sped up and kept going. They wanted no part of us and I don't blame them really – after all, we were three coach-loads of well-drunk West Ham fans. We piled back on and told the driver to follow that coach. We all laughed and I think the driver thought we were mad as he held us up to check his tyres or something. The excitement was over so we settled back for a drink and talk about the next game, which was Wolves at home. We hoped they would try and have a go back at us for the stunt and kicking they got on their turf. Only time would tell.

We got back to Mile End about 10.30 and we all headed off. I stayed at a mate's place for the night and joined some lads the next day for a Sunday drink. We met them at the back of Spitalfields market in a pub called the Ten Bells, famous as the boozer that Jack the Ripper used; it was called Jack the Ripper when I left England and was a bit of a tourist trap. First I went to Club Row to get another pair of Doctor Martens. We met the others and many looked like they had got a good kicking. It was a great day out but as for fighting we spoiled it ourselves by getting on the beer. We agreed there would be no more drinking till after the game, only the odd pint.

The Wolves game came around quickly and their fans bottled it. Hardly any showed, not the lads we wanted anyway. The game provided the highlight of the day, with a 1–0 victory for us. We had the Scousers next in the League Cup, a night game. They always brought a few down but seemed to sneak by all the time, not like Everton, who at least fronted. You only found out how many Liverpool fans were at the game when they scored and then they were all over the ground, mainly in the West Stand and a few on the South Bank. As far as fighting goes I saw a couple of little skirmishes after the game. A couple of Scousers got a quick kicking but I saw them being escorted to the station, so nothing major. We won the game 2 – 1. To have a go at Liverpool fans we had to take it up there, simple.

Crystal Palace was our next away game. Going over there was a pain in the arse, as you had to get a British Rail out to Norwood Junction – bit like the Yids in a way, only their fans were worse. There was the odd chance Millwall might meet you at London Bridge but this happened only a couple of times and they weren't mob-handed, only a few lads trying to pick up some stragglers and give them a going-over. Crystal Palace are much the same colour as West Ham and getting in their end was not a problem. Although they were South London and the accents sounded the same they were gypsies in our eyes, as were most clubs on the wrong side of the water. To say the Palace fans fought for their end would be a joke. Only when we scored our first goal could you see that it was nearly all West Ham fans. We won 3 – 0 and only a few minor scraps were going off, nothing much at all really. The whole day was wasted as far as fighting went, but once again we had proved that we could get into an away end without being noticed and take the piss. In fact, when the first goal went in, many Palace fans moved away from us. I think they were surprised at how many of us there were. To labour a point, if Eric Cantona did his kung-fu kick at the Chicken Run or even the Pop Side at Derby, or perhaps the Kippax, he would not have got out in one piece, as many fans will confirm.

The game over, we headed off towards the station. I saw a couple of Palace lads get a bit of a kicking, mainly from the younger ones, but as far as we were concerned it was a non-event. It proved one thing: that we were the kings of London and no one could touch us.

Sheffield United at home next and a non-event from their fans, which was a shame as we were dying to have a pop back at them. We even lost the game 2–1 and when they scored you could not see any fans around, a few in the seats only. It seems less and less fans were coming to Upton Park, so we would have to take it to them.

Huddersfield was next away and I gave it a miss. I never fancied it at all and I heard nothing went off up there; we even lost 1–0. I found out at the next game that a few of their fans had a go but got run easy.

Man City at home and not many came down. Those that did never had any trouble, the odd punch-up here and there but that was all. We lost 2 – 0 and were well pissed off, but that's West Ham. We had a couple of good games coming up, for the fans anyway.

Liverpool next and we decided to go up by coach. We could not charter from the firm in Mile End as the bottle-chucking affair at the Man U coach had been reported and the firm simply put their prices right up. We went with Laceys and at least there were no drink stops so we had to stay sober. About four coaches went up. We went by coach as the ground from Liverpool station is about a thirty-minute walk, maybe more, away from the ground. Unlike Manchester the locals would soon suss you out and attracting attention was something we did not want. We talked about going on their famous Kop end, but agreed you would need many thousands to make a dent in it. Four of us went on there, just to say we had been on the Kop. Their support at home was fanatical and the Kop was one of the best atmospheres I have ever felt, except for Wembley. It was a real mixed crowd, loads of older fans, many drunk, the place was alive with the crowd surging back and forth. On the away end the West Ham fans were trying a 'Bubbles' song but were soon shouted and whistled out. It was a shame they had never brought a load of these fans down to Upton Park. They scored and the place went mad. As it turned out, that was the only goal of the game and the Scousers left happy. Loads of cracks about cockneys, but we bit our tongues. Typical Scousers, gobby as always but when you are out numbered about four thousand to one, you take it on the chin. You would be stupid if you didn't.

Back on the coaches a few lads said they had a bit of a go in a pub near there. Nothing major and it was handbags we found out. Out of the two Liverpool teams, the Everton fans were the lads up for it. Their local derbys would have been good to see.

At our next home game we knew there would be some trouble: Arsenal were coming to Upton Park. Arsenal had won the double the season before and were only the second side to do so. Their hated rivals Tottenham were the first. Arsenal now had loads of fans on board – it's surprising what a bit of silverware does for a team's support.

If West Ham had had the success on the park that the fans had had off the park, who knows what would have happened on the hooligan front. I can say one thing about West Ham fans: they are loyal and if I was in a big off I would rather have them with me than anyone else. Maybe the Geordie lads and Man City lads were like that as well. The Sunderland fans were OK when they were down with us but they were a hard mob, something I saw at Wembley at the FA Cup in '73.

Back to Arsenal. They turned up in their thousands but were not organised at all. They just fronted up and offs were going on all over Green Street. Many an Arsenal lad copped a hiding that day and they filled the South Bank. Quite a few West Ham lads got a slapping in there and we wanted them bad. Our small mob was about a hundred strong and they gave us a kicking, nothing serious, more a case of damaged egos than anything else. They were well up for it and if they had been organised they probably could have taken our North Bank, but they seemed content with the away end. I got pulled by Old Bill, along with three other lads, and thrown out. No names taken, we were just told to fuck off. Not only had we copped a bit of a kicking, we had been thrown out of our own ground.

Well pissed off, we joined up with some other West Ham lads and decided to head off towards Liverpool Street station and wait there to see if we could pick some up. One thing about British Rail stations: you could get a beer when the pubs were shut, even if it was a lot more expensive. A few fans were coming through and we found out the game was a 0–0 draw and it was a boring game. An older Gooner fan had come into the buffet bar and filled us in on the game. He said he wanted to get away early, as the West Ham lads were potty – his exact words. He said many were leaving early. Little did he know he was talking to eight West Ham lads. Had he been twenty years younger he would have got a slap. More fans were coming through and going straight on the platforms. Then a mob of about thirty came on the concourse. A few headed into the bar where we were. We thought, here we go, grabbed ashtrays and bottles and waited. Three blokes came in, had a swift half, looked us over and left. Just as well, because there were now about sixty or seventy outside. We thought they were gonna tell them and we were ready. Then they all ran on to the platforms through the gates.

We went outside and heard the 'UNITED' chant getting closer. A mob of about one hundred West Ham lads came running up and headed in our direction. We were glad to see them but they thought we were Arsenal. We were getting ready to leg it, when one of the lads was screaming 'WE'RE WEST HAM, WE'RE WEST HAM!' They stopped and sussed us out. A couple of faces I knew from the ground and they knew us – they had been on the trip to WBA with us. We told them they had just missed a mob of Gooners that legged it when they heard them. They told us the Old Bill had it well sussed out at Green Street and they came up on the off chance of doing the same as us. Another load of about fifty came up and we all teamed up and decided to go down on the tube to look for them. We rode the tube up to Tottenham Court Road station and waited. A few trains came and went and there were no Gooners on board, only a few older fans and kids, no mob. They had disappeared; we could not believe it. We were well pissed off. They'd brought down such a big mob, and after the game they all vanished. To this day I don't know how they got away but they did it well. And the day had held so much promise too …

I gave the next away game a miss, Southampton at the Dell. I hated that place and their fans were a waste of time. The game was a 3–3 draw. Speaking to lads who went, they said it was basically a piss-take and there were only a few fights outside before kick-off, so I saved my money. We had the Geordie lads at Upton Park next. They nearly always put on a show, but not this time it seemed. They had no mob down at all and we owed them one for St James'. Only a few turned up though, and not the lads we wanted. Next time maybe; we wanted them bad and they knew it. Taking them up there would require a massive mob to make a dent in the Leazes End. Maybe next season.

One of the highlights of the season was coming up: the Yids away. We had heard they were getting it together and had put up a show last year inside the ground. Time would tell.

The plan was to meet at Liverpool Street station at midday. Word of this spread and we decided to go a bit later and stay away from the main mob and meet up in the ground. The trouble was, many lads thought the same and when we finally left the station about two hundred of us were going; no chance of sneaking in with this lot. Mainly older lads, they knew the score and we decide to go on the Paxton as we had heard the Yids were going to make a show of it. By the time we got there the place was crawling with Old Bill and we found out the West Ham lads were already in the ground.

We got in and half the Paxton was ours. The Totts again put up a show; we joined in and put on a massive charge at them. We went straight into them; they held and never ran. It was crazy, boots and fists flying everywhere. We were winning and Old Bill was trying to stop it. We surged again and I saw one Tott lad standing behind a crash barrier and kicking out at West Ham fans. He thought he was safe but was well hit when a lad did a flying kick at him from behind. He went forward and down and was set upon. He was trampled and St John's got him out after Old Bill dragged him clear. They were getting control now and we had run the Yids right over towards the corner section. We had two-thirds of the Paxton and they hated it.

More West Ham were on the Park Lane and when Clyde Best scored the only goal half the ground was West Ham. It kicked off in the Shelf and Old Bill was on the scene in a flash. Lads from both sides were being led away. We surged towards the Yids again but Old Bill kept us back. We would have them outside.

The game over, we tried one more charge at them. We got through and into them. This time they weren't standing. They had had enough but not us. We chased them outside and the West Ham lads who were on the Park Lane came round and straight into them. Some turned back into us; they were trapped. Old Bill were going mental, they had lost the plot and the Yids were getting a kicking. Loads fought back, they had no choice. One jumped me from behind and grabbed me round the neck. He pulled me down and I was sort of expecting to get a kicking but I got straight up and the lad who jumped me was getting it from three West Ham lads and I stuck a couple of boots into him as well. I never knew them but that was the good thing about us: we watched each other's backs, even if we didn't know them. They were West Ham and, like a family, we looked after our own. This was proven time and time again; we never let our own down, even if we got a kicking.

The Old Bill had it well sewn up now and were grabbing blokes from all over and getting them into vans and away. Loads of Yid fans were just laying there; they had been well done. We all headed off towards the station and jumped the train back to Liverpool Street. The day was ours and we done the Yids again on their manor.

As the train pulled in, a large mob of lads were waiting. We thought they were Totts and steamed at them and they charged at us. The poor ticket inspector legged it. The

'UNITED' chant went up. They were West Ham, the lads who had been on the Shelf. Again we nearly fought our own. We all laughed and headed off. Tales of blades being pulled from both sides were going around. I never saw any, though a couple of lads said a couple of Yids got slashed on the Shelf. I heard no more of it and nothing was in the papers, so I reckon it was all bullshit.

It was a good warm-up for our next game, which was Man U at Upton Park. We couldn't wait for it to come around. Some of our lads were going to the Blind Beggar on Sunday afternoon for a drink, so I stayed in the East End at a mate's place and joined them to arrange the next Saturday's entertainment. We all decided to meet up at the ground early and not bother meeting their train. We would meet at the Queens about 11 a.m. and take it as it came.

The day arrived and we met up with a few lads who had been up west the night before and had a couple of run-ins with some Man U fans, mainly lads working in London. About 12 o'clock a mob of fifty-odd came out of the station all geared up with colours and scarves. They crossed the road and started walking down towards the ground, all the time looking at us. We had about two hundred now and began taking the piss. They kept quiet and loads were hiding their scarves but they were walking right into some other West Ham lads who ran at them. They all spread and went different ways. Old Bill was soon there and a few were standing by them and talking and pointing in our direction. We had stayed put and took the piss some more. More Old Bill came and got between us and the station – a just-in-case measure, I reckon.

The Mancs were walked down towards the ground by a sole copper, but there were others near. Loads of lads made clucking noises like a chicken. They were keeping their heads down now, about two dozen of them. There were about fifty odd before but they were not hanging around. If that had been us we would have stuck together. More Mancs came out, mainly in threes and fours, and many were getting their scarves lifted and a touch up with the odd boot for their trouble. No main mob as yet and it was getting close to 2 p.m. We headed off to the South Bank. Old Bill were searching lads at random, mostly West Ham. The Mancs were already in and were standing next to the police dividing tunnel, as usual giving it all the gob. We had no hope of getting at them and only a few minor offs were going on. A couple of lads got grabbed by plain clothes Old Bill. They were quick to let you know who they were, as if they didn't a kicking was on the cards for sure. The Mancs were doing all the slagging and we were the ones getting lifted. I think the Old Bill were happy keeping them all together. If they were thrown out and allowed into Green Street alone it would have caused more bother by the lads who were already lifted. They had about a hundred of their main lads down and had gone in in small numbers and had formed up inside the ground. They never did this at any other ground and usually turned up, all singing and the usual gobbing off. It seemed that down here was not a place to take liberties and the softly-softly approach came into use. I can't say I blamed them – if you were an away fan, Upton Park was one of the least friendly places to visit.

The game was a great result for us on the field and we done them 3–0. Many lads left before the final whistle to get on to the tube station before the Old Bill escorted the Mancs up and locked the gates. Last time a small mob of ours did this they were turned over by Chelsea. We waited and took our chances at the end of the game. Old Bill escorted them out but only as far as Green Street, where a load went off to the coaches and the rest headed towards the station. With no police escort many Mancs hid their colours and tried to blend in. Loads were being picked off and there were small rucks going on all the way up to the station. They weren't interested and it was getting hard to find them. The lads on the platform turned a small mob over but again Old Bill was thick on the ground. Using plain clothes coppers was a first for us and many a lad got a pull and was searched and let go. It was like they were warning us, letting us know they were around. After so much anticipation, the day was a flop on the fan front.

I got the tube down to Stratford to hook up with the British Rail to Romford. At Stratford station a few other West Ham lads were on the platform. We wondered what was up and we soon found out about ten Mancs or Cockney Reds were in the buffet bar and they were waiting for them to come out. We told them they would be waiting all night so we went in for a look and a beer and sure enough there were about ten of them sitting down, all having a beer, giving it the gob about being robbed by the ref. For fuck's sake, it was 3 – 0, a convincing win. There were five of us and the lads outside, who seemed a bit reluctant to come in. We had enough and my mate chucked a chair into them. They were shocked and we steamed in and hit them with anything we had. They were cowering, and some were trying to get out. A couple did and went straight into the other lads. If any of you remember the buffet bar at Stratford station, or have been in it, you will know it is not the biggest and to have twenty-odd lads going off in there did not give you much room to move. It was all over in minutes. We had done them. Some had got away propelled by sheer fear; a couple were cowering against the wall with their arms covering their heads; the rest were well out of it. 'Not so gobby now, are we?' my mate was shouting as he laid the boot in. We pulled him out and got out of the station.

There is a pub called the Two Puddings in Stratford and we grabbed a pint in there before heading back to catch the train. Outside the station there was an ambulance and a couple of police vans. We went in and even bought tickets to Romford. We got back up on the platform and saw one Manc on a stretcher so we moved down the other end of the platform in case the staff at the bar saw us and pointed us out to the Old Bill. They had one of the lads who was outside before and he was being led off; the silly git must have hung around and got pulled.

At last the train came and we headed off. It had been close but we gave them a hiding. Those Mancs had all the gear – the Doctor Martens, the clothes; they had come dressed for the part and we served it up to them. One of our mates had a sore elbow; he reckoned he got hit with an ashtray by one of us. We all laughed and told him he shouldn't get in the way. We had a bit of a result, no major offs. The Mancs were getting cunning. We talked about the way they had sneaked in and reckoned we would have to get in the ground early next season – but that was next season.

Everton away was on the cards next and I didn't go and heard nothing, so I assume nothing went off, and we lost 2–1, so a trip and money saved. We had our friends Derby next and we had already talked about going on the West Side. We still wanted them and as far as we were concerned last season was not enough, we wanted to give them more. Many reckoned they would go on the Chicken Run. If they did they would get slaughtered on there with the mainly older West Ham on it. Any cheek and they would get stuck in for sure. We needn't have worried: hardly any showed and those that did were older fans and were mainly in the seats. It seems it was once bitten, twice shy. They liked giving it, but away they were nothing. We even heard Chelsea gave them a good kicking at Stamford Bridge. The game was a 3–3 draw.

The next game was sure to be a laugh: it was Ipswich at Portman Road. We had already talked about getting the Inter-city and booked during the week. It seems many other fans had the same idea. The railway bloke tried getting us on the special but we told him we weren't going for the football. It seems he had heard this before and gave us a strange look. We decided that for the extra few quid we would go first class.

Saturday came around and a massive West Ham mob was milling around. Most left on the special and about two hundred of us got the Inter-city. This brought the coppers around to us, the main mob had gone on the special and this lot were still here. They were puzzled and as we went through the gates our tickets were checked; they got a shock to find some of us were going first class. They did not know what to do. Some Old Bill travelled with the special but our mob threw them right out. We finally got off with no Old Bill. We weren't going to wreck the train – that would have brought attention to ourselves. Some of our mates took the piss out of us going first class and we told them British Rail had reserved the seats for us and we would see the common types at Ipswich. The difference between first and second class, apart from the price, is that the seats had little napkin head covers and you were in compartments. Apart from that, the food was the same and just as bad. We should have saved our money, because we stayed with the main mob of West Ham. The inspector told us we were in the wrong section and this brought laughs from our mates. We told him we wanted to see how the common man travelled. This brought more laughter, and all in all a good piss-take. The inspector just left shaking his head. Many played cards and three-card brag was the game most favoured. Many talked about what we would do when we got there. The special had already gone, so unless it was derailed the surprise was gone.

We got into Ipswich and there was a large Old Bill presence there. It was obvious that the first mob on the special had been through. We all got off and just walked up to have our tickets checked under the glare of Old Bill. We all met up outside and decide to split up to throw the police off. It was only Ipswich and their lads were not up for it. Old Bill were trying to herd us towards the ground, but about eighty lads broke away and started jogging into town. The Old Bill went mad; they didn't know what to do. We went straight into the ground and, as expected from their lads, it was a non-affair. We took their end again and we said we should chant 'Ipswich' as we wanted to stir the West Ham boys up. We did and they nearly ran at us. They were well up for it and the lads who went into town showed up. Nothing had happened, we found out, and we just went ahead and took the piss out of the locals. When the song 'I CAN'T READ, I CAN'T WRITE BUT I CAN DRIVE A TRACTOR' went up, the locals replied with some ditty about 'soap and water', meaning we were dirty cunts. Old Bill had us under wraps and at half-time anyone who went for a beer or a piss was watched all the way. This was the most police I had ever seen at a small match. They were everywhere and it was obvious that it was not for our protection. The game was over and we lost 1–0.

Well pissed off, we left with a police escort all the way to the station. We all started to jog and Old Bill were well pissed off too as they tried to keep up. Police vans and cars were racing to the front; it was more of a show of force than anything. Once again we walked all over Ipswich without a punch being thrown. The special was waiting and the lads piled in. We made our way into the buffet bar. Loads left to find an open pub. This confused Old Bill, but we were no trouble. The train was finally going and the lads who went looking for a pub just got on with a police escort. Nothing had gone off, we were told. Going by Inter-city once again had thrown the Old Bill.

To sum the day up, it was crap but we had a few laughs at the expense of the Ipswich fans. When we pulled into Liverpool Street loads of Old Bill were waiting and they were checking the tickets. There was no hassle at all and we went down on the tube and left.

I missed the next away game at Wolves, as I had to work. I heard from my mates that the subway trick nearly came off again but Old Bill were well clued up this time. It was more of a stand-off between the two sets of fans. I heard of only a few rucks going off, nothing major. We lost 1–0 and my mates said that just about summed it up.

We had the Palace next at home and, as expected, it was a no show from their lads. They had a few in the West Side and the seats who cheered when they scored but that was all we heard of them. The game was a boring 1–1 draw. Many of us decided to get the Inter-city up to Bramall Lane the following week. Some of us still owed them one and we hoped we would get a good away turnout.

We had about two hundred on the train and most knew

each other, if not by name then by sight. At Sheffield we made our way to the ground and linked up with about one hundred and fifty more, who came by coach or car. We went straight on to the Kop and stood in the middle, expecting them to run at us any second. But no, nothing. The kick-off and still nothing. They won the game 3–0 and we all left. We all felt disappointed that nothing went off, even with us taking the piss something shocking. We left and started to walk down the back of their end and there was a mob of about three hundred waiting. We all started running at them and as it was downhill we were soon in amongst them. I don't think they were expecting it, as only a few Old Bill were around and normally the away fans got a seeing-to and everyone up there went home happy. Not this time.

We ran straight into them, kicking and punching. They had a go back and stood for a short time but many legged it, mainly the kids who were just hanging on and not up for a ruck – not on a losing side, anyway. The Old Bill got caught short as well and more came in and settled it down. A few of their lads were on the ground and some were crying. We all legged it out and towards the station. We had a free run now and there were a few offs on the way back to the station. At the station the Old Bill was in force, as were loads of Blades fans. They were giving it all the gob behind Old Bill and some were spitting at us. We ran at them and they legged it. We could not get near them, as Old Bill was in the way. Many lads were searched and they were looking for an excuse to pull you. We decided to get on the train and sit it out. The police came on with the ticket inspectors, making sure we all had tickets and asked why we never took the special. Many said the special was cancelled, so it had to be this way. That seemed to calm them down and we finally got under way. The Sheffield United lads didn't expect us to have a go and they thought we would cop a bit of a slapping and be on our way. How wrong they were. Out of the two teams in Sheffield, United seemed to have the better lads and they were fucking terrible. No wonder they never showed away from home. A mate of ours got a thick ear. Not off the fans, but from Old Bill – they were well pissed off. I don't know what they did when teams like Man U, who always had a large away following, came to town; they must have walked all over the place.

The next few games were quiet on the fans front. Huddersfield at Upton Park, we won 3 – 0, then Leicester away and I gave it a miss, as it was normally a poor turnout from their lot. Later I got reports that they had a go and nearly ran West Ham with the numbers they had. That surprised me as they hardly brought any down to us. Maybe they were getting their act together. We lost the game as well, 2 – 0.

Next was Notts Forest at home. They brought a few to West Ham but we never saw them until they scored. We won 4 – 2. Sneaking into our ground seemed to be the trend. I gave Coventry a miss next, as it was a waste of time going there looking for their lads. The Old Bill were bad there as well. Our next away game was Chelsea at Stamford Bridge midweek. We looked forward to this one and as it was a Wednesday night many of us planned to meet up at the Rising Sun at the back of the Shed End.

Meeting up at Chelsea was not a good idea. Four of us got out at Broadway station and started to walk down towards the ground. We got jumped by some Chelsea lads who sussed us. Not a great mob but we got a bit of a kicking. We got away, mainly because Old Bill were on the plot and they wanted us to go on to the North Stand.

We didn't listen and went to the pub. That was mistake number two. The pub was packed with Chelsea lads and as we went in I got hit with a chair across the back and I went down. That's all I remember. I was taken to St John's and they were on my case and wanted me to go to hospital. I had a fair kicking and was hurting all over. I got a pair of black eyes, a thick lip that felt like it was six foot long, was sore all over and my back hurt like fuck. All I wanted to do was get into the game and find my mates. I didn't see them until after the game and they had a fair kicking as well. One mate involved had a badly cut forehead but refused to go to hospital to have stitches. The Chelsea lads had giving us a good seeing-to and they took us by surprise. We did not expect the pub to be full of them. Normally we walked all over them but we got cocky and paid the price. We never had the numbers and there is a degree of safety in numbers. To make matters worse, we lost 3–1 and some more West Ham lads were run after the game. I had never seen a Chelsea mob like it. They hit and ran at us all game and afterwards chased us back to the station. For once they got their act together and I won't take it away from them. We had a fair few on the North Stand, but they had the night. Maybe that was their secret: only good on night games. They done us well for a change and we hated it and they never let us forget for a few years to come.

We had Leeds at home the following Saturday and I had a quiet one on the Chicken Run, as did a few others. I was still sore and bruised from the kicking we got at Chelsea. Leeds had a few down and I just watched as a few offs went on in the South Bank.

1871–72

We had another night game on the Monday and it was a London derby. I wasn't going to sit back at this one. The Yids were coming and we hated them. As it was a night game, I met up with some mates at the Boleyn and we decided to go on to the South Bank. Nothing went off in a major way, due to a no-show from their boys. A load of older fans scattered around the ground, but that was it. We done them 2–0 and all in all it was a great game for us.

Stoke away next, another night game. It was a waste of time going up there on a Saturday, let alone midweek. The game was a 0–0 draw and I missed the next away game at Maine Road as well and heard a few tales of fights going on, mainly at the station. Most reckoned it was Man U boys. We lost 3–1 and we had the Scousers next, Liverpool at home.

They brought about three hundred down and went straight into the South Bank from the coaches. Hardly any came by train and they gobbed off all game right next to the police line. We ran at them once but Old Bill had it well sorted and loads of our lads were getting chucked out. They won 2–0 and we tried for them at the coaches but, once again, the Old Bill was thick on the plot.

We had one big one to go and that was Arsenal at Highbury. We were going for their North Bank again and it was common knowledge. We got to Arsenal around 1 o'clock about twenty-handed and teamed up with some more West Ham outside the ground. We went into their North Bank and we met up with about three hundred lads and one of the biggest Arsenal mobs I have seen. No sooner had we got in and joined up than they steamed us and it was toe to toe for a while. A lot of them were just standing off from us and spitting and taking the piss because they heard Chelsea had done us. Then a few of their lads came flying in. They were well up for it and it was on again.

They pushed us down the front and I copped a few boots around the top of the legs and a big hit in the back – by a flying kick, I was later told. I was sent sprawling and copped a bit of a kicking trying to get up. Some of us had split lips, it was nothing major but a bit of a touch-up all the same. Arsenal had turned the tables on us, we were outnumbered and they were well up for it. We would have done the same to them.

Loads of West Ham were on the Clock End and Old Bill wanted us to walk around and join them. Fuck that, we were staying and did so all game. When they scored they surged into us again and it was on. More kicks than anything else. They won 2–1 and when Brooking scored they surged into us again. There were loads of West Ham all over the ground. Had we been together things might have been different, who knows. Inside the ground, the day went to Arsenal, on the terraces and on the field, but outside they vanished. A few minor scuffles here and there but their main mob had gone. We had teamed up now and were nearly a thousand strong with no one to fight. I will never know why they had a go at us inside the ground and vanished when they had the numbers. We would have to wait till next season to find out.

Our last game at home and Southampton were down and as expected a waste of time as far as their fans went. I don't think I saw any at all and they done us 1–0 as well.

The season was over. There had been some great times and piss-takes. We copped a few hidings but gave more than we got. We had pulled some more stunts on away teams and at home it wasn't hard staying ahead of the Old Bill. For one season anyway Derby were league champions and Leeds won

1971–72

the FA Cup, beating Arsenal 1–0. We were nearly in the final of the League Cup, but we lost the semi-final after four matches with Stoke and one of the best penalty saves ever seen by Gordon Banks against Geoff Hurst. It seemed Chelsea were getting their act together and were doing something other than talking, as were Arsenal. Now to next season.

CHAPTER 7

1972–73

THE NEW SEASON was here and we were raring to go. A few old scores had to be settled and we could not wait. I had come out of my time now and was a fully qualified bricklayer. I had left the firm I served my apprenticeship with, and started working for a bloke whose base was at Camden Town, an Irish guy whose initials were E.G. He had work all over and the pay was much better – sixteen quid a day. Most lads I went to school with were still on much the same money as they were when they left school. I thank my old man for nagging me to get a trade, something I will never regret. The extra money allowed me to move into a bed-sit up Paddington way. I loved it and travelling to work was a lot easier with the tube stations very handy. And there was loads of work in London. The beer was dearer than the East End, but I met some great lads from all over the UK while I was up West. I still went down the East

End and met some mates to plan match days etc. Sunday afternoon was the popular time. I used to drink in a pub called the Mitre in Craven Terrace, a quiet little pub which had a downstairs bar and I met and got on with some Chelsea lads in there. They were into the football and we exchanged stories of past meetings. They reckoned West Ham were mental but we all agreed Chelsea were getting it together. They hated the Yids as well and could not wait for their game to come around.

Our first game was WBA away. I gave it a miss, as nothing seemed to be planned and I heard nothing about it. The game itself was a 0–0 draw, so all in all it was money saved. We had Coventry at home the following Monday and, as per usual, it was a no-show from their fans. We won 1–0 and that about summed it up. Next was Leicester at Upton Park and we done them 5–2. They had a few fans down but not the kind we were looking for. Wolves away next and I was going up. Four Midland teams in a row and this had to be the best chance to have some fun. Loads of West Ham went up, mainly by Inter-city, and the special ran as well.

We were going to put on a show of force with the numbers we had. The special left and our train went about thirty minutes later. This was good, as Old Bill would concentrate on the lads on the special and hopefully leave us alone. When we pulled in the Old Bill were waiting for us. It seemed they were getting clued up to the way we travelled. We gave them no bother but we were still under escort to the ground through the famous subway/underpass. We all looked and wondered if it was a trap as loads of lads were hanging around but most were lads from the special and teamed up with us. Old Bill was trying to get us on the away end and we weren't having it. We all started jogging towards the ground and we rushed the turnstiles to their North Bank. Many jumped them; Old Bill were trying to pull lads back, but had no hope. Not wearing scarves or colours helped that day and most got in. We reckoned we had about eight hundred on there and we charged towards the centre into the Wolves fans. Some stood; most legged it. Those who stood got a right kicking. Old Bill was soon in and many a lad was getting tugged out.

We all sang, 'WE TOOK THE NORTH BANK MOLINEUX AGAIN!' This upset them and loads of their fans ran at us and straight in. Old Bill was trying to form a line and weren't having much luck. With the help of the police we were shoved back a bit and had half of it. Loads of slagging went on. When they scored their first goal we charged them again, but with no luck. More lads were getting thrown out and they scored again, which sparked it off once more but it was all stand-off stuff. They ended up winning 3–0 and we were well pissed off.

Some of us left early and headed to the underpass where loads of West Ham had the same idea. Only trouble was Old Bill was a wake up to us and had a massive presence there – some with dogs, as mounted were useless in the subway. We weren't going to get our way and loads more of our lads now joined us. They tried moving us on and one copper set his dog on a lad and he was bitten, which sent us crazy and the dog, with his handler, got a touch-up. Funny when Old Bill are getting done how many appear out of nowhere. No one was nicked but the Old Bill went crazy, pulling their batons and pushing and hitting at us, keeping us back. The Wolves mob showed, being led by the Old Bill, who held them up and they soon disappeared. They were all front this time and we took the piss. Old Bill now had us moving and at the station they wanted us all on the special. Some lads were telling them they came by coach but they weren't having it. They wanted us away as soon as possible. Our train was waiting on the platform and we were made to get on. We could not even get a drink in the bars on the station.

Using the dog pissed us off and the lad who got bitten was well pissed off. He had been bitten on the inside of the thigh and we took the piss, saying that he had given the police dog rabies. A couple of lads had been hit at the initial off, but nothing major. Talk was about this and that and as more and more beer was drunk from the train bar the stories got bigger and bigger. All talk was on the Arsenal game away.

We had Liverpool midweek. Hardly any went up and we lost 3–2. The next game took some planning. Most of us agreed we would meet up at Mile End at 12 o'clock and go in force. We had copped a slapping the year before and we did not want a re-run. The day came and the station was packed. We left about 12.15. One load had already gone, made to leave by Old Bill, and as we left there were loads of lads still on the platform. Our carriage was packed, the whole train was nearly full of our lads; it was a good turnout.

At Tottenham Court Road station we changed and the lads from the earlier train were waiting. They told us they had run a small mob of Gooner fans already, so the surprise was gone but we had a large firm and more were coming. We went on to Arsenal station and all got out and started jogging to the North Bank. Old Bill was trying to get us on the Clock End, but we weren't moving. We got in – many jumped the turnstiles – and once inside we all gathered up and waited till most were in. Arsenal thought this was all the West Ham boys, they had no idea there was a large mob following or how many we were. They had a large mob settled on their North Bank and we just strolled on. Many thought we were Arsenal and started singing, 'COME ON ARSENAL!' Fuck it, we thought, we're close enough. The 'UNITED!' chant went up and we ran straight into them.

They were shocked and many a lad legged it, mainly the hangers-on. The main lads stood, but we done them. We had the numbers this time but we copped a few as well. It wasn't all our own way. The rest of the West Ham lads came on and joined us. Old Bill were fucked. We ran at them again and not many stood this time. It was chaos and I can say I never got hit or even landed a kick. Many others did from both sides, but the day was ours. We had taken their North Bank again and they weren't happy. We took the piss, chanting 'WEEDS, WEEDS', meaning that Leeds had done them in the FA Cup Final and they had bottled it. They tried having a go back but we steamed again and saw them off easily. They scored and we charged them but Old Bill soon sorted it and were throwing lads out all over. They won the game 1–0 – loads of us left early to try and catch them outside, but once again they left not mobbed up but just seemed to vanish. They were good at this; there was no point looking for them, as Old Bill was moving us on. We headed off and for once I left the lads and went up to Lancaster Gate station, where I went and had a pint in my new local. I saw a few Arsenal lads bring their scarves out on the train up West. They weren't real lads, they obviously thought it was safe to do so now. I laughed to myself. A good result and a bit of a payback from last season.

We had another big one coming up the next week. The Mancs at home, and they always brought down a crowd. I was working out at Welwyn Garden City, which was a joke. I had to catch the tube and then British Rail it out, something I wanted to avoid when living at Harold Hill. In the town centre is – or was – a pub called the Cherry Tree. It was a large pub at the end of the main road if I remember rightly and we used to have a lunchtime pint in there. Being Hertfordshire and Arsenal territory I got talking to some lads who reckoned Arsenal were gonna put a big show on at West Ham. They didn't know what team I followed and I said I liked Chelsea. They took the piss a bit. I didn't mind. If what they were saying was true and they seemed to know what the score was, then they would be in for a shock if they did come down mob-handed. I couldn't see it, but time would tell.

First the Mancs and I left about 11 o'clock to go down to the game. I met up with a lad who was hod-carrying for us, a big bloke from Barnsley who hated the Mancs and wanted to go to Upton Park but was dubious, because of his accent. I told him he would be all right with me. He was a Barnsley fan but he adopted us and went to many a game with us, home and away. His accent came in handy sometimes. When we were away up north we would get him to order the beers and we weren't sussed many a time till it was too late. My mates didn't know what to think of him. Would he stand in a ruck, would he bottle? They were friendly but offish towards him, and he knew it.

We rode down to Mile End and changed to the District line. Loads of Mancs were hiding their scarves and colours and as the train got to Upton Park we got out and they looked like any other fans. I met up with my mates and went straight on to the South Bank and waited. Sure enough, about half an hour before kick-off they started singing. We all ran at them, but they were on the other side of the police barrier and, as usual, were giving it all the gob. Half-time came and we went down below the stand for a beer and a piss. In the toilets my mate said something to one lad and this Manc bloke replied, thinking he was one of theirs with that accent, something about cockney bastards. He gave him the best headbutt I reckon I have ever seen, all in one motion, while having a piss. He just dropped this bloke and he was lying in the trough. A couple of his mates came to help and he hit them as well. They both fucked off and we got out and there they were, pointing at my mate. The Old Bill grabbed him and after a bit of a talking to they let him go. He said he was a Man U fan and the bloke he hit tried to grab hold of his dick, so he hit him.

He got away with it and he was escorted back to where the Man U fans were. We watched him and once he was amongst them the game kicked off. I wondered what he was doing but when they scored their second goal we found out. He was hitting into them on his own, screaming at them. Old Bill grabbed him and he was hauled out. My mates never doubted him again and Yorkie, as he shall be known, was a part of us. I didn't see him again till the Tuesday. He had been lifted and taken to court on the Monday and got a twenty-quid fine for being a public nuisance. They held him all weekend and he was well pissed off at the Mancs costing him twenty quid. It was a week's money for some. Not much went off after the game and the Mancs sneaked out the way they had come in. Not their biggest turnout, but they were spread all over the ground. The game was a 2–2 draw and that was it. I rode back up West and saw loads getting their scarves out of hiding, showing off again.

My local pub got a bit lively during the week. We were playing Chelsea the following week and the few Chelsea lads I knew who drank in there were asking all sorts of questions.

Like what time was I meeting my mates and was a big mob coming etc. They were sussing me out. I would know on Friday before the game what was happening. I planned to meet some lads at the Roundhouse in Barking, stay over at a mate's place and travel through with the lads. It was simpler to meet at Mile End at 11 a.m. and travel through and try and take the Shed End.

We met as arranged and loads of West Ham were already there. We hopped the tube and thought we would get on the Shed unnoticed with only a few hundred and see what happened. As soon as we came out of the Broadway station a mob of about our size met us. This was the Chelsea boys and they ran straight at us; it was obvious they were going to pick off West Ham fans as they came out of the station. They did not muck around and were hurling bottles and golf balls into us. We fought back. It was toe-to-toe stuff for a while and Chelsea were getting the better of it. I copped a good smack in the eye and it fucked me for a little while, long enough for them to lay the boot in. I was fucked and couldn't see. The Old Bill turned up; they weren't expecting any trouble so early and tried stopping it.

Loads more Chelsea joined in and we were copping a fair kicking. More West Ham came out of the station and ran straight in. Chelsea backed up and this seemed to put them off. Some lads of theirs were all for going at us again and cries of doing the Old Bill were going up from them. There weren't many at that time, but loads more came in. Chelsea had us on the back foot for a while and the numbers were pretty even. This was their lads and they were well up for it. More West Ham came out of the station and we had the better numbers by now, but they still did not run. This surprised us and we respected them for it, but we never showed it. Reorganised, we ran at them and Old Bill was powerless to stop us. They backed off now and about half of them bottled and the rest stood. We gave them a good slapping and they fought back, but in vain. They were back-pedalling now and we gave chase.

We met up with another mob of our lads outside the Shed. They had had a bit of a ruck with some Chelsea lads there and the Blues lads had gone into the ground. Old Bill weren't going to let us in and wanted us on the North Stand. A few lads got in but jumped the turnstiles back out as the Chelsea lads were waiting on the other side and they were copping a fair kicking. We were mad and wanted Chelsea bad but the Shed wasn't going to be the place. We all went on the North Stand and chants of 'WE'LL SEE YOU ALL OUTSIDE' were coming from both ends. We had about three thousand on the North Stand and talks of going across the pitch were on. I reckon Old Bill sussed this, as they put loads of coppers across the front of the stand. We saw none of their so-called North Stand boys, and if there were any around, they kept their heads down.

We won the game 3–1. A small mob on the Shed End went up and you could see Chelsea going for them. We all wanted to run on the pitch and join in, but Old Bill was pushing us back. A few got over the wall but were soon nabbed by the police. Loads of us left early to go to the Shed End; Old Bill had the road half blocked and we weren't going to get through. Chelsea came out and ran at us. The Old Bill was in the middle and for a while there was more talk and shouts to do them. They were in the way and we wanted each other. As expected bottles, golf balls and loads of other stuff was being chucked at us and we returned it. About four mounted came into it and one copper on a horse can split a crowd quite easily. This one was using the horse in a sideways motion and pushing us back, while his colleagues on foot were just pushing, with the odd kick thrown in. The horse's legs were getting a bit of a touch-up as well, but the copper stayed on. Not only did the Old Bill have us to deal with, but there were the Chelsea lads as well from the other side. I dunno why the Old Bill didn't leave us to it – we both wanted it.

It finally calmed down, with us being escorted back to the station. There was mostly Old Bill in front and loads behind in case the Chelsea lads tried it on again. This was their manor and for a change they weren't going to give it up. Many times people shouted that they were behind us; we turned, but nothing, just the coppers. Loads of Old Bill were at the station and we got on the trains and we were off. Many did not believe Chelsea stood, let alone fought. Some said that Millwall were with them but it was all shit; they were Chelsea and they were getting cunning. In the fight stakes it was about 50 – 50. Why they hesitated at the station I don't know. They could have finished us. We were glad the other lads joined in as numbers were getting to favour their side. Some of their lads ran, mainly wankers; every club had them, only Chelsea seemed to attract more. They dressed for it but didn't want to know when it came time for aggro; maybe it was the Kings Road image, I don't know. Chelsea fans come from all over and the football hooligan scene was quite fashionable at the time. Chelsea were getting their act together and we never underestimated them again. They had pulled a few cheeky tricks with us in the past. We only hoped they were as game when we played at Upton Park.

My eye was nearly closed and hurt like fuck. I went home, jumping off at Lancaster Gate and went into my local. A pint would kill the pain and I wanted to see the Chelsea lads who I had a beer with from time to time. My mate Yorkie was there and he said he was with the lads on the Shed End who got a slapping but nothing serious. The Chelsea boys came in a couple of pints later and they took the piss out of my eye. We talked about what had happened that day and they said there was a big off at Victoria station. About two hundred West Ham turned up and about the same Chelsea and it was on for young and old. Of course, Chelsea were on top till Old Bill stopped it – they would say that, funny. I quizzed them about Millwall being there and they said they never heard anything, so I guess it was all bullshit.

Only a few hours before we were bitter enemies and now, on neutral territory, we were having a pint. One lad was a chef and worked in the big Lyons hotel just up the road, so for a couple of pints we got an endless supply of red salmon in cans and all kinds of stuff. Sometimes on a Sunday he would tell us to come down – we could have a meal if it was his turn to cook the staff food. I was sad when he left; he went on to work on the cross-channel ferries. The money was better and he had the duty free handy. We saw him now and then but he seemed to drop out of the football scene. It was a couple of years later before I saw him again.

Newly promoted Norwich were next, at home, and we hoped they would not be like Ipswich and would bring down some lads, if they had any. A few did come down, mainly old ones wearing their bright scarves, and some were nicked by the younger lot. It wasn't hard to spot them with those colours. We done them 4–0 and that was Norwich out of the way.

The next big away game was at the Yids and we could not wait. The past couple of seasons they had been up for it and we hoped this time was no different. We planned to go on the Shelf and kick things off there. We knew Old Bill would have the Paxton tied up. About 200 of us met up on the Shelf at White Hart Lane and there were more coming on all the time. We could see a fair few of our lads on the Paxton already and the Yids were getting a few on as well. Nothing had gone off as yet and it took until they scored the only goal to kick it off. Like a signal, it was on.

We charged their lads and most bottled. This was not their main boys. We found out after that they were on the Paxton, where many a ruck was going on. The Yids had pulled one over on us again. They figured with a fair mob of older lads out of the way safely tucked up on the Shelf, they would have free rein with the younger lot, but they underestimated them. The average age on there was about 16 and most never gave a fuck and showed it. They gave nearly as good as they got but the Yids pushed them down towards the corner and loads of lads were getting pulled by Old Bill. They had half the Paxton but reclaimed it back with sheer numbers. We still tried, but most of all we fronted.

Outside the ground a few rucks were going on but most were stopped pretty quickly before it got out of hand. Our lot had not landed a punch or kick on any Yid and we went looking for them but could not find them. They did an Arsenal and vanished. At Bruce Grove station we caught a few but they jumped the tracks and got away. The Yids were getting clued up and their main boys were hard to find. They seemed to shake off the hangers-on fans and were putting themselves well about at home, but away they hadn't made an impact on us yet.

Newly promoted Birmingham City were due next at Upton Park and we did not know what to expect from their fans. We met up at the Queens as usual with many others and got a beer and stood outside. Old Bill hated this because the pub was too close to the station and any mob of away fans that came out could expect a hail of glasses lobbed at them when they came down the small hill and were nearly on top of us. The City fans came out, about two hundred of them. We could hear them on the platforms singing, 'CITY!' Loads of West Ham lads just waited. Out they came, scarves, the lot. No sooner had they got out than some of them were pushing kids and older fans around. One kid, about thirteen I reckon, fell over and got a bit of a kicking. We jumped the lads who were handing it out to the kid. We got a few hits in before they legged it across the road.

They were taking liberties and we, along with many others, ran after them. Glasses were being thrown at them and on the corner of the South Bank Road and Green Street more City fans from the coaches were waiting. So were a mob of our lads. They did not want to go up to the South Bank because of the lads there and they tried coming back up Green Street. I don't know where they were going but they ran into each other and we steamed right on. We had picked up a lot of lads on the run-down after them and the lads on the other side also ran into them. Not many fought, most just copped it, as simple as that. It was all right taking liberties with kids and old men, but when the proper fighting began they shite.

I got a few kicks in. Most were saved by mounted Old Bill and some on the ground who got them in the South Bank as quickly as possible. Many of our lads had their scarves and were burning them, spitting and jumping on them, anything to get a reaction out of them.

They had come down to take the piss in London but picked the wrong part. I heard the Yids and Chelsea gave them a good

The law take a firm grip on the hooligan element at Upton Park.

Cup Fever. A day those who were there will never forget, the day
West Ham brought the FA Cup back to town.

THE EMPIRE STADIUM, WEMBLEY

The Football Association
Challenge Cup
Competition

Final
Tie

SAT., MAY 3, 1975
KICK-OFF 3 p.m.
YOU ARE ADVISED TO TAKE UP
YOUR POSITION BY 2.30 p.m.

1. This ticket is not transferable.
2. The counterfoil must be retained for
at least 6 months.

CHAIRMAN
WEMBLEY STADIUM LTD.

TURNSTILES
H
ENTRANCE
58

WEST
STANDING
ENCLOSURE

STANDING
£1.50
TO BE RETAINED

SEE PLAN AND CONDITIONS ON BACK

Hail the heroes! *Above and below*: West Ham celebrate the cup victory.
Inset: a ticket from that memorable day.

We're West Ham, ain't we? The togetherness of the West Ham
supporters was admired and respected by rival fans.

West Ham fans abroad, for the European Cup Winners Campaign in 1976. For many, it was their first experience of travelling abroad with a football team.

Above left: We're on the beer and over here: in Eintracht for the semi finals in 1976.

Above right and below: The final in the Heysel Stadium in Brussels. Thousands travelled to Belgium to support their team.

Above: The Boleyn pub has become a famous landmark for fans due to its proximity to the ground.

Below: Visiting supporters all remember coming out of Upton Park station and passing the Queen's pub.

going over as well when they played them but this was only hearsay. Birmingham were supposed to be the lads in the Midlands; if that was their best, they were in trouble. Inside the ground they stayed close to Old Bill and only a few minor offs were going on. We beat them 2–0, so all in all they had a bad day.

I gave Ipswich away a miss next as nothing much happened up there and the game was a 1–1 draw. Sheffield Utd at Upton Park next and their fans were a no-show, as expected. We done them 3–1 on the pitch and that was the joy of the day, really. I missed the next four games home and away due to a death in my family. My mother had passed on and there were much more important things to do than football.

The next game back was Derby and I took the old man to try and get his mind straight on a few things and I reckoned watching West Ham would help. He was a life-long fan, as was his father before him. In fact, I reckoned I was conceived West Ham. Some of my mates joined me on the Chicken Run and the day cheered him up a bit.

Not long before we had been knocked out of the League Cup 2–1 by Stockport County and we knew there would be some mobs willing to take the piss. Derby had a few lads down, mainly in the West Side. I saw a couple of disturbances in the crowd but fighting wasn't on my mind. We lost 2 – 1 and afterwards I went back to Harold Hill and stayed the night. I had a drink with the old bloke on Sunday – at a pub called the Duck Wood Arms, I think – and I met up with some lads who I hadn't seen in a while, nearly all West Ham boys. The talk was of going to Goodison the next Saturday. I said I was up for it and these lads were getting a coach. I told them the Inter-city was the best way but they said getting to Euston from there was a bit of a hassle. I knew what they meant.

We took about three hundred up by Inter-city to Everton and the special had a fair load on as well. I don't know how many coaches but we would see when we got up there. Goodison is across Stanley Park from Anfield and we knew the Everton boys used this park to their advantage at the end of the games.

Old Bill made sure many got on buses to the ground and, once at the ground, tried getting us in the away end. Some lads had slipped off for a pint in the many pubs around the place. It was not the place to be short-handed if they were sussed. We went on to the away end, as the Everton home end would be near impossible to take unless you got there early and were well mobbed. About four to five hundred would make a dent in it, but we never found out. We won 2–1 and nothing happened in the ground except the usual piss-take from both sets of fans.

Once outside we knew Everton would be waiting at the park so we decide to go the other way around the ground and come at them where they least expected it. It worked for a short while. I think they reckoned we were more Everton fans coming to join in. We had about sixty and there were about one hundred-plus of them. No turning back, we went straight into them. This shook them and we had surprised them well, but it didn't last and soon the Scousers were handing it back. I got a touch-up, nothing major, and a few lads copped a bit, but we pulled one on them and it worked. Old Bill was caught short as well. You don't argue with Merseyside coppers. They have those big night sticks and knew how to use them. They got us apart and the Everton lads just left. We could not believe it. For a while they had us and if they had got us the way they wanted we would have been killed. In all fairness to their lads we surprised them, but they had the numbers and we weren't going to bottle. We could never have lived with ourselves if we had. We won the game 2–1 and had a great day out and a result on and off the pitch.

To take Everton on their manor you would need a massive mob. They were good and would shit on their cousins from across the park. It's funny: two teams from one area, same accents; one is all gob, like Liverpool, and the other isn't. Bit like Man City and Man U. The reds are the gobby ones while the City lads do most of their talking with their hands, not their mouths.

We had Newcastle next. Only a few coaches came down and most of their fans were spread all over the ground. No real lads to speak of. It was a shame, because Newcastle were always well up for it, one of the hardest lads around at home and never bottled away. Well, I had never seen them back down. The game was a 1–1 draw. I saw a couple of small fights outside. One-on-one stuff and it was a win for them and one was a win for us. Mainly older fans and not lads. Still, it was good to watch and as the Toon lad won his scrap we all booed. I reckon he thought we were gonna do him and he pissed off quick. The other one we cheered on like school kids and the Toon lost and Old Bill grabbed the West Ham bloke and led him away. It was funny to watch and the Toon lad was not seriously hurt, more damaged pride than anything, I reckon.

I gave the Leeds game away a miss. I wanted to spend some time with my old man, as me and my brothers took turns at seeing him at weekends. We had Stoke at home next and I convinced the old man to go with me and my brothers. I knew it would be a quiet one on the fan front. Not that the old man was an angel – he could look after himself, even if he was getting on a bit. Working all your life as a bricklayer kept you a bit fit and he was no exception. I met up with some mates who told me Leeds had run about two hundred of them with a large mob, and their Old Bill sorta helped them, but not many got a slapping and we lost 1–0. We won the Stoke game 3–2 and, as expected, it was a non-event from their fans.

I went to Southampton away next game. The Dell hadn't changed much and their fans weren't much better. A few were taking the piss because Stockport beat us, but we dealt with them. A couple got a smack, the others legged it. It was two days before Christmas and the place was freezing and a boring 0–0 draw had most of us wondering why we bothered at all.

Christmas came and went and on Boxing Day we had the Yids at home. They had loads of lads down, but all over the ground. You could see how many when they scored their first goal. The game was a 2–2 draw and loads were in the seats, older ones from their glory days. The South Bank had a few but they stayed tucked up mainly next to Old Bill. We could not find their lads. There were a couple of crowd disturbances in the West Stand. They had failed to come down with anyone capable of making a show. They were getting it together at home, but away, at least with us, it was a non-event.

I gave Leicester away a miss, as did many. It was New Year's Eve and it wasn't worth going up there. Their fans had the front but never the bottle and we lost 2–1, so it was money saved. The third round of the FA Cup was on us. We had drawn Port Vale. I gave it a miss as it was away; we got through 1–0, and I believe we were lucky. The FA Cup seems to lift lower-league teams, and they played their hearts out if the papers were anything to go by.

Our next home game was Liverpool and a few of their fans fronted, mainly by coach. A few small offs were going off all over. I wasn't involved in any, though it wasn't for want of trying. We lost 1–0 and you could see the turnout was weak when they scored. Maybe it was the time of year and most were skint and just getting over Christmas. I hated the Scousers, another team who were only good at home.

Old Trafford next and I didn't go. From what I heard, we had a piss-poor turnout, so no doubt the Mancs thought we were only good at home, I don't know. The next fixture we looked forward to was Chelsea at home and we were sure they would front after the stroke they pulled on us at Stamford Bridge. I hardly saw any fans come out of the station. They were around but not wearing colours; it was hard to find them. We decided to go on the South Bank early and see how many turned up. They had about three hundred down and they all had scarves on now. At about 2.30 we gave it a 'UNITED' chant in reply to their 'CHELSEA' and ran at them. They all scattered and loads jumped the fence and went into the West Side. Their main boys weren't around – or, if they were, they weren't game to have a go.

Once Chelsea were in the West Stand, down the corner bit near the South Bank, they started giving it all the gob. A few lads in that side had a go at them and they soon shut up. We done them 3–1 and nothing was heard from them all game. About twenty minutes to go and that section of ground was thinning out; they were skulking away early. Going after them on the tube would have been a waste of time as we could not find them at the ground. Their main lads had not shown and it was all a let-down.

The next game was new ground: it was Norwich away and I had never been before, only through it on the way to Ipswich. We took about four hundred away on the Inter-city and we had a good day. We got on their end and their fans had a bit of a go but soon legged it, mainly stand-off stuff and one bloke sorta fronted up as leader and urged us on. That was a mistake. We all steamed him and down he went. This fucked the rest and they had no stomach for a fight after that. We lost 1–0 and we all jogged back to the station looking for their mob, but there weren't any.

We had a good laugh on the train home, but when we pulled in we heard the chant 'TOTTENHAM'. The Yids were waiting for the train and we all piled off and gave it a 'UNITED'. This shook them, as we were obviously more than they had bargained for. We ran at the gate and they legged it. We got held up at the gates by Old Bill wanting to see tickets, along with the British Rail bloke. This was just delaying tactics, as a bloke on the train came round and checked them. It just enabled them to get away on the tube. We gave chase, but it was a waste of time. They had underestimated the numbers we had and clearly wanted a go at us, but it backfired.

The next few games were a waste of time as far as fans went. WBA at home and we won 2–1; Stoke away, we lost 2–0. I didn't go and I heard from those who did it was a waste of time. We had been knocked out of the FA Cup by Hull at their ground 1–0 and as far as cups were concerned it was a fucking shambles. First we got done by Port Vale in the League Cup and then Hull in the FA Cup.

We had Ipswich at Upton Park next and we lost 1–0. That about summed it up. I reckon the number of fans they had down you could count on one hand and they were in the seats.

Bramall Lane next on the cards and I never went. Some mates did and it kicked off again on their end; it was nothing serious and no one got really hurt. Man City was next at our ground and they had a fair few down, mainly by coach. Nothing went off between the fans; nothing ever did with Man City. A couple of punch-ups maybe, with older fans, but no major hooligan stuff.

We had the South London gypos next – Crystal Palace at Selhurst Park – and we had a run-in with some of their lads at London Bridge station. A mob of about forty was there and we turned up with about the same. They spotted us and starting chanting, 'EAGLES!' Fuck the chanting, we ran at them and they stood but they had no chance. One lad hit my mate with a bottle and he got a badly cut head. The Palace fan then tried to get away, but he was our target; he got a fair going-over and was left lying on the ground. I copped a whack in the nose, nothing major, I have had harder, but it made my nose bleed. Some of their lads were backing off now and Old Bill were grabbing blokes all over the place and keeping them apart. They were shouting that they had done West Ham and carrying on. We tried getting at them again but they stayed close to Old Bill. They had a bit of a result as far as they were concerned, but more of their lads had got a hiding than us and they still had to get the train to the ground. We tried getting on the same train, but the police weren't having any of it. Our mate was taken away and he had several stitches in his head. More of our lot came on and were keen to find out what the score was.

We finally got away and when we got to Norwood Junction there were about a hundred Palace fans waiting outside. One chant of 'UNITED!' and many fucked off. We got out and gave chase to the others. We caught a few, but they were mainly kids and we left them. I saw one lad crying and asking not to be hit. What a joke: he had all the gear, the bovver boots, the lot, but when it came down to it he shite. Why bother going if you were all show? We never found those lads from the station and all over the ground loads of rucks were going on. We won 3–1 and after the game we waited at London Bridge station to see if we could pick them up, but we never did find them.

The Toffees were next and we prayed they would bring down some lads. They normally did and loads of our lot went up West looking for them. A few got picked off as they came out of the station but nearer the game about three hundred were on the South Bank. We got in and ran straight at them. It was on; they stood, but not for long. We were giving them a good kicking and Old Bill moved in and yanked lads out all over, including me. The usual walk around and through the players' tunnel, name taken and what club did you support. Then we were let go with the warning that if we got caught on the South Bank again that day we would be nicked. The coppers at West Ham were a hard lot but there were some fair ones, better than any I've met in England with the exception of the Newcastle Old Bill. They just stopped you fighting, gave you a slap and left it at that. I went on the North Bank and just made kick-off.

We won 2–0 and during the game I saw loads of trouble on the South Bank and more and more lads getting the walk out. We looked for them after the game but many came by coach and picking them up on the tube was a non-event. I had noticed a few times on the tube to Lancaster Gate that, once past Liverpool Street, many fans were putting their colours on, thinking they were safe. I noticed it with Chelsea and a few other fans.

Newcastle at St James' was next and I didn't go. I was trying to save some money to go and work abroad in South Africa, where there was a building boom, as work was getting tight in London. I had met a couple of lads in my local who told me how good it was out there and I was keen to go. We won the St James' fixture 2–1 and fuck all of our lads went. Probably just as well, it was not a good place to be without a decent size crew and even then you would have to be careful.

Leeds next at our manor and they had a few down. They were in the semis of the FA Cup and went on to Wembley, only to lose to Second Division Sunderland, which was a game I went to and would have to rank as one of the greatest finals of all time. Most of the Leeds fans came by coach and we were picking a few up here and there as they came out of the tube. Mainly they were getting their scarves nicked and a couple of smacks off the younger fans. Leeds were another team who were all front at home and not much away – not with us, anyway. We heard they tried it on at Chelsea and got a right hiding, something I found out from some lads I knew who drank up my way. Their lot were on the South Bank and stayed near the Old Bill. When they scored we had a go at them but were soon kept apart. We tried them outside after, but most had left early and got to the safety of the coaches. The game was a 1–1 draw.

Easter was upon us and we had three games in as many days. Southampton at home, which we won 4–3 in a thrilling match, with Pop Robson getting a hat-trick. Derby away on the Easter Saturday. I never went and heard from those who did that Derby gave them a bit of a kicking. The game was a 1 – 1 draw and on Easter Monday we had Birmingham away again. I gave it a miss. Their fans never impressed me at our ground. We had heard loads of stories that mobs like Palace gave them a seeing-to on their manor, so I could not see the point really. I found out from some mates who did go that our lot had a big crew up there and they were well up for it. Oh well, what you lose on the swings, you make up on the merry-go-round. And the next game on the merry-go-round was coming to Upton Park.

Last game of the season and we had Arsenal. Being a London side, they had to come by tube and they had a couple of coaches down from supporters' clubs out in Hertfordshire way and further. About 2 o'clock a mob of about three hundred-odd came out of the tube. No chanting, they just came out, crossed the road and started walking down to the ground. We could not believe it – scarved up as well. We just gaped and when they were just about opposite us we hurled glasses into them and ran at them across the road. They started running but Old Bill on mounted horses started getting in our way. We got a couple and a few lads were getting pulled and taken away. The way they walked out seemed to be saying, 'We are here, come and get us.' We obliged and the front on them was something that got us by surprise. They got on the South Bank and they already had a fair few on there, lads who never had the front of the other lot. It was a stand-off for a while, till the game got under way and they scored and we surged into them. It was mental for a while but they stood and gave as good as they got. A few lads from both sides were getting tugged out now. They scored again and that was it, we surged into them once more and this time they backed off. Loads got a kicking, I copped a few boots and was spat on. This made us worse and loads of their lads were getting done. Some of ours copped it as well, it wasn't all one-way traffic. Old Bill had now got between us.

Brooking pulled one back and they had a go at us, something not many did at Upton Park. The police were now chucking loads out – my mate Yorkie got tugged and was let go after the usual name taking etc. The Arsenal boys were told to go home and not to hang around the ground as the gates were now closed. Yorkie told me many did this and legged it towards the station. Being thrown outside a ground with the turnstiles closed could be boring. The pubs shut early in those days and unless there were some other fans around, you just had to kill time. The game was over and we lost 2–1.

Loads of Arsenal had already gone, not as much front going as they had coming. The small mobs that were picked up in Green Street were given a bit of a touch-up before Old Bill stepped in. It was hit and run with them all the way along to the station. Loads rode the tube up to Tottenham Court Road station, where many changed to the Northern line. We chased a few but they had done their vanishing trick. They were good at that.

That was that. The end of the season. As I mentioned earlier, I went to Wembley that year to watch Sunderland play Leeds but more of that later. Next stop was South Africa, which meant I was going to miss a whole season. Sunderland were FA Cup winners that year and Liverpool won the title. It had not been a bad season as far as the football fans went. We finished sixth, our highest ever for ages, and had a shocking cup run in both FA and League Cups. Some London firms stood at home for a change and we gave loads of kickings out and got a fair few as well. Chelsea fans were picking their game up and were getting to be a decent force at home. The Yids were getting cunning at home and the Gunners had some front and had come a long way in a few years. I reckon winning the double helped them along. We heard some stories about clashes with their bitter rivals, the Yids. But West Ham were still a force to deal with. We pulled one on the Everton lot on their manor and would have done the Wolves the same again if the police hadn't looked after them. As for me, I was going overseas and my mate Yorkie was taking over my bedsitter while I was away. He nearly lived there anyway – mostly on game days, he kipped on the floor and the place was a home from home for him. So for the '73–'74 and the first half of the '74–'75 season I was abroad in South Africa. And then, as fate would have it, I had some time in Australia.

CHAPTER 8

1975

NINETEEN SEVENTY-FIVE was here. I had come back from abroad and had a great time. I went on to Oz with a girl I met over there and earned some great money. Oz was OK but getting results over there was bad – you had to wait till the Monday papers in those days. I got the odd letter from my mates. This was mainly when something happened at games like Man U going down at the hands of Denis Law, a United legend who was transferred to Man City and the last game of the season saw him score the goal which put United down – a cheeky back-heel. The Man U fans invaded the pitch at Maine Road afterwards. It was good to catch up with some mates and many a story was told about this game or that game.

A few lads had dropped out, some joined up in the army as work was scarce in England. A couple were banged up, though not for football violence. The old man had been to a few

games and some of the lads at Harold Hill went with him. So
as far as company was concerned he was in good hands. My
brother joined up in the army and I had to find somewhere
new to stay as my mate was living with his bird and it would
have been awkward living in a bedsit with three of us. I'd got
home for New Year and was dying to go to a match, but the
first game on the cards was Southampton in the FA Cup third
round at their ground, the Dell. As I'd just got back and I
knew what winter was like up there, I decided to give it a
miss. We won 2–1.

Next game was Leeds away and I gave that a miss as I was
trying to find a place to stay. I ended up in one of those one-
roomed hotels around Paddington way. There are hundreds
there and it was handy for the tube and most things. My
girlfriend was coming over in March so I needed to find
somewhere bigger but the hotel did for a while.

At last a home game, QPR and their support was good at
home, although they had no real lads, but away it was non-
existent. I got to the game and met up with old friends. Loads
of new faces around and it was great to catch up on some
stories. I was told a load of them went to White Hart Lane
when the Yids played Chelsea and stayed neutral; they were
only going to join in with the mob who started the trouble
first. It was the Yids and they done Chelsea bad, running them
on to the field. They were telling me it was mental that day
and the Yids were not the same mob they used to be and they
were well up for it. I dunno if they knew that they had West
Ham with them but Chelsea copped some kicking I was told,
though they got their own back at the Duck Pond.

The QPR game was a good one as far as football goes – but
for fans, nothing. I had never been so cold; I think I was

missing the sunshine. People were saying that your blood thins out. I reckon I had iced water in my veins, it took a while to adjust to the cold and the beer. The game was a 2–2 draw.

We had Swindon next in the FA Cup fourth round and the game ended in a 1–1 draw. Their support was terrible and the replay was four days off on their manor. I was going; it was only a bit over an hour from Paddington station and as I only lived around the corner it was handy for me. We got the Intercity about 5 p.m. I think and West Ham had a fair few going. A special was going as well and we hoped their fans would put on a show. We left before the special, which suited us well. If we kept schtumm getting off at their end we should be able to get around unnoticed. It was not to be. The Old Bill were a wake-up and insisted we get escorted to the ground. We all had a moan and some of the excuses the lads were giving made me laugh – 'I'm not interested in football' and the like.

Fashions had changed a bit and a lot of the younger lads were wearing these silky jackets with the Chinese writing on the back – kung-fu jackets – and platform heels were the rage. I never liked them and reckon Doctor Martens was the best boot around. I would not like to have an off wearing those great big high-heeled boots. Elton John made them popular after the movie *Tommy* and some wore them, but not many.

We slipped away at Swindon, about ten of us, and tried to find a pub, let things calm down and meet up later with the others. We found a boozer in town and a load of our lads who had the same idea were already in there. It was a mixed crowd. The game of Australian pool was taking over every pub in the land; this pub was no exception. Some of the lads were playing the locals for pints, beating them and letting them know. This ended up with one of their lads giving one of ours a right-hander. That was a mistake, because we went mad. My mate hit him with a pool cue and the balls were grabbed and thrown at them. There were a few in there, I don't know if they were football fans but who cared, they kicked it off and we were going to finish it. Ashtrays and glasses were chucked all over, it was like a wild west saloon for a while. The lad who kicked it all off was down and he copped a good kicking. The Old Bill arrived and it settled down. They held us and the publican did us a favour by telling them what happened.

The six of us were pulled in, along with the lad who started it and taken down the local nick. We were printed and had photos taken and held till the end of the game, taken back to the station and put on a train. We were told the publican did not want to lay charges and we could lay some against the lad who kicked it off but he would probably do the same and it would be morning before they sorted it. We were more or less being told to drop it. We didn't mind and no way we would lay charges. I think the Old Bill were just glad to see us go.

On the train we found out loads of lads were held in vans and were let go when the game was over. We won 2–1 and we were through to the fifth round. Not much went off at their ground and we found out a few of the locals fancied having a go but got a bit of a slapping, that's all.

Back in the league we had Carlisle next at home. From what my mates told me, they were hopeless at home so we weren't expecting a turnout from their lads – if, in fact, they had any.

Middlesbrough away was on the cards next. I did not go but a few lads told me only about three hundred went, mostly kids. A coach full of my mates teamed up with those up on the train and ran a massive mob of Boro after the game. Boro fans are like Everton in that they like to try it on in a big park near to the ground. My mates say Boro did this and it was bedlam for a while, with a lot of bricking going on that continued all along the back streets. Considering the numbers against the lads done well, one of those long, long days. Some of my mates still talk about that one today.

We had drawn QPR next in the FA Cup and we done them 2–1. It was a piss-poor turnout from their fans, mainly older ones in the seats. So we were through to the sixth round and we drew Arsenal at Highbury. We had Liverpool before that and a 0–0 draw and a poor turnout from their fans made it a bad day all round.

Wolves away next and I went up along with more West Ham than I have ever seen at their ground. We took their North Bank with sheer numbers and they weren't up for it at all. They even bottled on their favourite ambush trick. We heard Chelsea had pulled it on them and done them easy. We lost 3–1 and we went looking for their lads but they weren't around. They had bottled it.

Newcastle on our manor next and fuck all turned up. We even lost the game 1–0. There was a small presence in the West Stand; I saw nothing go off. On the tube back home I didn't see any, which was a shame as the Toon lads were always well up for a fight and always stood but not this time.

The Arsenal game in the cup came around and I jumped the tube down to Mile End to meet up with some mates. The whole of Mile End station was packed with our lads; it was going to be a big day. One trainload left and the second train pulled in to the platform, also filled. We were taking a massive load to Highbury and the plan was simple: take their North Bank.

At Highbury the Old Bill was telling everyone that away

fans must go on the Clock End and any away fans found on the North Bank would be thrown out. This never stopped us and we had about half of the North Bank. Arsenal knew we were there and when Alan Taylor scored his first of two, we all went up. We pushed into the Gooners, who were shocked at how many were on their end. Even the Old Bill could not believe it. We had about two-thirds of it now and hardly any major rucks were going on. The Arsenal fans went crazy for a while, after our goalkeeper Mervyn Day pulled down Arsenal's John Radford in the box. Much to our delight the ref denied the penalty. This pissed them off and a few golf balls came over, which surprised us, as the Gooners weren't known for lobbing things. Taylor put away his second and we went wild. We couldn't give a fuck about the Gooners, we were going into the semis and we could win Wembley at last, we hoped.

The trip home was knees-up all the way and only a few small rucks were going off. We had won the game into the semis and walked all over Arsenal's manor again. The whole day was a great success. I went down the East End that night and did not go back to my place till Monday.

My girlfriend was due over in a week and I was busy finding a bigger place. I got a bedsitter in Paddington which cost fifteen quid a week. When she came over I missed a few games and even took her to one. Not because I wanted to but because she wanted to see what West Ham was, the place she had heard so much about and that had lured me away from Australia.

I missed Burnley at home; we won 2–1. The Blades away, we lost 3–2, and Birmingham away, where a fair bit of trouble went on according to my mates. We drew 1–1.

We had Stoke at home next and I took my girlfriend to

that game knowing it would be quiet. I planned to meet my old man at the Boleyn and go to the game together. I treated us and we went into the East Stand seats. Taking girlfriends was not the done thing at West Ham but she wanted to see the place. The tube ride down woke her up: the scenery shocked her when the train travelled in the open. Some of my mates at the Queens wanted me to have a drink with them and talk about next week's game on Good Friday against Chelsea. I had the piss taken a bit about being under the thumb, but nothing serious.

We met the old man and had a drink and headed off to the East Stand. This was the first time I had ever been in the seats; it was the same for my old man, and he had been going off and on for forty years plus. It's funny sitting up there, though the language is just as bad as the standing area. The game was a 2–2 draw and that was the last time I took my girlfriend to football. She hated the East End and every time I took her down to see family or meet some mates and have a drink it was with reluctance. I suggested getting a flat down there but I was told she would be on the first plane home if I did.

Chelsea were next. They had a load down and as usual we never saw them until they were tucked up on the South Bank. I told my mates about the scarves coming out on the tube home and loads said we would ride the tube after to see if we could pick some up. In the South Bank we surged at Chelsea but they surged back and it was on for a while. Chelsea weren't backing down and Old Bill were giving loads of lads a tug out of the ground. With calm restored Chelsea scored and we were into them again while they were celebrating. We rushed them and it was boots and all. It settled a bit and became more of a stand-off. These lads weren't as gobby as the

1975

ones we were used to and they stood. Old Bill was trying to form a line between us but it was still going on, mostly kicks. We would try them outside. They won 1-0 and we left early in an attempt to get them.

Most of us went to Mile End where they would have to change, and loads more had the same idea. As the trains came in we could not find them and some lads were telling us it had kicked off outside the station in a big way. We had missed this and wanted to find them more than anything. Loads of us rode the tube up and looked for lads bringing their colours out, but only a few did, mainly older fans. Some of the younger ones were grabbing them and throwing them out at the next stop. They were scurrying out after them with the odd boot up the arse.

I got out at Queensway and had arranged to meet my girlfriend there in a pub opposite the park. The rest were going on to Victoria, about a hundred or so of them, to find the Chelsea lads.

Leicester away was next over the Easter period and most lads I knew were going down to Southend or Brighton; they reckoned it would be more of a laugh than Leicester. I heard nothing from the game and we lost 3-0. I missed the Derby away game, mainly due to the fact that I was working and we had lost a lot of time with the rain.

We had the semi-final of the cup next at Villa Park. I went with my mate in his motor and on the way we passed loads of coaches from both teams, giving the Ipswich ones the two-fingered salute and hitting the horn with a thumbs-up at the West Ham ones. We pulled into a motorway cafe for something to eat and we walked in on a load of Ipswich fans who were already in there. We never noticed their coach outside and we were wearing scarves for a change. It was the semi-final and we thought, fuck it, why not? We got some boos and hisses from this lot but no one made a move towards us. We sat and had breakfast, expecting them to have a go. They looked the part as well, but nothing. We would have been killed. There were five of us and loads of them but they stayed put. Had it been the other way round we would have given them a bit of a slap for sure. We left and laughed – what a mob of wankers, they could have had us easily.

As we pulled out we saw a coach-load of West Ham pulling in and we wondered should we stay and see what goes off but we thought, fuck it, there would be plenty going on at the ground with the amount of coaches going up.

Villa Park is a big ground with one of the biggest ends I have seen, the Holte End. It was intimidating compared to our North Bank or, say, the Shed, and we were on there along with thousands of West Ham lads. It seemed the whole East End was away for the day and I reckoned Ipswich was closed, with the amount they had there. There were loads of small rucks outside the ground and inside the numbers we had would have scared any mob. The whole game was an exciting 0–0 draw and if the truth be known Ipswich were the better side on the day – but that's cup football. After the game a massive mob of our lads tried a run at the Ipswich lot but they legged it back to the coaches. They did not want to know.

We had a replay on the following Wednesday at Stamford Bridge. All the way back we talked about the replay at the Duck Pond and what time we would meet up. We found out that some Ipswich fans got a kicking at Liverpool Street station and talk was a few lads had been nicked and charged. We had a quick trip home, only stopping once for some beers to drink on the drive back. We talked about following a coach-load into a motorway cafe and having a go, but we thought we had got away with it once, to try with so few lads would be stupid. We would have a go on Wednesday.

The day came and I went straight to Stamford Bridge from work and headed to the Rising Sun to meet up with some mates. It was about six o'clock when I got there and the place was packed inside and out. You had to squeeze through to get a beer and when I finally got one, talk was that Chelsea were going to front as they were the same colour as Ipswich. I reckoned this was bollocks. If they did show and put a good one in they would not let any carrot crunchers take the credit, they would want it. We filled the Shed End, a bit of a home away from home for us and the atmosphere at that game was unreal. A great game and we won 2–1.

We were going to Wembley. Our opponents were Fulham, who knocked us out of the League Cup early in the season. The funny thing was that Bobby Moore, the hero of West Ham, had gone to Fulham to play out his days. To us he was the king and one of the greatest ever. He had a shop across the road from the Boleyn and when he transferred someone bricked his shop window in. I reckoned that was real bad and I bet if that wanker ever told anyone about it he would have got a good kicking, West Ham fan or not.

I gave the Derby away match a miss; not many went. They won the league that season and beat us 1–0. All we could think of was Wembley. It had been ten years since we had played there and eleven since we won the FA Cup. Tickets were not a problem – my old man got me mine. He still had the contacts and it was sort of an early birthday present.

The last couple of games could not go fast enough.

Coventry at home, we lost 2−1 and a no-show from their lot of fans. Ipswich away was next and I didn't go; nothing ever happened up there except a piss-take and I was sick of seeing them after our semi win over them. They beat us 4−1 – a bit of payback but we didn't care.

One more to go before the big one and we had the Gooners at our ground. It was a night game and a poor turn out from their lot. We came across a few in the South Bank who had a go and one gave me a nice whack in the teeth. I saw him jump back and he was holding his hand. I reckoned it hurt him more than me. He got a going-over for his trouble and left me with sore front teeth for a while but that was basically it. We won the game 1−0, with Graham Paddon scoring the only goal.

All talk was of Wembley and the Cup; to say we were excited would be an understatement. We knew Fulham would be no trouble off the pitch as their fans weren't up to much. Some were saying Chelsea, their neighbours, were gonna team up with them. I knew that was bollocks as most Chelsea lads I knew hated them. I heard the Yids were coming as well. We didn't care on that day. Anyone was welcome to have a pop at us and would have got killed.

The third of May finally arrived and my girlfriend reckoned she never wanted to hear West Ham mentioned again; all the talk was about the game. I told her she could come and I would get a ticket from somewhere but she was not interested – thank fuck for that. I stayed over in the East End on the Friday night at a mate's place. We had a bit of a pub-crawl and ended in an old pub at the back of Limehouse called the Grapes, a place where Charles Dickens was supposed to have had the odd ale. We were going down to the Prospect of Whitby down on the water but the Grapes was as far as we got. Even in that old pub all attention was on the next day's final. For some of my mates it was the first time they would have seen West Ham at Wembley. I had been before with the old man and his brothers and saw '64, '65 and '66 – our own treble, if you believed East End folklore.

We decided to leave about 10 a.m. and have a look around the West End, have a couple of pints and then off to the big game. We ended up in Wards Irish House and by eleven the place was half full, mainly our fans. Some Irish lads were having a chat about great Irish players and the likes of George Best, who was brilliant. Things were fine until one Paddy said he bet we were glad that Bobby Moore was on the other side and that we had got rid of the thief (referring to the fit-up in the World Cup where he was accused – and later acquitted – of pinching some jewellery). The place fell quiet and, before anyone said anything, this lad, who was about thirty, came across and landed one of the best hits I've seen on this Paddy. He dropped like a sack of coal. A couple of his mates wanted to go on with it but ended up legging it out of the pub and leaving their mate on the deck. The funny thing was, he was wearing a West Ham rosette and said he was going to the game. That's how much respect Bobby Moore had with us, even though he was on the other side that day. What the Paddy said was bang out of order and one of the other blokes lifted his ticket to the game.

We got out of there just in time. As we left the Old Bill were coming in with the blokes who legged it out. They had grassed us up and we went straight into the tube and away. On the trip to Wembley the trains were packed with both sets of fans and it was mostly a piss-take. The odd bloke was grabbed and given a bollocking. We heard a few lads had a go but never saw much ourselves. This was one day we again wore scarves and whatever else we could get our hands on.

There was no point going into the Greyhound pub as it was packed and the queues to get a beer were out of the door. If you ever went to Wembley to watch your team in a final you will know there was nothing like walking up Olympic Way, or Wembley Way as we called it. The twin towers looming, the atmosphere really got you going. The funny thing was, the following week I would be working next door on the Conference Centre.

We got into the ground and it seemed like the whole ground was West Ham. Fulham had a lot there but we outnumbered them easily. The game itself was a bad one and our hero Alan 'Sparrow' Taylor scored the two goals that won us the cup. He had scored two in the quarter- and semi-finals and now two on the big day; he was the hero. When Billy Bonds lifted the cup the cheering was unbelievable and we went mad and invaded the pitch, something not done at Wembley. I have read it was done to have a go at the Fulham fans. This was not true, we were simply ecstatic that we finally had won something. We took the piss out of the Fulham lot, but that was all. We were finally herded back on to the terraces and the lap of honour was done. The roar was something I never forgot. I had been to other cup finals, to watch other teams, but that day was different. We finally left and headed back to the East End. We mixed with loads of Fulham fans and on any other day they would have got a hiding but they were saying well done and we just took the piss. Had we lost, things would have been different and I reckoned it would have been mass riots.

I did not go home till the Monday afternoon and then I was

still pissed. I had Tuesday off and went back to work on Wednesday. The season over, we finished thirteenth and had won the FA Cup. Derby had won the title. Our first game next season was against them in the Charity Shield at Wembley. What a contrast that day was.

CHAPTER 9

1975-76

WE KNEW DERBY had a go at home but their form away from home, as far as fans were concerned, was terrible. I could remember only once that they had a decent crew down and then they had got a fair kicking.

We had arranged to meet up at Mile End about 11 o'clock. When we got on to the station the place was packed and already a few trains had gone. We finally met up, about thirty of us, and joined another load of lads on their way to the game. Loads more got on at Liverpool Street station and a lot of new faces were around. When we changed to the Northern line we had our first off with the Derby lot. About twenty of them had a go at some lads in our carriage, not knowing it was full of West Ham. They were all scarved up and started whacking into these lads, all around the 18 mark. Their fans were blokes and it was a fucking liberty as far as we were concerned. We charged up the end of the carriage at them and some lads came through the connecting doors to join us. They had seen what was going on and felt the same. They tried having a go but we kicked the shit out of them and many were just crouching between the seats and our lads were jumping on the seats and stamping on them. They were well fucked and a couple were relieved of their tickets and thrown off at the next stop.

We talked to some lads who had been up the West End the night before and they told us there were loads of Derby down and some were taking liberties all over, having a go in most pubs and at anyone who got in their way. We got to Wembley and joined up with some West Ham who were on the early trains. They told us a mob of about five hundred Derby had run them back to the station and were down by Wembley Way.

We had about the same number and word soon got around. A load of lads piled out of the pub and linked up with us and another load of our lads came out of the station and we moved off. It's a short walk down to Wembley, mostly downhill and we all started jogging down towards where the Derby lot were supposed to be. Old Bill on mounteds kept up with us and as we turned into Olympic Way we saw them about halfway up towards the ground. They were urging us on and when they saw the mob we had they all started legging it to the ground. We kept running at them and caught a few who had no go in them at all but still got a kicking. Anyway, we caught a lot by the steps and steamed straight into them. Old Bill was everywhere but they could not stop us. One Derby lad pulled a hammer out and was waving it wildly. It was lucky Old Bill grabbed him before us. He still copped a few boots for his trouble. I went to help my mate who was being held by a Derby fan in a head-lock and couldn't move. I hit the cunt and he let my mate go. We both jumped on him and a couple of mates came over to help.

I copped a big hit in the back and went down. It must have been a flying kick or something because it knocked me head over arse. I copped a few boots while I was down, mainly on my hands as I was trying to get up and shield my head at the same time. No sooner had I got up than I copped a hit in the forehead and I went down. That's all I remember except coming to with some ambulance guys over me. I had been hit with something and had a massive lump on my forehead. It felt like someone had stuck a huge rock on there and the skin felt all tight and it hurt like fuck. The ambulance guys reckoned I should go to hospital for observation as I had been knocked out. I told them no way – I would go after the match. It was not every day your team plays at Wembley and I wasn't going to miss it. A couple of my mates hung around and saw me into the ground. I felt a bit groggy but I didn't care. My mates told me they had done the Derby lads and a few were carted off in ambulances. One reckoned I was hit with a length of pipe. I don't know, but it knocked me silly.

At the back of West Ham's support inside Wembley Stadium a feud erupted amongst much older fans. Gangs of Stratford, Canning Town, Mile End fought with each other. Nobody could say how it started as things got thrown and people got pushed into. The feuding would start, stop, then restart. When these old disputes raged up you did your best to keep away and let it sort itself.

We lost the game 2–0 and after the game loads of our lads went around to storm the Derby fans' end. We failed to get all the way inside their end and enraged Derby came out fighting with half the Midlands alongside them. A massive ruck was going on and we were getting the better of it. I did not do much as I felt terrible and all I wanted to do was piss off home. We finally got on the tube and my head was splitting. There were loads of rucks going on, both on and off the train, and, from what I remember, the Derby lads got a good hiding. Loads of my mates were going up the West End to find some more and wanted me to come but I gave it a miss. I was in no state to fight anyone and I headed home. At Paddington station I collapsed and woke up in hospital. I was kept in for two days, I had concussion and they decided to keep me a bit longer because of the size of the lump on my head. When they kept you in intensive care for observation, especially when you were unconscious, you were allowed nothing to eat, as food built up your blood pressure. A small glass of water was all you were allowed. They let my girlfriend know I was in there but I don't even remember her being there.

I missed a couple of games and I made the Burnley at home next which we won 3 – 2. Alf Garnett did a walk around the pitch before kick-off, with a rattle and billboard saying 'Up the Hammers' and dressed like he'd just stepped out of the TV show. A lot of new faces were around now. I suppose it goes with a bit of success.

We had the Yids on the Monday after. Fuck all of their lads showed and we done them 1 – 0. I wasn't going to go to many away games this season as my girlfriend was getting pissed off at me. Here she was, all the way from Oz and getting stuck in London while I was off all over the country.

QPR at Loftus Road next and I met my mates at the Springbok Arms pub, in South Africa Road, I think it was called, near their ground. As I walked in I saw a load of faces I knew. Then, one mate of my mine started shouting at me and calling me a cunt and hit me in the face with an empty glass. I was shocked and they knew it, as the look on my face would have told them. I found no blood or cuts – the pint glass was plastic. It was a wind-up, something I did not need after the Derby affair. The pub brought out plastic pint glasses on match days and they were hard to break. If you wanted a light and keg it was poured for you and you weren't allowed the bottle. The pool table was off-limits on game days and plastic ashtrays and water jugs became common in most pubs around the grounds in London.

We went on their end and Old Bill were asking all kinds of questions, like who was the team trainer and only stuff a QPR fan would know. If you didn't know you were walked up the other end, and many were. We stayed on the covered end. QPR scored first and it was nearly on but if you looked like trouble you were grabbed and thrown out. In the second half, Billy Jenning drew us level with a goal scored from a tight angle at the away end. Half the Loftus Road end went up and Old Bill were pissed off. They thought they had most of us on the away end but half the home end was ours. Our lads were getting picked out and taken outside. One good thing at QPR: that fucking drum had gone. I reckon the home fans were jack of it as well.

I missed the next three games as I spent some time working every day I could. I was going back to Oz with my girlfriend and we wanted to save some money. I limited myself to only a few away games, ones where I knew there would be some action.

The next home game I went to was Everton at home. Our first loss of the season: they scored from the halfway line with Mervyn Day being well off his line. Fuck all of their fans turned out and apart from the odd fan getting a touch-up, that was about it.

The next game I went to was against Man U at our ground. They had come straight back up into Division One after them taking the drop a couple of seasons ago. I'll say one thing for them: in Division Two they were still pulling massive crowds. We reckoned they would get fifty thousand-plus for two dogs having a fuck in the street in Manchester as there was fuck all else to do. But for now they were coming to our manor and, such was the notoriety of Man U's Red Army fans, the borough of Newham drew up battle plans to tackle it. Transport unions held meetings, all police leave was cancelled, shop shutters went up and all the pubs agreed to remain shut for the day, while all throughout the week there had been talk of the tubes not running. Man U fans had made a mess of some grounds when the team was in the Second Division, and smashed up a couple of tubes as well. Local police reports revealed arrests at Upton Park were up 50 per cent from the previous season's figures. Two sets of fans with growing reputations were about to confirm people's worst fears.

The day came and the tubes did run, and on the trip down there were hundreds of them, all age groups and as usual giving it all the patter about how great they were.

I got out at Upton Park and I saw a massive load of our lads outside the Queens market. The Mancs came out all scarved up and singing. No one moved and most of them saw the crowd and went across the road. As they came down the small hill the West Ham lads ran at them. They scattered and many a ruck was going on. I belted one bloke who was having a go at a younger lad and I copped a couple of boots as well. Most legged it towards the ground and as they were going they were running the gauntlet of our fans having a go at them. We went round to the South Bank and a massive load of West Ham were on there already and the Mancs were pouring in. They had two groups, one down near the Chicken Run and the other near the corner on the West Side. We had a go at the mob of about two hundred near the Chicken Run. We steamed into them, pushing right down the front, and many legged it over into the Chicken Run. Some stood and were singing, 'MANCHESTER LA, LA, LA', to which we gave it the 'MUNICH, MUNICH '58' chant. That got them going and it was off again. A load of their lads were being led away with cut heads and holding their faces. They had got a good slapping.

The game started. We scored first and went crazy. The mob near the West Side had a go at us and it was back on. Lads came from all over the South Bank, and more joined us from the little door that adjoins the West Side and steamed in. They were fucked and many, in fact nearly all, jumped on to the pitch to get away. The game was stopped for twenty minutes while Old Bill tried to get things in order. They were put in the West Side and stayed there near the South Bank corner all game. Some of their lot from the other corner were jumping out of the Chicken Run and running over to join their main mob. It seemed they had got a slapping in there as well from the older fans. I later learned the game was two minutes away from being abandoned by the ref.

The game restarted and they drew level. We hadn't realised how many they had. There were still loads on the South Bank who had been keeping their heads down but now were all cheering. We grabbed a couple and gave them a touch-up. One of them was calling out, 'Police, police!' He got some more for his trouble but a lot more were pissed off at him being a grass.

We learned of a large mob of Mancs outside who were locked out, and attempted to break through a big wooden door, and word was going around that Chelsea were helping us as well. I never saw any Chelsea lads or heard them, but they were welcome as they had the numbers.

The majority of the Mancs came by coach and over a hundred coaches were parked up at Central Park Road and it was there we would go for them. Alan Taylor scored and again he won the game for us. It seemed he was now scoring when it was most needed, as he had during the FA Cup run and now again today. We went mad and loads of our lads were singing, 'EAST LONDON LA, LA, LA' in reply to the Mancs, who had gone all quiet. The game over, we all moved off to where the coaches were parked. The mob of Mancs who were outside had gone and we all ran to the left of the South Bank and joined up with a fair crew from the North Bank, running across Barking Road and in the back way to the coaches. Getting in from the other end of the street would have been impossible as a massive Old Bill presence was blocking the road but we hadn't pulled this stunt for quite a while and it caught them off guard. Loads of Mancs were trying to get in the coaches and a few coach windows were going in. I saw a bloke who lived in one of the terraced houses nearby come out with a hammer in his hand as loads of fans were trampling over his tiny front yard. The hammer looked liked one of those panel pin ones and he stood there holding it like he just won a cup or something. A couple of lads said, 'Have him,' and he bolted back in the house. He had done his brave act and now it was time to give it a miss.

As the Mancs were trying to get on the coaches we kicked the fuck out of them. Many went down and their mates just trampled over them to get on. I grabbed one bloke and tried pulling him back and copped an elbow in the mouth. That shook me up. The Manc didn't want to have a go but in fear of not getting away he lashed out and I copped it. I had a bit of a split lip, nothing serious. I was more upset that I had been hit at all.

The mounted Old Bill were now on the plot. Some coach drivers would not open their doors as they were scared we might get on. I bet they were popular on the trip home. Things calmed a little and Old Bill were chasing us out. We all ran past the road-block towards the station, a massive mob looking for them but only the odd few were being picked up and mainly by scarf hunters whose tactics were to grab the scarf, give a kick or a hit and leg it. We had turned them over well, in and out of the ground. Instead of waiting for them to sneak into the South Bank we got in first and called their bluff. The Old Bill were also bluffed again at the coaches.

I rode the tube home with loads of lads looking for the so-called Cockney Red lads, who weren't really cockney. It was just assumed if you were not from the north and you were from London then you were a cockney. Nothing could be further from the truth. Most of these southern-based Manc lads were from Essex or Kent and did not live in London at all. They just grabbed the name and I think they reckoned it gave them some prestige. It counted for nothing with us and I know firms like Chelsea and the Yids didn't care either. They mastered the art of gobbing off and were experts at vanishing when they wanted to. They were hard lads to find and having a southern accent and no colours, it was hard to pick them. I saw a mob of them once at Victoria station. There were about fifty of them and we ran at them alongside some Chelsea lads, who also hated them. The scarves were hidden and they legged it. Probably getting the

British Rail home to some small southern town where they stand the dead up in bus stops to make the place look busy. They have the cheek to call themselves cockneys. Most of them would not know where the Bow Bells were and if asked most would say Bow and be wrong.

I jumped off at Lancaster Gate and called it a day. It had been a great result for us on and off the park but we had the return on their manor yet and we hoped we would have a big turnout.

I missed a load of games from then on and went back about four or five weeks later. We had the Arsenal at home and I wasn't going to miss it. At least, that's what I thought on the tube down. My Yorkie mate and I got a kicking from a load of Gooners that got on at Tottenham Court Road station. Some of them knew us and before we knew it they were into us and we got a fair kicking. I was bruised all over and my legs were killing me. My mate got hit with something and had a badly split head. They chucked us off at the next stop and I could hear the cheers from them. They had a result and were happy. My mate needed stitches so we went back to Paddington and gave the game a miss. We won as well, 1–0.

I had copped a good whack in the shins and was limping for a week. My ankle was swollen where I think the Gooners had jumped on me. My girlfriend was well pissed off and asked me to give the football up – this fell on deaf ears as I could never do that, I was enjoying it too much. She could not believe me – if getting your head kicked in was fun then she reckoned I was mad. I did agree to limit my games, though.

I went to the Villa away game – about thirty of us joined up with some other lads and got the Inter-city up. We went on their end and went to the back of the stand to get a beer. We found the main Villa lads and loads of other fans had a bingo club under the Holte End and used to play bingo before a game. We reckoned it was one of the funniest things we have seen and talked about gate crashing it but we let them get on with it. Even today when I meet up with a Villa fan, I ask him if they still play bingo. I normally get a yes and then he realises I am taking the piss. During the game lads were calling out, 'Five and nine, the Brighton line', a bingo call used in London, as the fare in the early days was five shillings and nine pence. Cries of 'Two fat ladies' rang out; and a general piss-take was going on. I dunno how many the Holte End holds but it's massive and the ground was packed, over 50,000 that day. We lost 4–1. Even when Billy Jenning scored we all went up and cheered and no one had a go at us. There was only about one hundred to one hundred and fifty of us and we would have been killed if they did, but nothing. We couldn't believe it.

The next one was Liverpool in the League and the following week we had them in the cup. Round about Christmas we topped the League for a week and this brought fans from all over, some who hadn't been in ages and the hangers-on, who seem to only follow successful sides. Liverpool done us 4-0 easy, which began a big slide for us. Toshack got a hat-trick and Keegan got the fourth. That pairing was great to watch and took many a team apart. Their fans were non-existent. The following week we played them again and in the papers they said the BBC were going to follow the cup holders all the way as we were favourites to go on to back-to-back finals. The Scousers stopped that: they done us 2 – 0 with Toshack and Keegan scoring again.

The bulk of their fans were in the seats in the East Stand up the North Bank End. I saw a few little groups but for a cup match, their turnout was shocking. It seemed getting any mob down to us was becoming a problem.

Before this season the Mancs were dropping how many they brought down. After one season in Division Two, walking over lower sides seemed to give them enough courage to bring a decent mob down to us. It seemed we had to take it away and, the way Old Bill was watching us, it was getting hard.

We had the Yids next on their manor and most of us met up under the main stand. We knew the Old Bill would be watching the stations. Once inside we got a beer and looked around. There were loads of familiar faces and a casual nod here and there and you knew it would kick off soon. As it turned out the Yids kicked it off. A massive mob of them came charging past us and on to the Paxton but there was no one there. We all steamed after them and came up behind them. They were fucked and most jumped on to the pitch to escape. The few who didn't got a kicking and that incident even made the London *Times* newspaper, a rarity for such an upper-class paper in those days. We were called working-class thugs who terrorised the innocent at White Hart Lane. What a load of shit! It just goes to show, no matter how good the paper is, the people who write for them are all fucking bullshitters. The Yids kicked it off; we finished it. Simple. We had most of the Paxton. Only in the corner where the stand is, where you can walk around to the other end, there was the odd off. We drew 1–1 and that was about it. The massive mob that had charged past us had gone and outside there were a couple of rucks here and there, but Old Bill had it quickly sorted.

We went to Coventry next, and as my girlfriend's aunts and relations had originally come from that way, we decided on having a weekend away. She could look them up and I could go

to the match. We left on the Friday and got into a Bed &
Breakfast. I met her aunts and relations and couldn't wait to get
away. They had arranged a look around for her while I was
going to the match.

I went into the pub at the back of the West Stand, I think it
was called the Mercer Arms or the Sky Blues. About 12.30 p.m.
some familiar faces came in. They had come up by car and the
train was yet to arrive. A few were surprised to see me there
before them and we had a few beers and waited on the rest
from the train. We went into their end and stood to the left
behind the goal. We were all chanting and taking the piss and
a few of their lads fronted us. When they found we weren't
going to back down they backed off. I followed a couple of our
lads up to the back of the City mob and two of them just
pushed into them. One was lifted, the other got away. Their
fans, apart from surging forward when being pushed, did
nothing. We lost 2–0.

I went to the Leeds game at home and hardly any of their
fans fronted. Another team who brought fuck all down to us.
The next game was the Mancs away. My mate was going home
to Barnsley with his girlfriend and wanted me to come. We
would leave on Friday and travel through on the Saturday. This
was a good idea and I took my girlfriend along as well. We got
a Bed & Breakfast and he stayed at his folks' place in a little
place called Stains Cross, just outside Barnsley.

We left next morning and got to Old Trafford about 1.00
p.m. We met up with some lads we knew but it looked like a
poor turnout from our lads. I met a couple of our lads who
came up by car and they were wearing a Manc scarf; they
weren't taking any chances. I don't know how many times we
were asked for a light or what time it was, but my mate did

most of the talking and so far we weren't sussed. About thirty-odd faces I knew from West Ham turned up and started talking to the lads who came by car. We joined them and went in the bit of the ground in the corner known (by the locals) as 'Alchys' corner'. We never had the numbers to try the Scoreboard End. Even before the game started we were sussed and lads jumped us from all over. I got hit by a bloke doing one of those flying kung-fu kicks and went down the steps that lead down to the front. I copped a fair few kicks on the way and the other lads got bit of a slapping as well. I was out of it. I dunno if I hit my head on the steps or got booted but I was as shaky as fuck. My Yorkie mate had a busted nose and some of the lads were upset. The Old Bill put us in the older side stand and I was taken to a St John's bloke, as were a couple of others.

I was out of it and my mate said we were off back home. I don't even remember the trip back but next morning I had the worst headache I ever had and I had bruises all over. They had got some back and I reckon if we had the numbers that day, at least three hundred, we could have had a bit of a go but beating the Mancs at home was an awesome task. My girlfriend was pissed off coming all that way and staying in the B&B all the time. We lost 4–0 I found out later. Some of the lads reckoned we were grassed by the blokes who came up in the car and were wearing the Mancs scarves. I didn't believe it as I had seen these lads with us before and they had stood many a time. I reckon it was just sour grapes. If you are gonna give it you gotta take it.

I went to the next home game against Birmingham and went with the old man and my brothers. I met up with some mates in the Boleyn and they were telling me they got a bit more of a going-over, including the lads who the others reckoned had grassed. No serious injuries, more of a small kicking and they reckon they got off light as Old Bill sorta saved them for once. They said they were glad to see them. They had seen me on a St John's stretcher and wanted to know how I was. It turned out I got a fair kicking as I went down the steps and was trampled on. A couple of mates got it bad as well trying to help me out. Yorkie, who drove us up, got a couple of black eyes as well as a busted nose.

I went on the Chicken Run that day. There were some City fans on the South Bank and there was some crowd disturbance, but I don't know what went on. My old man told me to get over there, which surprised me. There wasn't much he didn't know and I forgot he kept in touch with a lot of his mates, normally down the Lane (Petticoat) on a Sunday. Some of his mates' sons knocked around with us. We lost 2–1 and I went home.

My old man wanted me to go out his way for the night but I could imagine what my girlfriend would think if I never fronted home and as we didn't have a phone I gave it a miss. In fact, I gave a few more games a miss, including Leeds and Newcastle away. A lot of lads were getting pissed off with the way the team was going and we were in a bad slump. We escaped relegation but the way the team was playing was shocking and crowds had dropped right down. One game at home, against Wolves I think, we only got a bit over 16,000 and they were nearly all West Ham fans. However we were doing well in Europe and were into the quarter-finals of the ECWC and the crowds were up around the 38,0000 to 40,000 mark for these games. It seemed we were only concentrating on Europe and I wanted to go over a couple of times but there was no way my girlfriend was going to let me go on my own. I told her if we made the final

I was going. As it turned out she wasn't around anyway. Her mate from Oz came over and they went off on one of those European coach tours for six weeks. Which was just as well, as we made it through.

First we had Arsenal at Highbury and by rights the Gooners should have kicked our heads in. We were about one hundred strong on the North Bank and we even baited them with songs like 'WE'VE TAKEN THE NORTH BANK HIGHBURY AGAIN!' And still nothing. They done us 6–1 on the pitch and we all went home well pissed off.

We had made the semis and we were up against the mighty Eintracht Frankfurt. It was a two-match semi and we lost the first one on their ground 2–1. We played them at our ground in April and we done them 3–1 in a great match where Trevor Brooking scored two and Keith Robson the other.

I went to the last home game of the season against Villa, a 2–2 draw and most talk was on the final at the Heysel Stadium in Brussels, which was home ground for the team we were playing, Anderlecht. We finished eighteenth that season and had lost the grip on the cup and the Yids done us in the League Cup replay at our ground. Liverpool won the League title and Southampton won the cup. More on that later. I'll cover what went on in the ECWC in the next chapter.

We moved into the next season, 1976–77. I only went to a few games as I got engaged in the off-season. We planned to move to Australia to live and saving money was the main priority.

I was going to Charlton to see us play in the League Cup, third round. I hadn't been to the Valley in years. At London Bridge station Old Bill were everywhere it seemed. A few lads had told me that some Millwall lads had jumped some West

Ham scarvers on the train, not realising that it was full of our lads with the usual no colours. They got a hiding, during which the train door was opened and one was thrown out of the train into the path of another train. I have read it was at New Cross tube station but fighting someone and opening a tube door at the same time and then throwing him out doesn't add up with me. Also, why were all the Old Bill at the British Rail station? Millwall were hated more than the Yids but killing someone was lifting the game a little. I gave a few games a miss from then on. My mates were telling me Old Bill were thick on the plot about it and were coming down heavy at home and nicking lads for anything. Not just throwing them out, but charging them and getting them before a magistrate. As I was going to Oz I didn't need the trouble.

I got home and my fiancée was worried. She had heard someone had been killed and she was worried it could have been me. My days of going to matches were slowing down. I went to Bristol City away and took my fiancée with me. I wanted to look up some people that my mum stayed with during the war when she was evacuated as a kid. We left on the Friday night and stayed in a Bed & Breakfast in a place called Coronation Road. The place I went to see the other people at was called Wrington and it was not far outside Bristol. I never even made the match as I got stuck in the town on the Saturday in a pub called the Pin and Cushion, I think, and ended up well out of it after trying the local scrumpy. The game was a 1–1 draw and I heard from my mates that the locals were well up for it. They could have bombed the place and I wouldn't have known.

The next game I went to was the Yids at Upton Park and to our surprise they came with a massive mob and went on the

North Bank and had half of it and they weren't moving. Most expected them on the South Bank but they came in force and went on the other end and ran the lads who were on there. They got half of it back but loads got done. We had a big one with them outside on Green Street as well and it took Old Bill to get between us and pull it up. They meant business for a change and had totally surprised us. In all fairness I would say the day was theirs but they weren't getting away lightly. That was the last time someone pulled that on us and on the tube back loads were going to Liverpool Street station to have another go. I went home and I heard it was a fucking big off as well, with the Yids getting the upper hand. To hear that from my mates I knew there would be some truth in it. We hated the Yids and to admit getting done by them was something we did not do lightly. We would get our own back on their manor soon. In fact, that was the next game I went to: the Yids at White Hart Lane.

I met up with some mates at Liverpool Street and you would think I had been away for years. We decided to try the Paxton but first we would have a beer under the stand and see what happened. There were loads of West Ham under there and we had a massive presence on their manor. A huge mob came through like they did the season before, only this time they went straight into us. It was on, and I copped a whack in the mouth from someone and felt blood coming out of my lip. It was split wide open and I was getting a kicking, as were many. The Yids had done it again. The Old Bill calmed it down and lads were getting pulled. My top lip felt like it was on fire. A copper grabbed me and I thought I was nicked. Instead, he was taking me out for some attention. He saw what my lip was like and decided that my day was over.

I was taken away by ambulance and at hospital I had 18 stitches put in my lip. It felt like it was six feet in front of me. I was asked what happened and told them I fell. I was told it was more than likely a knife or sharp blade that had done me, as the split was cut so clean. I was dirty on this. I knew of lads who carried blades and had felt them before, when my elbow was slashed, but this was close. A bit higher and my eye would have been gone. I reckon knives are the lowest thing going. I had many a kicking and gave as many, but never pulled a knife. I've chucked things and even hit people with ashtrays, but I never carried a knife. I had seen a couple of times when other fans had pulled them and waved them around and hesitated. That was the mistake: if you're gonna carry one and pull it, make sure you use it, because in the cases I had seen the other fans got a good going-over.

I got a lift home by Old Bill and they wanted to know what had happened. I told them I didn't know and if I did I would tell them. They used the bit about getting compensation if they brought the bloke to trial, but it never worked. I don't know to this day who shived me.

The end of January that year l left for Australia. And the trouble I had getting out was unreal.

CHAPTER 10

The ECWC Final

THE ECWC FINAL was a day I will never forget. The trip itself was a good laugh on the way over and when we left Victoria station the whole place was claret and blue. Three ferries were going over along with three bus-loads of local Old Bill to help out the local police. We found out afterwards that ten thousand had made the journey. It seemed like twice as many and I saw faces I hadn't seen for a long time. Our ferry was held up as the company's flag was taken down and an English flag put in its place with crossed hammers. The skipper of the boat wasn't going to budge until it was fixed and when we finally got under way the bars were opened. Only plastic glasses were allowed. I don't know why, we were all West Ham fans.

I got some food and I saw my mate, one of the Chelsea lads I used to drink with. He was working on the boat in the kitchens as a chef and when he saw me and Yorkie he gave us the 'sshhhh' sign. We laughed. We weren't going to grass him up and he told us to find a seat in the cafe and he would bring us something to eat out, which he did for free. We asked him to join us at the game but he declined. He reckoned with so many of us it was a bit dodgy for him if someone recognised him. He told us the ship's staff were all told to be on alert and at the sign of any trouble they were to close the bars down. He told us what to expect from the Anderlecht fans as he had been to a few of their home games and warned they were nothing much but liked carrying knives. We passed this around to our lot, who in turn did the same. By the time we docked there was talk of a massive mob of their fans armed with blades – that's how much the rumour got out of control.

Customs were real slow and most lads were let through. Our Old Bill, who were over with us, were picking lads at random to have their passport checked. You were searched and if you had a overnight bag it was turned over. I was one who was picked for this treatment and I was asked what the purpose of my visit was. I thought, he's joking, ain't he, but told them I'd come to watch football. Some said to declare war and other smart remarks. They were held up a bit longer. The Belgian police looked the part: riot shields, helmets, the lot. Standing beside our coppers it looked funny, but after the game I knew which lot I preferred.

Getting to the ground was a laugh. Many got a bus into the city and then walked; some got the train. We jumped a cab and went straight there. Heysel Stadium was quite large, bigger than our ground with the ends being open and no roof, and crowd segregation was a joke. No wonder there was so many fans killed by the Scousers later. If that had been us that day or even Everton, Man U or even Millwall, I reckon it would have been worse.

We were there because we were in the final and we were even wearing colours. We weren't looking for trouble but we heard a few cafe bars had been turned over by our lot when locals had a go and expected us to back down. They picked the wrong lads.

The game started and it was like a home game. You could not hear their lads and we scored first. Patsy Holland, a local lad from Poplar, started the proceedings. Frank Lampard's dodgy back-pass allowed them the equaliser just before half-time. No sooner had the second half started than Anderlecht went in front. Then Keith Robson pulled one back – 2 – 2 – and the cockneys were in song. Then came the dodgiest of penalties after Holland robbed Resenbrink. It was 3 – 2 before Van der Elst, who we were later to buy, finally killed us off with goal number four. We had been done and we were gutted. Loads left before they lifted the cup.

Outside, the Belgian coppers were pushing things along, hitting lads across the legs like we were cattle and shouting in Flemish at us. I saw three of them giving a lad of about fourteen or fifteen a right going-over, I mean boots and all, and when a couple of our Old Bill tried to stop it they were pushed away and threatened with batons. One of our coppers was slapped across the legs with a truncheon and that was sort of a signal. If the Old Bill were having a go at each other, then fuck, why not us. Only trouble was the Anderlecht fans were still inside celebrating their win so our attentions turned to Old Bill.

That was the first time I had a taste of tear gas and I hope it was the last. Lads were going mental and my eyes were stinging like fuck. Loads had hankies and their shirts held over their mouths. I got my eyes washed – with coke, I think – and I helped another lad wash his with beer. Our lot were chucking anything they could find at the plod, who were now forming a line, with their shields as protection. Many were getting nicked and I got a tug and was dragged off. I do mean dragged as well, and thrown into a van and left with some other lads.

About an hour went past and we could hear things were quieter now and many of our mob had finally been herded off. They finally let us out one by one and our ferry tickets were taken, along with any cash we had. They ripped up my tickets and did the same to the next lad. There were four of us who got this treatment and we were shown the way we had to go. Only thing was, we could not get on the ferry as we had no tickets and no cash and one ferry had already gone. I had about fifty quid lifted by their Old Bill and the lad I was with reckoned he only had about twenty on him. We told our coppers about it and we tried getting the ferry company to let us on by taking our names and address. They weren't having it and we were told to go to the British Consul. Only trouble was, it was about 11.30 p.m. by now, so we stayed in the ferry terminal till morning, walked into the town and finally found the Consul.

Once inside we told them what had happened and it seemed a few more were caught like this as well. We had to hang around for about two hours while we finally got a one-way ticket home to Victoria and two quid each for the journey. The conditions were that they take your passport off you at immigration and you had writing on every page in bold red IMMIGRATION OFFICER SEE INSIDE. I finally got home and my passport was nabbed at Customs.

Which brings me to the English police. I was nicked in 1976 on the Friday between the FA Cup Final between Man U and Southampton. I was having a drink with a bloke from Carlisle and his bird in the Charles Dickens Tavern in Paddington. My mate's bird was wearing one of those vertical striped college scarves in red and white. She knew nothing about football and her boyfriend was not an active fan, more into the odd game at Fulham or QPR. He was not into the terrace scene in any way. While we were in the pub a load of Mancs came in, got a beer and spotted the scarf she was wearing. They started taking the piss and thought she was a Southampton fan. It ended up with my mate dropping one of them and a few smashed glasses urged us on. I chucked a chair at them and it missed and hit a fag machine on the wall which got knocked off. A couple of other lads in there helped out and we ran the rest out. Outside one clocked me one in the nose, not hard but enough to make it bleed. My mate's bird gave me her scarf to wipe the blood off and we moved off to another pub we used, called the Polly Perkins, up the back of Paddington.

As we walked in I still had the scarf and I got whacked in the side of the head with a punch from, I was later told, a lad who thought we were Mancs because of the scarf. We nearly got a kicking as my mate was trying to calm things down but his accent wasn't helping. Some lads in there knew us and told this small mob we were locals. They were Chelsea lads looking for Man U fans who came down early and thought we were some. We had a pint and these lads left and we soon followed and walked down Praed Street and there the Old Bill pulled us over and asked about the incident in the Charles Dickens. The landlord had called them and we were taken to Paddington Green station. I still remember the copper's name, a smug young cunt in plain clothes. He must have thought he had Lord Lucan, the way he carried on.

We told our stories, which were backed up by the publican, but the fag machine was damaged and someone had to pay. And that someone was me. I was printed and had my photo taken, and they tried throwing everything at me from burglaries to handbag snatching. Trying to clear the books up and they thought I would do. My mate and his bird were let go with no charges and I was charged with causing malicious damage. As this was my first offence I wasn't worried but they refused me bail and I spent the weekend in Paddington Green nick. I was taken to Marylebone court on Monday, and I pleaded guilty. The police gave their version and it was nothing like what happened at all. I was shocked. They said I was an active football hooligan and asked for the matter to be adjourned and for me be held on remand while their enquiries continued. Now, I had pleaded guilty, but that clearly wasn't enough for them.

The magistrate asked if they had any evidence about the matters raised and the Old Bill said it was ongoing. The magistrate fined me fifty quid, ordered me to pay the damage for the fag machine, one hundred and twenty quid, which was a joke as it only fell on the floor. But the fags went missing and I had to pay, so someone scored at my expense. I was also put on probation as it was a first offence and given time to pay as well. I had to report to a probation officer down the East End about eight hundred yards past Mile End tube station. My fiancée was back now and I took her along as the officer wanted to see how my home life was, which I reckoned didn't concern her. She asked how I got my scar. I told her how but not where and *she* told *me* White Hart Lane. She had slipped up and knew it and became very coy. It seemed the Old Bill had done some homework on me. In fact, she was a Yid fan and every time I had to see her she kept trying to bring up the football to see if I was still going. It didn't matter, I hardly went now, but she never stopped asking if I had applied to emigrate to Oz.

I thought there would be no trouble. I had an Aussie fiancée, had a place to live when I got there and her old man was a bricklayer also and I had a job. So I was right as far as I was concerned. They knocked me back and would only issue a twelve month visa, after which I would have to apply again. We told them we would be married by then but it didn't matter, they still could refuse me.

I had to get my passport back for them to give me a visa. I went to Petty France, the passport office then if I remember rightly. I had to make an application to get it and had to go upstairs. Then they dug it out and I had to go back downstairs. We paid the money owed and I got the passport. In the lift down the civil servant who had my file was with us and I noticed he had every address I had lived at for the past couple of years on the front of the folder. I asked where he got them from and he pulled the file to his chest and just tapped his nose and smiled, like he was saying, 'You don't need to know.' This shocked me and my fiancée, as some of those places listed we were only at a couple of weeks before moving on. They had the lot. With my passport back I ripped the front page out and applied for a new one, explaining that it had been damaged at a party. I did not want to give Aussie House a passport with red writing all over it.

I got my new one and applied for my visa and got knocked back, because I had a record. One mark on my name. I couldn't believe it. Here was a country founded on convicts and I had one small mark and it was a knock back. My fiancée got her parents on the case. They lobbied their local MP and finally I got my visa but I had to have a medical first and pay my own fare. I had to prove I could do it. It cost me £317.50 one way. They wanted me to get a return, as if they were expecting me not to meet my visa conditions. We objected and after threats of going to the MP again they buckled. I passed my medical and when we finally left to go to Oz at Heathrow I was turned over by Customs – what for I don't know. I was leaving, not coming in. My fiancée was left alone. We talked about it on the plane and could not work it out.

It all clicked some years later when I was doing some brickwork for a bloke who was an ex-copper in the West Country and came out to Oz and joined up with the NSW (New South Wales) police. He jacked it in and now owns several ice cream vans and he reckons he's never looked back. We talked about the football. He was a Plymouth fan but mainly based in Bristol. He told me every time a lad got pulled and their name was taken it was forwarded on to Scotland Yard and it was all collated there and many a time they had photographers down taking pictures in and out of the grounds. I realised now that the Old Bill had files on all of us and maybe even photos. Something I confirmed when I came back in 1981 for my father's funeral. I was again turned over at Customs and held up. I had the same treatment at Hong Kong, where we went for a week's holiday. The customs went through me again. I have since become an Aussie citizen and now have two passports. We went to Hong Kong again before it was handed over and I used my Aussie passport – nothing, straight through, which proves to me that Big Brother is watching you all the time.

So if there are any lads out there who have been thrown out of a ground and had their names taken, do not think you got away with it, because it's recorded somewhere. I know, believe me.

CHAPTER 11

Other Games

I WENT TO OTHER games aside from West Ham. A few times I went to England v Scotland, both home and away. I've been to an old firm derby in Glasgow and in '70 and '73 I saw two FA Cup Finals between teams I had no connection with.

The Chelsea v Leeds final was a boring game and we had tickets in the stand opposite the steps at Wembley. To say the Chelsea lads had a result would be an understatement. Outside I saw loads of Leeds fan being run by them, loads of small offs where the Leeds lads stood but in the end were swamped by the Chelsea lads. They were well at it that day and the lads from up north went home with some sore reminders of London.

The other final I went to was Leeds v Sunderland and I was with the Mackems. They are a passionate lot and to me it was one of the greatest finals ever. Jim Montgomery playing a blinder, making two incredible saves. They won 1–0, with Ian Portfield scoring the winner. Before the game the Leeds lads, who had a fair crew, had a go at the Mackems outside the Greyhound. The Mackems knocked the shit out of them. I have seen Newcastle lads in action and have been on the receiving end as well and these lads were much the same. Not one of them backed down – and Leeds had the numbers, too. It was like that all the way up to the ground: Leeds lads having a pop at a couple of Mackems and getting their heads kicked in. Not many of the Yorkshire lads hung around after the game. They all vanished with their tails between their legs.

Another game I went to was the old firm meeting in Glasgow, Rangers v Celtic at Ibrox. I took my girlfriend with me to a place called Largs where I had mates living, lads who I had worked with in London. Largs is a small town and the locals were quick to tell you that Lou Macari's parents owned the local chippie. It was sort of an honour for them. The Jocks are a funny race but if you are on the right side of them then you are OK. There's always one or two that will tell you about their history, especially if you are English. If they won a darts championship against England it would be written down as folklore and ten songs would be written about it.

I had never drunk so much in my life. I love a good session any time but they don't know when to stop. They would have a gut full of beer and then get on to a cheap South African wine, called llanlick or llanie by the locals.

Largs was a nice place and we had a drink on a little island off the coast, where at closing time you were sort of kicked off. We went to Greenock up the road a bit and what a difference: the place was a shithole, and that's putting it nicely.

The day of the game arrived and I joined my mates for the train ride into Glasgow. They were already on the drink and were sharing a bottle of rum. I gave that a miss. We ended up at a place call Brigdon Cross, I think. All I remember of the place was that loads of roads all met up there and the pubs were all full of Rangers fans, like my mates. Loads of Celtic fans walked through and past and the insults were going back and forward. There was the odd punch-up, but most were happy with name calling, singing about King Billy and getting drunk. I could never understand why a mob of fans so loyal to the Union Jack and hating the Catholics had a Dutch hunchback who lived in Ireland as their hero. I knew the story of the Boyne as I had been told many times by, I reckon, every Rangers lad I met.

I saw a few rucks at the ground and one particularly nasty one, with lads from both sides. They were using anything they could and it was pure hatred from both sides. In the ground itself the atmosphere was incredible. There was a load of black lads together singing, 'I'D RATHER BE A DARKIE THAN A TIM!' I laughed at that.

The game over, we headed off. Loads of fights outside but no real big mob fights and it seemed everyone was shouting at each other. This was different, this wasn't just football hatred, it was much, much deeper, the Catholic/Protestant thing, which never really bothered me. I was Church of England but the times I had been to church I could count on one hand. One thing I learned in Glasgow is that the people there have the biggest chip on their shoulder I have ever seen. They are the same out here: very 'cliquey'.

The England vs Scotland game was different. I was with the same lads who lived in Largs, only I was going back that

OTHER GAMES

day. I think I was one of about a dozen English fans there and I had no bother at all, just a lot of piss-taking. A few younger lads tried it on but the lads I was with told them to fuck off and they did. I don't know what would have happened if England had scored but Dalglish nutmegged Clemence for the first and the Jocks were happy. They sang all day, only stopping to have a drink. Alcohol was banned at these games from the vendors at the game but many had half bottles of Scotch they'd sneaked in. Being the smaller size and sort of flat shaped, they fitted nicely down the front of your trousers.

Scotland won, everyone was happy and I headed off to the station to go home. All the way to London, the Jocks were singing and carrying on and when we pulled in many were staggering off the train. I had a few myself; it was the only thing keeping me sane with that lot.

The game at Wembley we flogged the sweaties 5–1, and easy as well. It certainly upset their fans. They were chucking cans at the players and anybody else. In London they boarded up the statue of Eros, as having a couple of hundred drunken Jocks hanging over it would have snapped it for sure. The Jocks came down in numbers and at the time they reckoned some eighty thousand were living in London. The dole system up there was different and after a couple of weeks you were off 'the brew' as they called it. Such restrictions weren't applied down in England, so many moved. I knew loads of Jock families in London who were signing on and working on the lump or cash in hand. Some were decent blokes but when an England vs Scotland game came around, they changed. That said, they never got away with their antics down our way. Loads lived in the Salvation Army home in Garford

Street in Poplar near the dock gates. Up the West End they overtook the place. Having a mob of eighty thousand based in London is some handy team.

They always carried on that the English never showed. Not many cared while they were making a spectacle of themselves up west. If they tried down our manor, or say Millwall's or even the Yids', it would have been different. Of late, from what I read and see in the media, the English lads are having a go back.

Some lads reckon London firms always shit it. Bring them down Plaistow or the Old Kent Road and see what happens. Since the movie *Braveheart*, have you noticed the Jocks all wearing the blue face paint and mimicking Aussie/Yank Mel Gibson? If you watched that film properly it shows them having a win or two but finally getting stuffed by the English. Why? Because they sold out for the English shilling. Ask any Jock, next time he has a pop at you about Bannockburn or some other skirmish, why they sold out their own kind. It normally shuts them up, or gets you a smack in the mouth if they think they are good enough. In fact it was an Englishman who invented the kilt and the ancient Greeks who invented the bagpipes. Even golf was invented by a Dutchman – it was called kolf. And I reckon the only way penicillin was invented by a Jock was because he was too tight to throw some rotten bread away. I don't mind the Jocks, but fuck, they go on. The Kiwis are a bit the same. If a Kiwi person did something good, fuck, they let you know, same as the Jocks.

You have to feel a bit sorry for the real Man U fans as well. It's unreal the way people have jumped on their bandwagon. Go into any internet chatroom and you find many who support Man U but have never been to the ground, let alone know anything about the club. I doubt it will ever happen, but if my team was ever as good at buying trophies as the Mancs then I would feel sorry for them. I wouldn't want the bystanders hanging on. We had a few in 1975 and I missed 1980 but I imagine there were some then.

A team like Man U, or Arsenal, and throw Chelsea into it, should be winning week-in-week-out with the squads they have got. The modern player is not a ninety-minute player. I will give you an example. Malcolm MacDonald, or Super Mac as he was known, was banging goals in regularly. A move to the Arsenal and what does he do? They trained him to be in the centre and take crosses on his left foot and hopefully score. Where would the Mancs be without Beckham? Most of their game is based around the way he can cross a ball. Take him out and the team falters. The time they had players like Cole and Yorke, for the money they cost they should have been able to bang a couple every week but most times they were subbed and on comes a red-nosed paper boy and ex-Millwall cunt and they pull them through. If blokes like Fergie or Taggart have their way the game will go the way of the Yanks with their grid iron – change sides when you are defending and vice versa.

The game is too big now and has come a long way. I love the pay TV. Being so far away I can watch a lot of games. Many an ex-pat will agree with me about the benefits, I'm sure, but it's ruining the game, with players wanting more and more. Fair enough, if the big companies are cashing in on them, why not? They don't play all their life. The game's gone soft. They talk about blokes like Roy Keane being a nutter and a hard man, but all he does is go in a bit harder than most. Nobby Stiles, or even Norman 'bite yer ankles' Hunter, would have been red-carded every game if they were playing today.

Man U claim to have won the treble. Not so, they have won three cups. The proper treble has never been done. I know now they say the League Cup doesn't count. Teams like them should join a Euro league and the sooner they form it the better. To miss out on competing in the FA Cup was a shocker and I know many of their fans agree. The oldest competition in the world and they travel halfway round the world to compete in a Mickey Mouse competition to help Taggart's ego.

If the truth be known, Lazio are the champs of Europe, as they won the Euro Super Cup, doing the Mancs 1 – 0. Ask any Manc and he will tell you that it doesn't count. Had it been the other way round and the Mancs had won, God knows what they would have said. Alex Ferguson getting a knighthood for having enough money available to buy the best and picking up three cups in one season is wrong. Ten years ago he was nearly sacked until they opened the cheque book. Players like Bobby Moore, who lifted his country's only World Cup, only gets an OBE. It's all wrong.

We, the people who have supported the game for years, don't count. They don't want the hooligans, only the family who are gonna buy a repro shirt and all the other goodies that go with it. I'm told around Bethnal Green its all Man U and Arsenal shirts now. I don't think I ever had a repro shirt as a kid; they weren't around. West Ham was the last club in England not to have advertising around the ground and in its match day programme. Haven't things changed? I love the West Ham sponsors – the very same brand of footwear the coppers used to make you take off if they were steel toe-capped are now the sponsors of the shirts.

How long will it be before someone goes off his head with a gun at a game? The Hillsborough disaster was bad; the fences put up by the authorities killed the fans. The police had a lot to answer for on that, but they were never really taken to account.

The First Division attendances are well up now because people are sick of paying though the nose to follow their club. Me, if West Ham went all the way down I would still support them and many would, it's bred into you. Changing teams from season to season really annoys me. I don't know how you could do it but then again I'm one of the old fans.

I don't care what they say, the game's not getting any better. Football hooliganism has always been around. The hooligans won't stop, it will be harder for them but can you imagine a steward trying to chuck you out twenty years ago? He would have got killed. There will still be trouble inside stations, same as pubs. So as far as I'm concerned, the all-seater killed the game and with it some good terrace culture. But then again, as I said, I'm an older fan now, who cares about my opinion? One day you will be an older fan too. Scary, ain't it?

CHAPTER 12

The Mobs

THE MANY FIRMS we have had fights with over the early years are all different and we had different results at some grounds and we got a hiding at others. So I will try and give my thoughts on the lads we had a go with over these short, but as far as I'm concerned, great years.

CHELSEA

The lads at Chelsea, the main boys, are a loyal lot and have stuck by their team through thick and thin. The trouble with the Chelsea boys was that they had a load of hangers-on who were all part of the scene and dressed for it as well. The problem was when it came to a big ruck, many of these fringe lads legged it, leaving the main mob to cop it or leg it as well. I have met a few Chelsea lads and they are sound blokes, like the one-armed man and the twins. Another mate of theirs we called Lurch because of his size and features. We had a go with them at the so-called Cockney Reds and ran them. Many of our lads called Babs the Fugitive because like the TV show we were always looking for the one-armed man.

When Chelsea took the drop many of their fans left and the crowd figures showed it. They were lucky to pull 15,000 at Stamford Bridge. Also, in those days, having links with the National Front and mobs like that didn't help. I mean, Asians weren't welcome anywhere in those days, in the skinhead scene in particular, but we accepted blacks down West Ham and I had many a good mate who was black. Not all our fans accepted them, but at match days they were accepted and many stood with us through thick and thin.

When Chelsea went down, their main lads were still active and had a few good run-ins, like when they turned Notts Forest over – in '77, I think. They pulled a few good moves against us and at the night game I mentioned earlier they had the night, I would say. Many times we have walked all over their manor and there was nothing they could do.

I saw their lads give the Leeds fans a good slapping in 1970 and at the replay I was told they did Leeds again, before Fulham made it into the Premiership. I remember people were saying then, if Fulham ever did, Chelsea will lose half their fans. I don't reckon they will as they hate Fulham, and I know in '75 when we played Fulham at Wembley many a Chelsea lad was hoping we would win. Chelsea then had a strong following and one thing we learned was not to underestimate them. They took some liberties on our manor and nearly got away with it.

TOTTENHAM HOTSPUR (THE YIDS)

The Yids were a funny lot. Many of their fans were still living in their glory days, when they did the double. They pulled some good moves, but most times it backfired. I have never liked them and, after getting cut by them, I hated them even more. They changed things at football, the way they changed ends. I don't know if it was because they weren't up for it but it was a good move. I reckon the Yids would have had more success had they been on the tube line.

One night at Liverpool Street station we met about ten of them in the buffet bar and they were there for the same reason as us, to wait for Chelsea lads coming back from Ipswich. I met Sammy Skys and he wasn't a bad bloke. Some of the hangers-on I wasn't keen on and I reckon the feeling was mutual. We were bitter enemies but that night there was no aggro between us; it was a sort of stand-off. The Chelsea train pulled in and loads got off. We just stayed put and hoped none of them would come in. There were about twenty of us and a whole train-load of their boys. We would have been killed, but they went straight into the tube, chanting all the way. The Yids always had a go at their ground but nothing much happened outside; they just seemed to vanish. That said, they were getting their act together when I left England.

ARSENAL

Every gunner a runner. Never a truer word has been spoken I reckon. They have a huge support now and are a massive club but only a couple of times have they stood. The number of times we took their North Bank was a joke. Even when we had only a small crew on there, they did nothing and I have never seen a mob vanish like them. They are one of the trendy clubs now, along with Chelsea and the Mancs. Their run-ins with the Yids, their neighbours and most bitter rivals, were legendary but we never saw much of it. We have had a few run-ins with smaller mobs and have been done, but, as for being a big firm, forget it. I had been told that at Wembley in 1980 the West Ham lads had a field day with them but I got that second-hand and as I wasn't there I can't comment. If past performances are anything to go by, then I believe it.

MILLWALL

Without a doubt the one team following who we loved to hate was Millwall. Although I have never been directly involved in any of the games played, I have come across a few run-ins with their fans and I recall a few run-ins with them at away games but never at Upton Park. The closest they got to Green Street is where the tube lines crossed at Whitechapel and many times we heard they were waiting at the Whitechapel for the passing West Ham tube. Many a lad was ready for them and we would go down there and wait for them but nothing ever came of it. Funny enough, whenever Chelsea were game on the day there were always rumours that Millwall was there with them. Maybe it was true, I don't know, but that did not stop us – we looked down on them both with contempt. That said, many other teams feared them.

The history of the two clubs goes way back to the docks and beyond when Millwall were in fact an East End team, with their ground on the Isle of Dogs. Then they moved over the water to South London. With Millwall I never came up against a large mob in those days. It was mainly little firms like ours and normally on other teams' manors, such as Chelsea or the Yids.

Without a doubt they were a game bunch but I doubt if they could have taken it to a team week in, week out in the old First

Division as we did in those days. We were the guv'nors and they resented living in our shadows for so long. This was a fact proved on their manor and ours when they were promoted to the First Division in the Eighties. The infamous Harry Cripps testimonial game, in which many watched the fighting on the terraces rather than the game, will go down as one of football's most violent clashes ever. Eye-witnesses to that game will tell you that many a hard lad on both sides that day recalled never ever seeing anything like it. Put simply, the two teams' supporters hated each other and always will.

FULHAM
Forget them, simple.

QPR
You went because it was another London club to take but it was not a ground you relished going to. Not because of any fans, but because of that bloody drum. It was many seasons before it got silenced.

EVERTON
Some hard lads who didn't mind a scrap, when they brought the numbers down or on their manor. You needed a fair crew to make a dent in them. Stay away from the park outside their ground – many a firm has fallen foul there.

LIVERPOOL
At home they were awesome but their travelling support to Upton Park in those days was shit. They only brought numbers down to us a few times, and most went in the seats. The gobbiest of the two Merseyside teams and the weaker, in those days.

MANCHESTER CITY

The true fans from Manchester and I had a lot of time for them.
Like us, they hated their red cousins. The Kippax boys are a mad
lot and I was glad we got on with them as I heard many a story
of crews falling foul of them, including United. I dunno if the
feeling is still the same but I'm told that in the mid-Eighties
they were looked after again on our manor.

MANCHESTER UNITED

If ever a team had the worst hangers-on, it's them. It was bad
back in those days and I imagine its fucking worse now. They
have some solid lads and always bring a great mob down,
anywhere they go, but ask any Man U fan now, the older kind,
and most will be quick to point out that they have been a life-
long fan or have followed them for ten years or so. They are
quick to defend themselves so as not to be pointed out as glory-
hunters. They done us well in 1967 but since then things have
changed. They have given us a few good kickings on their
manor and any firm who reckons they run the Stretford End in
those days was a liar. They were hard to beat at home and had
the numbers. It's a shame tiny mobs who call themselves the
Cockney Reds and other little mobs around the country fuck it
up for them. On any football special you went on in those days,
how many of them did you see? It was all chartered coaches
from their fan clubs all over the place and mainly for their
safety. They were good at giving it all the gob but when trouble
started they were the first to leg it. I don't think the real Mancs
even like them, but they can have them. I'm sure London firms
don't want them.

THE MIDLAND FIRMS

A fucking joke the lot of them. Only Wolves with their underpass or subway trick had any bottle and when that was sussed it never came to much again. Aston Villa are better at playing bingo and WBA are worse than Fulham. Birmingham had a bit of a go at our ground, mainly showing off I think, as they had just come up. They did not do it again. As for Coventry, why the place was rebuilt I'll never know. Their fans must be the most gutless I have ever seen and I believe the Yids gave them a good going-over at Wembley when they won the cup.

LEEDS

Leeds had a good firm and were hard to beat on their Spion Kop. Now and then you would see a few lads away, but not many. At home the Old Bill was to their advantage and the Leeds coppers are one of the worst. I saw them get a good hiding in '70 and '73 from Chelsea and the Mackems, but most of their hate is saved for Man U. They played up a bit in the Euro Cup Final, mainly chucking seats in the ground at foreign fans. Let's face it, the foreign mob aren't much, are they?

SHEFFIELD UNITED AND WEDNESDAY

Out of the two my money is on United, as they have had a go at us but only on their manor and never brought any away. Wednesday were rubbish home or away, simple as that.

IPSWICH AND NORWICH

Both rubbish at home and away. Take any sort of firm there and the carrot crunchers want a straightener with you.

DERBY COUNTY

Had their nutters at their ground and have surprised many a team. They brought it down to us once at Upton Park and they had a go at Wembley in the Charity Shield. Many a firm has been caught up there and they are not to be taken lightly.

NEWCASTLE

The Geordies are one of the most loyal lot of fans I have come across. I have never seen them back down and they always stood by their mates. At St James' Park it would take a small army to turn them over and they don't shy from anyone. If Newcastle was on the outskirts of London, things would have been different in the smoke – on the fan front, anyway. I have a lot of respect for the Toon lads, but only in the sense that they stick together and back each other up.

SUNDERLAND

I have never had a run-in with the Mackems but saw them in action against Leeds in the FA Cup in 1973 and they were the same as the Toons. They stood and never backed down. I suppose with the teams only being twenty-five to thirty miles apart, it is not surprising. The Mackems in the real old days were what the Mancs are today – comparing money and club size, that is. They have a loyal following. I have heard the Roker Roar, and it is a roar, let me tell you. Their end was a bit like Chelsea's, with a sort of tin shed on it at the back; I can't remember the name. Not a ground to take the piss – about the same with St James' Park.

MIDDLESBROUGH

Nothing like the Mackems or the Toons. I can't think of anything positive to say about them. When they were managed by Jack Charlton they played the most boring football away from home. Jack's plan was hold them in defence, stick one up front and get a draw away from home, or maybe nick a lucky goal. That about sums them up and their fans were non-existent down at our ground.

I won't go on and name every team, because maybe one game some team brought down a small mob and did something that hardly rates a mention. In those days the Mile End Mafia or the Willesden Whites and a few other gangs were running around. There were some wild times and if your opinion differs it depends on where you were standing or what view you had. As I've said before, I only wrote what I saw, simple.

THE MOBS

In The Know

IS AT www.network54.com/forum/181218

Have a look when you are on the net, it is the best site around dealing with football fans, and the culture in general.

Cheers,
Micky

ALSO BY CASS PENNANT

CASS

The life story of one of the hardest men in Britain. This bestselling book tells Cass's amazing story – how he saved Frank Bruno from a knife attack, was shot three times in the chest and kept fighting, and went on to be the alleged leader of the notorious West Ham 'InterCity Firm'.

Paperback price £5.99 (incl. p and p)

CONGRATULATIONS
YOU HAVE JUST MET THE I.C.F

For the first time ever, all the faces of the West Ham firm reveal their memories of the battles, the violence, the run-ins with the law and all that came with it. Cass has used his unique position as a West Ham insider to create a stunningly dramatic book that is a must read for die-hard football fans and social historians alike.

Hardback price £15.99 (incl. p and p)

Available in all good bookshops. To order your copies direct send a cheque or credit card details to: John Blake Publishing Ltd, 3 Bramber Court, 2 Bramber Road, London W14 9PB.
Alternatively, call us on 020 7381 0666.